QUEST FOR FAILURE:

A Study of William Faulkner

QUEST FOR FAILURE:

A Study of William Faulkner

)))))))))))))))))))))))))))))))))))<<<<<<<<<<<<<<<<<<<<<<<<<<<<<<<

By WALTER J. SLATOFF

Cornell University

Cornell University Press

ITHACA, NEW YORK

This work has been brought to
publication with the assistance of
a grant from the Ford Foundation.

CORNELL UNIVERSITY PRESS

First published 1960

PRINTED IN THE UNITED STATES OF AMERICA
BY THE VAIL-BALLOU PRESS, INC.

To Jimmy

Acknowledgments

TO Robert Adams, John Arthos, Anthony Caputi, Arthur Eastman, Lee Gerlach, Jóhann Hannesson, David Novarr, Warner Rice, William Sale, Jr., John Senior, Alan Swallow, and Austin Warren, I wish to express my gratitude for their various kinds of assistance and encouragement and to thank them and other friends and associates for patiently listening to me talk so much about Faulkner. I am grateful also for the help provided by the Grant-in-Aid Fund of the English Department of Cornell University.

For permission to quote I am indebted to the following: to Random House for works by William Faulkner as here listed— *Absalom, Absalom! As I Lay Dying, Collected Stories of William Faulkner, A Fable, Go Down, Moses, The Hamlet, Intruder in the Dust, Light in August, Pylon, Requiem for a Nun, Sanctuary, The Sound and the Fury, The Town, The Unvanquished, The Wild Palms,* and *The Faulkner Reader;* to Dent & Sons for Joseph Conrad's *Youth and Two Other Stories;* to Kenkyusha Ltd. for *Faulkner at Nagano,* edited by Robert A. Jelliffe; to *The Reporter* and Irving Howe for the latter's article "Thirteen Who Mutinied: Faulkner's First World War"; to the *New York Times* and Harvey Breit for the latter's article "A Walk with Faulkner"; to *PMLA* and C. Hugh Holman for the latter's article "The Unity of Faulkner's *Light in August*"; and to Michigan

State College Press for *William Faulkner: Two Decades of Criticism*, edited by F. J. Hoffman and O. W. Vickery. Parts of this book appeared originally in *Twentieth Century Literature* under the title "The Edge of Order: The Pattern of Faulkner's Rhetoric"; these are reprinted with the kind permission of the editors.

WALTER J. SLATOFF

Ithaca, New York
January 1960

References and Abbreviations

THE abbreviations and editions of Faulkner's works used in this study are as follows. All the editions are published at New York by Random House unless otherwise noted. *AA: Absalom, Absalom!* (Modern Library, 1951); *AILD: As I Lay Dying* (Modern Library, 1946); *CS: Collected Stories* (1950); *F: A Fable* (1954); *GDM: Go Down, Moses* (1942); *H: The Hamlet* (1940); *ID: Intruder in the Dust* (1948); *LIA: Light in August* (Modern Library, 1950); *MCS: Mirrors of Chartres Street* (Minneapolis: Faulkner Studies, 1953); *P: Pylon* (New York: Harrison Smith and Robert Haas, 1935); *RN: Requiem for a Nun* (1950); *S: Sanctuary* (Modern Library, 1932); *SF: The Sound and the Fury* (Modern Library, 1946); *T: The Town* (1957); *U: The Unvanquished* (1938); *WP: The Wild Palms* (1939).

Contents

QUEST FOR FAILURE:

A Study of William Faulkner

Introduction

IN William Faulkner's short story "Delta Autumn," Ike Mc-
Caslin says that "the heart dont always have time to bother
with thinking up words that fit together" (*GDM*, 348). In
Absalom, Absalom! when Charles Bon leaves for college, Faulkner describes him as "almost touching the answer, aware of the
jigsaw puzzle picture integers of it waiting, almost lurking, just
beyond his reach, inextricable, jumbled, and unrecognizable yet
on the point of falling into pattern which would reveal to him
at once, like a flash of light, the meaning of his whole life"
(p. 313). The integers never do fall into place for Charles Bon.
Much the same can be said about Benjy and Quentin Compson,
Darl Bundren, Gail Hightower, Thomas Sutpen, and numerous
other characters in Faulkner's novels.

Every Faulkner novel in some way provides the reader with
the problem of fitting pieces together, and many readers of
Faulkner feel with respect to the meanings of the novels much
as Charles Bon did about the meaning of his life. Much Faulkner
criticism has been devoted to explaining, both in particular
novels and in his works in general, how the pieces do fit together, the patterns of meaning they do form. A good many
such patterns have been discovered and offered as the essential
meanings of the novels and of Faulkner's vision as a whole. Indeed, so many and such varied and divergent patterns have been

offered that viewed in a body they do not so much clarify the works as provide a puzzle of their own.

Most simply stated, this book is about some important ways in which Faulkner's words and larger units of language and thought do and do not fit together. It advances the thesis that a crucial aspect of Faulkner's work is the number and variety of things in it which do not fit together or which are yoked by a relationship which does not resemble a fitting marriage nearly so much as it does that between Houston and his wife in *The Hamlet*, who are "chained irrevocably . . . not by love but by implacable constancy and invincible repudiation" (*H*, 237).

I suppose some readers may find this a thesis-ridden book; if it is, I believe it has been made so by the compelling quality of the thesis itself, rather than by my own efforts to prove it, for, in fact, I did not set out with a thesis in mind but with quite another intention. That this was true, that my conclusions were, in a sense, unsought, makes me more confident of their validity. For most novels, and especially those of Faulkner, are so rich and varied that seekers will usually find in them what they are looking for. At the same time, as with many unforeseen journeys, this one has involved certain changes in direction and requires some explanation.

My initial intention was a comparatively limited one. I wanted to see what I could discover about Faulkner's fictional world by giving it the kind of close textual scrutiny that most critics now give to poetry and that some critics have given to individual novels. This sort of examination of Faulkner seemed particularly necessary in view of the wide differences of opinion among critics over almost every aspect of his work. And since it appeared that "evidence" for almost any interpretation of Faulkner could be found in the novels, I felt that the most pressing question we had to ask about his works was not what was discoverable in them, but what was persistent in them. Therefore I set out to discover and trace the most persistent elements in Faulkner's moment-to-moment presentation of experience, those things which he emphasized consistently throughout his works.

Although I began without any firm preconceptions as to what sorts of elements I would find, my examination was governed largely by the notion that a fictional world is in great part ordered and characterized by the modes of perception and thought embodied in it. These modes at once shape and are evident in the rhetoric which presents that world. Thus the experience of encountering a fictional world, in part, seems comparable to having a guide through the real world who subtly and irresistibly commands one to note color at one point, to compare two velocities at another, to ignore a vase of flowers and instead watch a heel crush a cigarette butt, to be blind to the shape of a man's face but to note how still it is or how sullen. That guide becomes, in effect, the sensory and cognitive apparatus through which one perceives the world. The presence of a guide, a selective mind, means continual imposition of form and continual interpretation. I assumed that, by investigating the kinds of things the guide most persistently emphasized and the kinds of relationships he habitually pointed out, one would come to understand a good deal about the kind of experience one had had and about the shape of the fictional world one had encountered. I assumed, also, of course, that such an investigation would provide some insight into Faulkner's vision and view of life and into the workings of his mind, but my chief concern, at first, was the surface and texture of his fictional world rather than the vision or mind which lay behind it.

As I continued, however, to trace the persistent elements of Faulkner's rhetoric and perception, the particular aspects of experience which he stressed continually, I became increasingly aware of something much more significant and pervasive. This was Faulkner's fascination with a certain kind of relationship, a relationship which seemed to dominate his presentation regardless of the sorts of experiences or entities he was dealing with. And the more I investigated this relationship, the more I became interested in the problem of Faulkner's coherence and in what I have called his "polar imagination" and "quest for failure." I came to feel, finally, that these aspects of his work were the most crucial.

This gradual shift in focus and intention has made for certain problems of presentation. On the one hand, my central thesis, as finally developed, does not require the extensive and detailed descriptions of surface and texture demanded by my original intentions, nor are all aspects of these descriptions directly relevant to my thesis. On the other hand, I believe that these descriptions have value, in themselves, as studies in the lineaments of a fictional world and as experiments with a method of examining fiction. To have reshaped them in such a way as to give the most direct and efficient support to my final conclusions would have been to strip them of much of their independent value. I compromised, of course, by reshaping them a little. The persistent elements, then, described in Part I and to some extent in Part II, should be viewed not simply as evidence supporting a larger thesis but also as aspects of Faulkner's presentation which in their own right have much to do with the shape and impact of his fictional world.

The reader, at times, especially in Part I, may become impatient with the amount of evidence I present. My concern with the persistence of elements and with the texture of Faulkner's world, however, makes copious illustration necessary. Furthermore, the always unsafe assumption that a few illustrations are representative is especially dangerous when considering Faulkner's works, which already have provided "evidence" to support so many divergent interpretations. I cannot underscore this too heavily. Recent interpretation of Faulkner has been generally perceptive, intelligent, and provocative, but far too much of it has rested upon extremely limited evidence. If I am even partially correct about the essential nature of Faulkner's art, interpreters of his work must pay peculiarly careful attention to the adequacy of their evidence. If I am entirely correct, even that may not be sufficient.

PART I

Persistent Patterns of
Rhetoric and Perception

Motion and Immobility

WHEN we try deliberately to remember or describe a fictional world, we are most likely to think primarily of its broad general structure and outline, of the remarkable events which have occurred in it, of the unusual people who have inhabited it, and of the striking peculiarities of the vision which created it. We tend, as we usually do in recalling our experience of the real world, to overlook our moment-to-moment process of perception and sensation which more than anything else gives our experience its body and texture and much of its particular flavor. And we tend to forget that this moment-to-moment experience is largely the experience of encountering a world already perceived, perceived not only in its main outlines but in all its detail. Thus we sometimes speak of a work of fiction as a "slice of life," forgetting that there is inevitably a high degree of selection, both conscious and unconscious, and therefore form and interpretation, in the construction of every sentence, in the mention, to say nothing of the description, of every object, action, or state of mind—forgetting that the mention of a cigarette butt or of the odor of armpits is no less a selection, has nothing more or less to do with reality, than the mention of a lover's sigh or of the odor of a rose, and that even when a novelist says merely a character "did not move" he has made a choice to tell us this and not something else and that he has chosen one out of numerous ways to express it.

But even if we are not usually aware of this moment-to-moment process of selection and arrangement, it seems safe to assume that it has much to do with determining the nature of a fictional world and the kind of impact it has upon us. And it seems safe to assume, also, that a study of that process will reveal much about the creator of such a world.

In this and the next three chapters I shall attempt to describe some of the most persistent emphases and patterns in Faulkner's moment-to-moment presentation of experience, emphases and patterns which, as much as anything else, I believe, provide the body, texture, and flavor of the fictional world we recognize as William Faulkner's.

In describing a facial expression of Byron Bunch during a conversation with Hightower in *Light in August,* Faulkner is not content simply to note, "He grimaces faintly," or even to add, "It is not a smile. His upper lip just lifts momentarily." He goes on to report "the movement, even the surface wrinkling, travelling no further and vanishing almost at once" (pp. 67–68). During that conversation Faulkner notes six times that Hightower is motionless. When Byron tells Hightower that Joe Christmas is part Negro, Faulkner writes:

He [Hightower] does not move. For a moment longer he does not move. Then there seems to come over his whole body, as if its parts were mobile like face features, that shrinking and denial, and Byron sees that the still, flaccid, big face is suddenly slick with sweat. [p. 78]

When Joe Christmas tells the waitress, Bobbie, about his Negro blood, we find again an emphasis upon movement and a contrast of immobility and motion.

Then she lay perfectly still, with a different stillness. . . . He lay peacefully too, his hand slow up and down her flank. "You're what?" she said.

"I think I got some nigger blood in me." . . . his hand slow and unceasing. . . .

She did not move. She said at once: "You're lying."

"All right," he said, not moving, his hand not ceasing. [p. 171]

When Jody Varner signs a contract with Ab Snopes in *The Hamlet*, Faulkner places immobility and motion in antithesis by describing "one broad black-haired hand motionless and heavy as a ham of meat on the paper and the pen in the other tracing the words of the contract in his heavy deliberate sprawling script" (p. 14).

In *Pylon*, Shumann, the racing pilot, and the reporter are on a moving train:

The reporter did not move yet and the brightness and intensity and gravity had not altered as he watched the deliberate, unhurried, slightly awkward movement of the pen across the blank signature line. . . . But he did not move even then; it was not until the pen without stopping dropped down to the third line and was writing again that he leaned and stopped it with his hand. [p. 212]

A few lines later, Faulkner notes again that the reporter did not move. He then reports that "the train began to slow; . . . the vineshrouded station flowed up, slowing; it would not quite pass" (p. 213).

In *The Hamlet*, Ratliff and Flem Snopes are bargaining:

And he [Ratliff] saw it—an instant, a second of a new and completer stillness and immobility touch the blank face. . . . For that instant even the jaw had stopped chewing, though it began again almost at once. . . . Ratliff had not moved. And now just for another instant Ratliff believed he saw the jaw stop. . . . And then he knew that the jaw had stopped chewing. It did not move at all during the full minute while the broad impenetrable face hung suspended like a balloon above the soiled dog-eared paper. [pp. 96–97]

In *As I Lay Dying*, when Addie Bundren dies, Dewey Dell leans above the bed, "the fan still moving like it has for ten days." She begins to keen,

the fan still moving steadily up and down. . . . Then she flings herself across Addie Bundren's knees, clutching her, shaking her with
the furious strength of the young before sprawling suddenly across
the handful of rotten bones that Addie Bundren left, . . . the fan
in one hand still beating with expiring breath into the quilt. [p. 372]

Eventually the fan becomes "motionless on the fading quilt."
When her father tells her she might as well lay out supper, she
"does not move." Then she "rises, heaving to her feet" (p. 374).

Pa "stands over the bed, dangle-armed, humped, motionless.
He raises his hand to his head, scouring his hair. . . . He comes
nearer and rubs his hand, palm and back, on his thigh and lays
it on her face and then on the hump of quilt where her hands
are." He tries to smooth the quilt with clumsy motions and
finally "desists, his hand falling to his side and stroking itself
again, palm and back, on his thigh" (p. 375).

Vardaman "begins to move slowly backward from the bed
. . . his pale face fading into the dusk like a piece of paper
pasted on a failing wall, and so out of the door" (p. 372). Once
outside he begins to run: "I run . . . to the edge of the porch
and stop." He thinks of his mother's death in terms of a race:
"And now she is getting so far ahead I cannot catch her." He
"jump[s] from the porch, running. The top of the barn comes
swooping up out of the twilight" (p. 376). In the barn he
touches Jewel's horse: "The life in him runs under the skin,
under my hands. . . . I can smell the life running up from
under my hands, up my arms" (pp. 376–377). He finds a stick
and "run[s] across the lot and into the road," in order to punish
the horses of Dr. Peabody, whom he blames for his mother's
death. The horses watch as "I run up, beginning to jerk back."
They rear and plunge as he strikes them. "I run this way and
that as they rear and jerk at the hitch-rein." Then the horses
wheel

in a long lunge, the buggy wheeling on to two wheels and motionless
like it is nailed to the ground and the horses motionless like they are
nailed by the hind feet to the center of a whirling-plate.

I run in the dust. I cannot see, running in the sucking dust where the buggy vanishes tilted on two wheels. I strike, the stick hitting into the ground, bouncing, striking into the dust and then into the air again and the dust sucking on down the road faster than if a car was in it. [p. 377]

He goes back to the barn and "run[s]" at a cow. "She jumps back and whirls away and stops, watching me. She moans. She goes on to the path and stands there, looking up the path." He watches as Cash "comes to the hill, limping," "comes down the path stiffly," and "turns and limps up the path" (p. 378). After the funeral service:

Motionless, the tall buzzards hang in soaring circles, the clouds giving them an illusion of retrograde.

Motionless, wooden-backed, wooden-faced, he [Jewel] shapes the horse in a rigid stoop like a hawk, hook-winged. They are waiting for us, ready for the moving of it [Addie's body]. [p. 406]

These are a few illustrations of Faulkner's emphasis upon motion, immobility, and velocity, and of his antithesis of motion and immobility. They might be replaced by many hundreds of others. Chosen largely for their brevity and explicitness, they are by no means the most striking examples; nor do they begin to suggest the persistence of this emphasis throughout his works or the power he often achieves by it. Yet even in these few illustrations we may notice that the description of motion is not merely embellishment but an integral part of his presentation. Faulkner has not simply called to our attention the movements of his characters, though certainly he has done that, but he has to a large extent made motion and immobility part of the very form and texture of experiences and events.

The emphasis on motion is most striking, as might be expected, in those works which are built primarily around protracted physical movements such as journeys, races, pursuits, and flights: *As I Lay Dying, Light in August,*[1] *Pylon,* the "Old

[1] The remarkable persistence and intensity of Faulkner's emphasis on motion in *Light in August* becomes apparent when one compares Faulkner's description of Lena Grove's journey with the somewhat similar

Man" sections of *The Wild Palms*, "Retreat" and "Raid" from *The Unvanquished*, "The Long Summer" from *The Hamlet*, "The Old People" and "The Bear" from *Go Down, Moses*, "Red Leaves," "A Courtship," "Fox Hunt," and "The Hound." These works testify most dramatically and completely to the persistence and strength of this emphasis. Not only are they thematically and symbolically heavily dependent upon movements, but almost every page of them will supply examples of Faulkner's descriptive focus upon motion, immobility, and velocity. From a rhetorical point of view it would be most effective to dwell upon these works or to focus upon a single one of them like "Red Leaves" in which virtually every event, internal and external, is rendered as motion, but the most conclusive evidence of Faulkner's preoccupation with motion is his persistent emphasis upon it even in those works where there is least need for it.

In *The Sound and the Fury*, for example, where the themes and plot would seem to demand little focus upon characters' movements, and where the first person points of view might be expected to make such narration difficult, we still find an immense concern with motion. Indeed, we receive almost as full an account of Benjy's and Quentin's movements as we do of their thoughts and emotions. The novel begins with Benjy moving about the Compson grounds, watching the movements of the players on the golf course. It ends with his carriage ride with Luster, an unforgettable description of motion and sound.

Quentin seems almost as obsessed with motion as he does with his relationship to his sister. When he looks out of his window he watches the students "running for chapel . . . the same books and flapping collars flushing past like debris on a flood." He notes Spoade in the middle of the runners "like a terrapin in a street full of scuttering dead leaves . . . moving at his customary unhurried walk. . . . The others passed him run-

---

journeys of Tess in Thomas Hardy's *Tess of the D'Urbervilles* and Hetty in George Eliot's *Adam Bede*.

ning, but he never increased his pace at all" (pp. 97–98). About
to leave the building, he watches the movements of his shadow:
"The shadow hadn't quite cleared the stoop. I stopped inside
the door, watching the shadow move. It moved almost per-
ceptibly, creeping back inside the door, driving the shadow
back into the door" (p. 100). Immediately following this his
mind moves to Caddy's wedding, which he visualizes almost
entirely as a running:

> Only she was running already when I heard it. In the mirror she
> was running before I knew what it was. That quick, her train caught
> up over her arm she ran out of the mirror like a cloud, her veil swirl-
> ing in long glints her heels brittle and fast clutching her dress onto
> her shoulder with the other hand, running out of the mirror. . . .
> Then she was across the porch I couldn't hear her heels then in the
> moonlight like a cloud, the floating shadow of the veil running across
> the grass, into the bellowing. She ran out of her dress, clutching her
> bridal, running into the bellowing. [pp. 100–101]

Throughout he has an intense awareness of his own movements:

> She moved along just under my elbow. We went on. . . . She
> moved along just under my elbow. . . . Then I ran.
> I ran fast, not looking back. . . . I ran on.
> A lane turned from the road. I entered it and after awhile I slowed
> to a fast walk. . . . I slowed still more, my shadow pacing me, drag-
> ging its head through the weeds that hid the fence. [pp. 151–152]

Jason's movements about town and his desperate chase of
Quentin fill a large part of the narration and description of the
sections devoted to him. Dilsey's movements are described with
particularly painstaking detail (e.g., pp. 287–288).

In *Absalom, Absalom!* the narrative emphasis on motion is
less continuous than in any other longer work, especially in
those sections narrated by Rosa Coldfield, whose preoccupation
with internal states is such that she is largely blind to external
ones. Yet her own physical and mental condition, and that of
most of the other characters, is often rendered as a dynamic

immobility, a running without movement,[2] and the notion of simultaneous movement and immobility is perhaps the metaphorical matrix of the entire work. Then, too, much of Sutpen's history is the narration of movement. This history, so far as we are acquainted with it, begins with the wagon trip from West Virginia, "an attenuation from a kind of furious inertness and patient immobility, . . . a sort of dreamy and destinationless locomotion . . . during which they did not seem to progress at all" (p. 224). At the end of his life he stands motionless after learning of his failure to produce a son. He "didn't move at all" while the terrified midwife wants to run but cannot move. When Sutpen leaves, "she found out that she could move, get up, run out of the cabin and into the weeds, running——" (p. 286). Then Sutpen's body lies outside the cabin while Wash, who has killed him, decides not to flee,

it seeming to him probably that he had no less to run from than he had to run to; that if he ran he would be fleeing merely one set of bragging and evil shadows for another, . . . too old to run far even if he were to run who could never escape them, no matter how much or how far he ran; a man past sixty could not be expected to run that far. [pp. 289–290]

Sutpen bequeaths to one son "flesh and bone and spirit . . . which sprang in quiet peace and contentment and ran in steady even though monotonous sunlight," and to another that which "sprang in hatred and outrage and unforgiving and ran in shadow" (pp. 317–318).

Charlotte and Harry's rebellion against convention and respectability in *The Wild Palms* is not a stand, but a flight, a literal and spiritual running away. At the end Charlotte sits "all day long in a new cheap beach chair facing the water . . . not doing anything, just sitting there in that complete immobility, . . . that complete immobile abstraction from which even pain and terror are absent" (p. 5). Harry is "seen usually walking

[2] See especially pp. 137–142.

barefoot along the beach at tide-edge . . . passing the immobile woman in the beach chair with no sign from her, no movement of the head or perhaps even of the eyes." [3]

In *Intruder in the Dust,* in which much of the dialogue takes place in moving vehicles, the narration and description of motion is so persistent that it is difficult to decide upon specific examples. Especially vivid, however, are the description of the sheriff's arrival back in town after discovering the evidence which clears Lucas (pp. 180–183), and the description of the mob's flight:

the Square not empty yet, . . . the khaki and denim and the printed cotton streaming into it and across it toward the parked cars and trucks, clotting and crowding at the doors while one by one they crawled and climbed into the seats and beds and cabs; already starters were whining and engines catching and racing and idling and gears scraping and grinding while the passengers still hurried toward them and now not one but five or six at once backed away from the curb and turned and straightened out with people still running toward them and scrambling aboard, . . . watching them condense into four streams into the four main streets leading out of town in the four directions, already going fast even before they were out of the Square, the faces for one last moment more looking not back but out, . . . vanishing rapidly in profile and seeming already to be travelling much faster than the vehicle which bore them. [4]

One of the most delightful passages in Faulkner and one completely dominated by motion, is his description of Miss Habersham's effort to drive her truck through one of these streams of fleeing cars (pp. 187–188).

The problems of the exhausted and overstimulated Charlie when he gets home after the flight of the mob are all related to movement. He has the problem of accepting the fact that the crowd "ran," a word he repeats again and again, the problem of

[3] Pages 5–6. Compare the emphasis on motion in the hospital scene (pp. 295–307) with that in the hospital scene in Dos Passos, *Manhattan Transfer* (New York: Harper, 1925), pp. 5–10.

[4] *ID,* 184. Compare the description of the square on pp. 235–238 and in *Sanctuary,* pp. 132–133, where the emphasis is upon much slower motion.

moving his own exhausted body, and the problem of the movement of his overstimulated mind, which is still deeply involved
in the unfinished adventure:

. . . the need not to finish anything but just to keep moving not
even to remain where they were but just desperately to keep up with
it like having to run on a treadmill not because you wanted to be
where the treadmill was but simply not to be flung pell mell still running frantically backward off the whole stage out of sight, and not
waiting static for the moment to flow back into him again and explode
him up into motion but rather already in endless motion like the
treadmill's endless band, . . . safe only so long as he did not move.
So he moved. . . . [pp. 197–198]

Especially noteworthy in *Requiem for a Nun* is the fifty-page
section called "The Jail," in which history, progress, and change
are rendered primarily by means of metaphors of motion and
stasis and by sharp antitheses of motion and immobility. For
example, in 1861,

The destiny of the land, the nation, the South, the State, the County,
was already whirling into the plunge of its precipice . . . and now
not only the jail but the town too hung without motion in a tideless
backwash: the plunging body advanced far enough now into space
as to have lost all sense of motion, weightless and immobile upon the
light pressure of invisible air. [pp. 229–230]

In *A Fable*, which is in its entirety as much a pageant and
procession as a novel and in which motion and immobility play
a large thematic and symbolic role, the opening chapter is a
particularly good example of how completely narrative and
description can be dominated by reports of motion, immobility,
and relative velocity.

So far I have focused chiefly upon Faulkner's extended narration and description of motion and have kept in the background
the most striking aspect of his emphasis upon motion—his
imagery. I have done so because I have wished, above all, to
suggest the continuousness and persistence of Faulkner's con-

cern with motion and the degree to which it is a part of the texture of his world and not merely an intermittent phenomenon.

In a highly compressed image such as "empty carcasses [of hogs] immobilised by the heels in attitudes of frantic running" (*ID*, 4), the antithesis of motion and immobility is more tense and striking than it would be in more extended description. It seems likely, however, that the cumulative effect of the looser but generally pervasive sorts of antithesis may be just as great or greater.

Faulkner's images, however, do present the most dramatic testimony to his preoccupation with motion and to his tendency to juxtapose or simultaneously suggest motion and immobility. Numerous critics have been impressed by the prevalence of images of stasis or arrested motion, and certainly such images are an important and characteristic part of his style and vision. One cannot read very far in Faulkner without coming upon an image of a frozen action. The image may present a literal suspension of movement, as in this passage from *The Hamlet*.

For an instant Varner did not move at all, his leg still extended, the plug and the severed chew in one hand and the knife in the other just about to enter his pocket. None of them moved in fact, looking quietly and attentively at their hands or at wherever their eyes had been when Varner interrupted himself. [p. 62]

Or the primary purpose of the image may be symbolic:

the beast the plow and the man integrated in one foundationed into the frozen wave of their furrow tremendous with effort yet at the same time vacant of progress, ponderable immovable and immobile like groups of wrestling statuary set against the land's immensity. [*ID*, 147]

It is important to recognize, however, that images such as these, while exceedingly common, are merely extreme examples of the same kind of perception which persistently informs Faulkner's description and imagery and that they are only one variety in an incredibly large class of images which involve a similar sort of antithesis and tension.

The opposition may simply be between the relative velocities of two objects, entities, or actions:

Already running, he passed another Negro. The two men, the one motionless and the other running, looked for an instant at each other. [CS, 331]

My entire being seemed to run at blind full tilt into something monstrous and immobile. [AA, 139]

He was working fast, yet thinking went slow enough. [LIA, 351]

It may be between the apparent and actual velocities of a single entity or unit:

Without ceasing to run she appeared to pause. [S, 56]

He turned into the road at that slow and ponderous gallop, the two of them, man and beast, leaning a little stiffly forward as though in some juggernautish simulation of terrific speed although the actual speed itself was absent. [LIA, 176]

A most remarkable number of horses, mules, wagons, buggies, motor vehicles, and trains are similarly described.

The engine is in sight now. . . . It has an effect of terrific nomotion. Yet it does move, creeping terrifically up and over the crest of the grade. . . . He watches the engine approach and pass him, laboring, crawling. . . . It passes; his eye moves on, watching the cars as they in turn crawl up and over the crest, when for the second time that afternoon he sees a man materialize apparently out of the air, in the act of running.[5]

Very often, as in the last illustration or in the image of the immobile frantically running hogs, the tension becomes extreme because the image opposes suggestions not simply of immobility and motion but of immobility and violent or "terrific" motion or effort to move:

[5] LIA, 386. See also, for example, LIA, 7; SF, 143; AILD, 345–346, 377, 413; S, 162–163; AA, 224–225; U, 111–112; GDM, 320–322; ID, 184.

It [the horse] slowed into the curb and stopped. . . . Yet still the rider leaned forward in the arrested saddle, in the attitude of terrific speed. [*LIA*, 183]

Motionless, facing one another like the first position of a dance, they stood in a mounting terrific muscular hiatus. [*S*, 114]

electric furious immobile urgency. [*AA*, 160]

On numerous occasions the opposed suggestions are confined in phrases like "poised and swooping immobility" (*P*, 77), "terrific immobility" (*P*, 64), or "dynamic immobility" (*AILD*, 392), where the antithesis achieves the compactness and tension of the oxymoron.

In most of the illustrations so far, the actions described have been physical ones. Faulkner's treatment of psychological events and his figurative language are characterized by a similar emphasis on motion and a similar tendency to place motion and immobility or differing velocities in tense antithesis. Quentin Compson describes his mental and sensory experience in a schoolroom:

Then the minds would go away, and after a while I'd be afraid I had gotten behind and I'd count fast and fold down another finger, then I'd be afraid I was going too fast and I'd slow up, then I'd get afraid and count fast again. So I never could come out even with the bell, and the released surging of feet moving already . . . and my insides would move, sitting still. *Moving sitting still.*[6]

A remarkable number of important psychological experiences are rendered in almost identical terms. In the scene in *Light in August* describing Joe's discovery that the waitress is about to flee, we read that when he sees her packed luggage "perhaps looking saw once, faster than thought" (p. 186). A moment later, in referring to the same event, Faulkner writes that Joe

[6] *SF*, 107. For comparable scenes which lack an emphasis on motion, see James Joyce, *A Portrait of the Artist as a Young Man* (New York: Modern Library, 1928), pp. 7-8, 48, 51, 56.

had looked at the piled luggage "while thought went faster
than seeing," an interesting reversal of terms, about which I shall
have more to say later. In the same scene Joe is described as
"running . . . as a man might run far ahead of himself and
his knowing in the act of stopping stock still," and a moment
later we read that "though Joe had not moved since he entered,
he was still running. When Max touched his shoulder he turned
as if he had been halted in midstride" (p. 187).

In *Absalom, Absalom!* Rosa Coldfield attempts to communicate a crucial experience in much the same way. She describes
Clytie's face as "stopping me dead (not my body: it still advanced, ran on: but I, myself, that deep existence which we
lead." Clytie emanates a "furious yet absolutely rocklike and
immobile antagonism," and her body "without moving . . .
seemed to elongate and project upward something" (p. 137). A
little later we read, "Then she touched me, and then I did stop
dead. Possibly even then my body did not stop, since I seemed
to be aware of it thrusting blindly still against the solid yet im-
ponderable weight . . . of that will to bar me from the stairs"
(p. 139). The two women are then placed in an opposition in
which each is described in terms suggesting simultaneous motion
and immobility: "We just stood there—I motionless in the attitude and action of running, she rigid in that furious immobility" (p. 140). A moment later, having run upstairs, she sees
Judith: "and I stopped in running's midstride again though my
body, blind unsentient barrow of deluded clay and breath, still
advanced" (p. 142).

In *Sanctuary* many of Temple's responses are similarly described, although in her case it is her body which usually remains immobile while her self or spirit runs on. At one point
she stands and "watch[es] herself run out of her body" (p.
109). An especially intriguing description of this sort of condition is that of the reporter in *Pylon* as "apparently having already rushed on and out of his precarious body so that only the
shell glared back" (p. 220).

Faulkner often uses similar metaphors to render the actions of minds and senses. Shumann, the pilot in *Pylon*, looks at a note "with that baffled immobility behind which the mind flicks and darts like a terrier inside a fence" (p. 215). The Negro in "Red Leaves" "looked this way and that continuously . . . as though sight never quite caught up with looking" (*CS*, 339). A character in *The Wild Palms* is described as feeling and hearing the "cogs" of his mind, "clicking, going fast; he felt a need for terrific haste in order to keep up, a premonition that the final cog would click and the bell of comprehension ring and he would not be quite near enough to see and hear" (pp. 11–12).

The phantasies and confusions of characters are frequently built upon figures of motion. Examples have already been given for Vardaman and Quentin.[7] In Horace Benbow's phantasy about Little Belle in *Sanctuary* she is "bound naked on her back on a flat car moving at speed through a black tunnel, the blackness streaming in rigid threads overhead" (p. 268). The confusions and symbols of Wash Jones in *Absalom, Absalom!* (p. 287) and of Hightower in *Light in August* primarily involve figures on galloping horses. Even in the pulpit Hightower "couldn't get religion and that galloping cavalry and his dead grandfather shot from the galloping horse untangled from one another" (p. 53). For Faulkner, too, it seems clear, the figure on the galloping horse is an important and disturbing, and perhaps not entirely bridled, symbol.

Death and the decay of the body and even of the world are frequently presented in metaphors of motion and velocity:

The body still ran, still retained a similitude of power and even speed, would even run on for yards and perhaps even miles, and then for years in a gnawing burrow of worms, but that which tasted air and drank the sun was dead. [*P*, 182]

the friction of the earth on its axis, approaching that moment when it must decide to turn on or to remain forever still: a motionless ball in cooling space. [*S*, 267]

[7] See above, pp. 10, 13, 19.

Conditions and actions of man's moral as well as psychological and physical being are similarly rendered. Moral weakness is almost always dramatized as a fleeing or running away. Here is Brown, finally compelled to face Lena, from whom he has already once fled,

holding his eyes up to hers like two beasts about to break. . . . Yet still she could watch his mind darting and darting, . . . watched him fumble and flee and tack until at last all that remained in him of pride . . . fled from him. [*LIA*, 376]

After this he again takes to flight. In the face of Charlotte's "unwinking yellow stare" Wilbourne "seemed to blunder and fumble like a moth, a rabbit caught in the glare of a torch" (*WP*, 87). Sutpen becomes bogged down "in his morality which had all the parts but which refused to run, to move" (*AA*, 279).

In a number of cases great segments of the life experience of an individual or group are rendered as motion or flight. In *Light in August*, after Joe Christmas has left McEachern's and has been betrayed by the waitress, "he entered the street which was to run for fifteen years" (p. 195). Faulkner repeats the metaphor eight times in three pages. The passage ends: "But the street ran on: catlike. . . . But the street ran on in its moods and phases, always empty: he might have seen himself as in numberless avatars, in silence, doomed with motion." [8]

Rosa Coldfield of *Absalom, Absalom!* describes a period of her life as a "dream-state in which you run without moving from a terror in which you cannot believe" (p. 142). Ab Snopes's son is described as

moving, running, outside the house, toward the stable: this the old habit, the old blood which he had not been permitted to choose for himself, . . . which had run for so long (and who knew where, battening on what of outrage and savagery and lust) before it came to him. [*CS*, 21]

[8] *LIA*, 197. See also Gavin Stevens' "explanation" of Joe's life and behavior, p. 393.

In the section of *Requiem for a Nun* called "The Jail," history itself is presented largely as a velocity. Even cotton becomes "petty globules of Motion" (p. 227). The existence of the old jail amid the rush of progress is

like the track-walker in the tunnel, the thunder of the express mounting behind him, who finds himself opposite a niche or crack exactly his size in the wall's living and impregnable rock, and steps into it, inviolable and secure while destruction roars past and on and away, grooved ineluctably to the spidery rails of its destiny and destination. [p. 248]

At the end of "Carcassonne," which may be read as an allegory of the body and soul or of the struggle of the artist, Faulkner writes:

I want to perform something bold and tragical and austere, . . . me on a buckskin pony with eyes like blue electricity and a mane like tangled fire, galloping up the hill and right off into the high heaven of the world. Still galloping, the horse soars outward; still galloping, it thunders up the long blue hill of heaven, its tossing mane in golden swirls like fire. Steed and rider thunder on, thunder punily diminishing: a dying star upon the immensity of darkness and of silence within which, steadfast, fading, deepbreasted and grave of flank, muses the dark and tragic figure of the Earth, his mother. [CS, 899–900]

One way of regarding Faulkner's emphasis upon motion is to think of it as choreography and to see Faulkner as presenting in great measure a dance,[9] a dance not only of humans, but of mules, buggies, planes, and trains, and even involving entities like vernal equinoxes which come with "galloping fury" and winds which run back and forth "like a drove of bridleless horses in an empty plain" (*WP*, 313) and including even the earth itself, spinning, slowing, or racing toward destruction. It is a relatively simple and stylized dance, many of whose

[9] For a report of an actual dance interpretation of *As I Lay Dying*, see Truman Capote, "Faulkner Dances," *Theatre Arts*, XXXIII (April, 1949), 49.

effects depend merely upon the juxtaposition of immobile bodies and moving ones and upon tableau, sometimes peaceful, more often full of muscular tension. At times the dance is macabre or violent. On occasion we may feel we are watching Apache dancers in a pseudo-French night club in New York:

He came toward her, lifting his hand. . . . He gripped her arm, slowly. . . .

Slowly he drew her out of the door. . . . Motionless, facing one another like the first position of a dance, they stood in a mounting terrific muscular hiatus.

With scarce any movement at all he flung her aside in a complete revolution that fetched her up against the table, her arm flung back for balance, her body bent and her hand fumbling behind her among the soiled dishes, watching him across the inert body of the child. He walked toward her. "Stand back," she said, lifting her hand slightly, bringing the butcher knife into view. . . . He came steadily toward her, then she struck at him with the knife.

He caught her wrist. She began to struggle. He . . . caught her other hand as it flicked at his face, and holding both wrists in one hand, he slapped her . . . first on one cheek, then the other, rocking her head from side to side. . . . He released her. She stumbled backward against the table and caught up the child and half crouched between the table and the wall, watching him as he turned and left the room. [S, 113–114]

At its best and most powerful, however, the dance achieves the simplicity, stylization, and dignity of ritual, as in parts of the chapter in *Light in August* describing the last flight and death of Joe Christmas, or throughout "Red Leaves" and "The Bear."

Then he saw the bear. It did not emerge, appear: it was just there, immobile, fixed in the green and winkless noon's hot dappling, not as big as he had dreamed it but as big as he had expected, bigger, dimensionless against the dappled obscurity, looking at him. Then it moved. It crossed the glade without haste, walking for an instant into the sun's full glare and out of it, and stopped again and looked back at him across one shoulder. Then it was gone. It didn't walk into the woods. It faded, sank back into the wilderness without motion as he had watched a fish, a huge old bass, sink back into the dark depths of its pool and vanish without even any movement of its fins. [*GDM*, 209]

The presence of this "dance," I believe, accounts for much of Faulkner's power. It does so by virtue of its continual stimulation of kinesthetic and motor responses in the reader. And the stimulation of these responses undoubtedly is greatly responsible for the high degree of empathy which Faulkner's works produce, a matter I shall speak more of later.[10]

Faulkner's emphasis on motion and immobility is, in its own right, a significant aspect of his presentation and has much to do with the shape and impact of his fictional world. But it also forms part of a more general and even more important emphasis, that upon quiescence and turbulence of any sort. Furthermore, his treatment of motion reveals other important aspects of his presentation: his tendency to describe things in rather simple, generalized, and dramatic terms; his tendency to use sharp and tense antithesis; and his tendency to provide opposed and even contradictory suggestions. One effect of these tendencies is to make us respond quite similarly to a surprising variety of objects and events: for example, to an engine moving up a hill (with "an effect of terrific nomotion"); to the carcasses of hogs ("immobilised in attitudes of frantic running"); to Quentin's feelings as school is let out ("moving sitting still");

[10] A number of critics have testified to this empathetic effect. See, for example, Richard H. Rovere, "Introduction," in *LIA*, vi–viii; Malcolm Cowley, *The Portable Faulkner* (New York: Viking Press, 1946), p. 80. Although the precise causes and nature of empathy are unknown, there is general agreement that the phnomenon is largely dependent upon the motor senses and that kinesthetic imagery is capable of affecting those senses and evoking empathetic responses. See Herbert S. Langfeld, *The Aesthetic Attitude* (New York: Harcourt, Brace, 1920), chs. v, vi, pp. 109–154; Clarence DeWitt Thorpe, "Some Notices of Empathy before Lipps," *Papers of the Michigan Academy of Sciences, Literature and the Arts*, XXIII (1937), 525–533; Richard H. Fogle, "Empathetic Imagery in Keats and Shelley," *PMLA*, LXI (1946), 163–191.

and to Rosa Coldfield's deep sense of shock over Henry's shoot-
ing of Charles Bon ("motionless in the attitude and action of
running"). Although our comprehension of these objects and
events is not reduced entirely to a sense of tension between conflicting forces (since we do have other information about their
nature), this sense of tension is undoubtedly the dominant part
of our response. Faulkner's shift, in describing a single event,
from "looking saw once, faster than thought" to "thought went
faster than seeing" suggests that, at times at least, he is concerned chiefly with that sense of tension.

My discussion and illustrations have emphasized the antithesis
of motion and immobility and of differing velocities, and I
shall later make much of Faulkner's general use of antithesis, but
this should not be allowed to obscure the importance of his
concern with motion per se, the remarkable extent to which he
transforms life, virtually all aspects of life, external and internal,
into motion. Faulkner's artistic aims are far more complex than
those he attributes to Charlotte Rittenmeyer, who has become
a sculptress of sorts, but surely he is not speaking of her alone
when he writes:

There was a narrow finger of beach with a buck standing on it, pink
in the Sunday dawn, its head up, watching them for an instant before
it whirled, its white scut arcing in long bounds while Charlotte,
springing from the car . . . ran to the water's edge, squealing.
"That's what I was trying to make!" she cried. "Not the animals, the
dogs and deer and horses: the motion, the speed." [WP, 99–100]

« 2 »

Sound and Silence

ANOTHER persistent element in Faulkner's writing is his emphasis upon sound and silence. It, too, forms part of the more general emphasis on quiescence and turbulence, and it, too, reveals Faulkner's tendency to juxtapose opposites and to make opposing or contradictory suggestions. Although not as utterly pervasive as his emphasis on motion, his concern with sound and silence is nevertheless striking, and significantly helps to shape his fictional world.

Common throughout most of his works are descriptions of the sounds of the natural world. These may be brief: "palm fronds clashing with their wild dry bitter sound" (WP, 8); "somewhere in the swamp a bird sang" (S, 116). Or they may be extended as in the following description from The Hamlet, in which Faulkner alternates sound and silence and also uses concepts and terms of motion, immobility, and velocity.

Now he had the booming of the frogs to guide him, blending and fading then rising again in choral climax, each separate voice not a single note but an octave, almost a chord, in bass, growing louder and louder and nearer and nearer, then ceasing abruptly too into a second of frozen immobility followed by a swift random patter of small splashes like hands striking the water. [pp. 264–265]

Motion also plays a large part in this description from The Sound and the Fury:

27

A pair of jaybirds came up from nowhere, whirled up on the blast [of wind] like gaudy scraps of cloth or paper and lodged in the mulberries, where they swung in raucous tilt and recover, screaming into the wind that ripped their harsh cries onward and away like scraps of paper or of cloth in turn. Then three more joined them and they swung and tilted in the wrung branches for a time, screaming. [p. 282]

In sharp tonal contrast is this passage from *As I Lay Dying:*

Before us the thick dark current runs. It talks up to us in a murmur become ceaseless and myriad. . . .

It clucks and murmurs among the spokes and about the mules' knees. . . . Through the undergrowth it goes with a plaintive sound, a musing sound. . . . [It is] a scene of immense yet circumscribed desolation filled with the voice of the waste and mournful water.[1]

Especially prominent in Faulkner's world are the sounds of animals:

I hear the cow a long time, clopping on the street. Then she comes into the square. She goes across the square, her head down   clopping   . She lows. There was nothing in the square before she lowed, but it wasn't empty. Now it is empty after she lowed. She goes on clopping   . She lows.[2]

The bloodhounds assigned to catch Joe Christmas in *Light in August* are first described as "yap[ing]," "snuffing loudly," and "whimpering" (p. 259). Thinking they have cornered Joe, "they bayed . . . with the passionate abandon of two baritones singing Italian opera" (p. 260). Later, the dogs become lost:

They were not baying now, with pride and assurance and perhaps pleasure. The sound which they now made was a longdrawn and hopeless wailing, while steadily the men shouted at them. But appar-

[1] Pages 438–439. Compare the description of Dilsey's song: "something without particular tune or words, repetitive, mournful and plaintive, austere." The stove fills the room with "murmurous minors of the fire" (*SF*, 286).

[2] *AILD*, 525. The unusual typography follows the text.

ently the animals could not hear either. Both voices were distinguish-
able, yet the bell-like and abject wailing seemed to come from a single
throat, as though the two beasts crouched flank to flank. After a while
the men found them so, crouched in a ditch. By that time their voices
sounded almost like the voices of children.[3]

The sounds of wagons and other vehicles are frequently emphasized or noted. In the following illustration from *Light in
August* Faulkner again presents sounds as having motion and
velocity:

After a while she began to hear the wagon. She heard it for some time.
Then it came into sight, mounting the hill.

The sharp and brittle crack and clatter of its weathered and ungreased wood and metal is slow and terrific: a series of dry sluggish
reports carrying for a half mile across the hot still pinewiney silence
of the August afternoon. . . . As though out of some trivial and unimportant region beyond even distance, the sound of it seems to come
slow and terrific and without meaning, as though it were a ghost
travelling a half mile ahead of its own shape. "That far within my
hearing before my seeing," Lena thinks.[4]

Again and again Faulkner emphasizes sounds which generally
fill the air, like those of bells, chimes, church choirs, sirens, and
amplifiers. In the description from *The Sound and the Fury*
which follows, note that the italicized fragment of consciousness
also has to do with sound, Benjy's only way of expressing his
misery about Caddy's wedding:

The chimes began again, the half hour. I stood in the belly of my
shadow and listened to the strokes spaced and tranquil along the sunlight, among the thin, still little leaves. Spaced and peaceful and serene, with that quality of autumn always in bells even in the month
of brides. *Lying on the ground under the window bellowing.* . . .
The chimes ceased. [p. 119]

[3] Pages 260–261. For other varied descriptions of the sounds of the
natural world, see *SF*, 134, 141, 142; *AILD*, 378, 462; *S*, 2–5, 243; *LIA*, 200,
343; *WP*, 71–72, 281–282; *H*, 207, 286; *GDM*, 240, 353; *ID*, 99–100.

[4] *LIA*, 7. See also pp. 9, 10, 24, 25. For other reports on the sounds of
wagons, see *AILD*, 413, 462; *H*, 183.

In the following briefer descriptions of the sounds of bells, among the many from the same work,[5] observe the ways in which Faulkner gives the sounds solidity.

It was a while before the last stroke ceased vibrating. It stayed in the air, more felt than heard, for a long time. [p. 98]

The three quarters began. The first note sounded, measured and tranquil, serenely peremptory, emptying the unhurried silence for the next one. [p. 194]

The bells were ringing again, high in the scudding sunlight in bright disorderly tatters of sound. [p. 320]

The fire siren in *Light in August* is described as "mounting to a slow and sustained scream that seemed at last to pass beyond the realm of hearing, into that of sense, like soundless vibration" (p. 402). On the following page Faulkner reminds us of the siren three times and, after describing the death of Joe Christmas, ends the chapter: "Again from the town, deadened a little by the walls, the scream of the siren mounted toward its unbelievable crescendo, passing out of the realm of hearing" (p. 407). Amplified music or voices receive emphatic mention in *As I Lay Dying*,[6] *Sanctuary*,[7] and *Intruder in the Dust*[8] and in *Pylon* become an important narrative and symbolic motif.[9]

These are a few of the kinds of sounds which Faulkner emphasizes throughout his works. The sounds which most often claim Faulkner's attention are those of the human voice. I will say nothing here about the astonishing frequency with which he describes these as quiet, for this will be apparent shortly when I consider his emphasis on quiescence and turbulence. An example of his presentation of unquiet voices is the following passage from *Light in August*. McEachern has just caught

---

[5] See, for example, pp. 100, 115, 194, 308, 317, 321. See also *LIA*, 260; *AA*, 31, 343.

[6] See pp. 512, 529, 530, 532.   [7] See pp. 133, 242.

[8] See pp. 236–238.

[9] See, for example, pp. 23, 25, 26, 28, 29, 30, 31, 37, 39.

Joe and the waitress in a dance hall. Note the heightening of intensity achieved by the spatializing term "into" and by the emphasis upon contrasting silence and peace.

"Away, Jezebel!" he said. His voice thundered, into the shocked silence, the shocked surrounding faces beneath the kerosene lamps, into the ceased music, into the peaceful moonlit night of young summer. "Away harlot!" [p. 178]

The loudness is further emphasized by the statement which immediately follows: "Perhaps it did not seem to him that he had been moving fast nor that his voice was loud." A moment later Faulkner focuses upon the sounds of the waitress:

Joe was breathing hard. He could hear it, and also something else, thin and shrill and far away. He seemed to listen to it for a long time before he recognized it for a voice, a woman's voice. He looked and saw two men holding her, . . . her mouth a small jagged hole filled with shrieking. "Calling me a harlot!" she screamed, wrenching at the men who held her. "That old son of a bitch! Let go! Let go!" Then her voice stopped making words again and just screamed. [pp. 178–179]

Soon after this we hear Joe's voice in a description which contrasts motion and immobility and quiescence and turbulence, as well as sound and silence.

"Get out of here!" Joe shouted. He whirled, swinging the chair; yet his face was still quite calm. "Back!" he said, though no one had moved toward him at all. They were all as still and silent as the man on the floor. [p. 179]

On numerous occasions an action or series of actions is rendered entirely from an auditory point of view.

So he didn't move. He lay with his eyes closed, his breathing gentle and peaceful, and heard them one by one leave the tent. He listened to the breakfast sounds from the table beneath the tarpaulin and heard them depart—the horses, the dogs, the last voice until it died away and there was only the sound of the negroes clearing breakfast

away. After a while he might possibly even hear the first faint clear
cry of the first hound ring through the wet woods.

. . . . .

Afterward it seemed to him that he had begun to hear the approaching
boat almost immediately, . . . the mounting snarl of the outboard
engine, increasing, nearer and nearer and louder and louder then cut
short off, ceasing with the absolute instantaneity of a blown out
candle, into the lap and plop of the water under the bows as the skiff
slid into the bank.[10]

Later, when "the mounting then fading whine of the motor"
dies away, the tent holds only "silence and the sound of rain"
(*GDM*, 364).

In each of Faulkner's works particular sounds, or sometimes
absences of sound, become important narrative or symbolic
motifs. In *The Sound and the Fury*, for example, Benjy's
whimpering and bellowing are not only the primary clue to his
own state of mind and his principal means of communicating,
but, as Lawrance Thompson suggests,[11] they also give us insight
into the moral nature of the other characters. In the same
work, time, mortality, and irrevocability are audibly symbolized
throughout by the ticking of Quentin's watch and the sounds of
other time indicators. Other important recurrent sounds are the
music of the carnival band and Dilsey's singing. In *As I Lay
Dying*, Jewel's almost unbroken, tense silence becomes as loud
a testament to his torment as Benjy's roars do to his. The recurrent dry sound of the corn shucks rattling in *Sanctuary* is
symbolic of the hollowness and sterility of the characters and
their lives. Church music and the sounds of insects are prominent in *Light in August*. In *Pylon* "the voice of the amplifier,
apocryphal, sourceless, inhuman, ubiquitous and beyond weari-

---

[10] *GDM*, 355–356; for other examples see *SF*, 259; *S*, 59, 97, 120–121;
LIA, 89–91, 144; *WP*, 70; *U*, 31–37, 94; *H*, 59, 60; *ID*, 102–103. Faulkner
characters are sometimes described as hearing their thinking or listening
to sounds within their bodies. See, for example, *LIA*, 25; *AA*, 329; *H*, 107.

[11] "Mirror Analogues in *The Sound and the Fury*," *English Institute
Essays* (New York: Columbia University Press, 1952), pp. 83–106.

ness or fatigue" (p. 39) becomes a persistent symbol of the mechanical world which has grown out of the wasteland. In *The Wild Palms*, "the palm fronds clashing with their wild dry bitter sound" (p. 8) become a symbol and mocker of Charlotte and Harry's failure. Throughout Chapter 5 the wind, "risible and chuckling," serves as a jeering chorus. In *The Hamlet*, Mink Snopes cannot escape the sound of the gunshot when he killed Houston nor the cry of the hound, "ringing, deep, resonant and filled with grief" (p. 256). Ab and Flem Snopes are characterized by their silences, I. O. Snopes by his noisiness. In *Intruder in the Dust* sound along with motion becomes a symbol of the evils of progress:

but mostly and above all the motion and the noise, the radios and the automobiles—the jukeboxes in the drugstore and the poolhall and the cafe and the bellowing amplifiers on the outside walls not only of the record-and-sheetmusic store but the army-and-navy supply store and both feed stores . . . not to mention the ones which would be running in the apartments and the homes . . . so that nowhere inside the town's uttermost ultimate corporate rim should man woman or child citizen or guest or stranger be threatened with one second of silence. pp. [237–238]

In *Requiem for a Nun* progress is often characterized as a "roar."

These are a few varied examples which may give some indication of the persistence of Faulkner's attention to sound and silence. As in his treatment of motion, however, what is most striking is his tendency to present the opposed conditions as existing simultaneously, or to suggest them simultaneously.

Again and again Faulkner seems to conceive of silence as a space, a container for sound or action. Silence remains even while the sounds are occurring. Not infrequently, this view receives direct expression. In *Light in August*, for example, Faulkner speaks of a "silence filled with the puny voices of men" (p. 259). In *Sanctuary*, Temple Drake is described as "voiding the words like hot silent bubbles into the bright silence" (p. 122).

Often sound is not only encased in silence but seems the intruder into, or violator of, silence. In one of Faulkner's earliest
essays he plays with this idea directly. From a violin bow "there
arose a sound . . . which silence itself, seemed to find strange
and hard to digest: toying with it when the bow ceased" (*MCS*,
19–20). The jabbering of Ab Snopes's daughters in *The Hamlet*
is likened to the "sound . . . emitted by two enormous birds;
as if the aghast and amazed solitude of some inaccessible and
empty marsh or desert were being invaded and steadily violated
by the constant bickering of the two last survivors of a lost
species which had established residence in it" (p. 54). The
silence of the forest in *Go Down, Moses* is described as "musing
downward upon this puny evanescent clutter of human sojourn
which after a single brief week would vanish" (p. 353).

In some of these last illustrations both sound and silence take
on spatial and almost palpable qualities which intensify the
sense of their conflict and simultaneous existence and which add
contradictory suggestions of simultaneous substance and lack of
substance. On numerous occasions Faulkner carries this even
further. In *The Hamlet*, for example, Mink Snopes is tormented
by a "tremendous silence" which

roared down about him and, still roaring, began to stiffen like cement,
not only in his hearing but in his lungs, his breathing, inside and without him too, solidifying from tree-trunk to tree-trunk, among which
the shattered echoes of the shot died away in strangling murmurs,
caught in that cooling solidity before they had had time to cease.
[p. 264]

Here we have not only the opposed suggestions of silence and
roaring but the paradox of an insubstantial entity stiffening and
solidifying and beyond this the paradox of sounds dying away
and yet being caught before they had time to cease—and
caught, we must remember, in a silence.

In *Pylon* the notion of substantial sound is carried to the
point where our presumable knowledge of how congealed
sounds look is supposed to enable us to visualize more clearly

an image which is visual to begin with. Moreover, the congealed sounds are used to describe a condition already described as silent. And the silence itself is paradoxical, since we expect planes to make noise: "The four machines [planes] seemed to hover like dragonflies silently in vacuum . . . with now a quality trivial, random, almost like notes of music—a harp, say —as the sun glinted and lost them" (p. 233). This sort of image is extended still further, impossible as it may seem, by Darl, in *As I Lay Dying:*

Cash labors about the trestles, moving back and forth, lifting and placing the planks with long clattering reverberations in the dead air as though he were lifting and dropping them at the bottom of an invisible well, the sounds ceasing without departing, as if any movement might dislodge them from the immediate air in reverberant repetition. . . .

The air smells like sulphur. Upon the impalpable plane of it their shadows form as upon a wall, as though like sound they had not gone very far away in falling but had merely congealed for a moment, immediate and musing. [p. 392]

Here, in addition to the contradictory suggestions of "sounds ceasing without departing," an image of substantialized sound is used to help us visualize shadows which have fallen upon an impalpable entity.

We have just seen a variety of illustrations suggesting the simultaneous existence of sound and silence. Very frequently, just as Faulkner gives maximum simultaneity and compression to motion and immobility in images like "dynamic immobility," he compresses the suggestions of sound and silence to the condition of maximum tension provided by the oxymoron. Thus again and again in his works we find phrases like "crashing silently," "exploded soundlessly," "silence . . . roared," "clashing soundlessly," "soundless yelling," "quiet thunderclap," and "thunderous silence." The frequent notations that a character heard or listened to silence is a more devious form of this oxymoron, as are the phrases "soundless and involved arpeggio"

(*SF*, 293) and "rising inflection of a risible silence" (*WP*, 7). On at least three occasions, Faulkner sets up, in effect, a double oxymoron.

They walked on in silence again; it was as though the silence were the dialogue and the actual speech the soliloquy, the marshalling of thought. [*P*, 172]

Moving, he made no sound at all; the released door yawned and clapped against the jamb, but it made no sound either; it was as though sound and silence had become inverted. She could hear silence in a thick rustling as he moved toward her through it, thrusting it aside. [*S*, 121–122]

shaping the soundless words in the pattering silence. [*CS*, 899]

This juxtaposition of sound and silence, and the sense of silence as a container for sound and of sound as a kind of entity which intrudes upon a vast background silence is not merely a matter of intermittent images. Often it is a far more pervasive condition. At times, silence becomes as much a part of the setting in Faulkner's world as Egdon Heath is in Hardy's. It becomes, in effect, a more or less permanent part of the scenery or background for sound and action, at once intensifying and muting it.

This sense of a pervasive silence is perhaps most strong in parts of *Light in August*. The conversation of Hightower and Bunch early in the book is a good example. On page 78 we read that Hightower's "voice sounds light, trivial, like a thistle bloom falling into silence without a sound." On the same page Faulkner reports, "The sound of music from the distant church has long since ceased. Now there is no sound in the room save the steady shrilling of insects and the monotonous sound of Byron's voice." On the following page we read that Byron "ceases. Then there is no sound in the room save the insects. Beyond the open window the steady insects pulse and beat, drowsy and myriad." On page 87 we again read that "Byron's voice ceases. Its flat, inflectionless, countrybred singsong dies into silence." In the next chapter the sounds of the drunken Brown seem to occur in this same silence:

He [Christmas] heard Brown before he saw him. He heard Byron approach the door and then blunder into it. . . . Brown was breathing heavily. . . . Brown began to sing in a saccharine and nasal tenor. . . . "Shut it," Christmas said. He did not move and his voice was not raised. Yet Brown ceased at once. . . . Then he let go of the door and Christmas heard him stumble into the room; a moment later he blundered into something. There was an interval filled with hard, labored breathing. Then Brown fell to the floor with a tremendous clatter, striking the cot on which Christmas lay and filling the room with loud and idiot laughter. [p. 89]

After Christmas has quieted Brown, he stands over the cot, "his own breathing so quiet, so calm, as to make no sound even to himself. . . . Brown breathed quieter now. . . . While Christmas watched, he began to snore." Christmas lights a cigarette and snaps the match toward the door. "Then he was listening for the light, trivial sound which the dead match would make when it struck the floor; and then it seemed to him that he heard it" (p. 91).

In the opening pages of *Sanctuary* the scene of Benbow and Popeye at the spring is encased in silence: "Somewhere, hidden and secret yet nearby, a bird sang three notes and ceased" (p. 1). When Benbow rose from his drink he saw the "reflection of Popeye's straw hat, though he had heard no sound" (p. 1). Popeye stands in "sunny silence."

Behind him the bird sang again, three bars in monotonous repetition: a sound meaningless and profound out of a suspirant and peaceful following silence which seemed to isolate the spot, and out of which a moment later came the sound of an automobile passing along a road and dying away. [p. 2]

They squatted so, facing one another across the spring, for two hours. Now and then the bird sang back in the swamp, as though it were worked by a clock; twice more invisible automobiles passed along the highway and died away. Again the bird sang. [p. 3]

This casing of silence is also particularly effective in the final chapter of *The Wild Palms*. Not only does Wilbourne feel "globed in silence," but the silence throughout the chapter is such that the various carefully described sounds of the wind and water become a terrifyingly vivid presence. In the hospital corridor it is silent enough for us to hear the rubber wheels of the stretcher "making a sucking sound on the floor" (p. 294), to hear "the tinkle of the bells, the immediate sibilance of rubber heels and starched skirts, the querulous murmur of voices about nothing" (pp. 299–300). The jail is silent enough so that the cigarette paper parts "suddenly between his hands with an almost audible report" (p. 309). The silence of the deserted Sutpen mansion in *Absalom, Absalom!* is such that Quentin "almost believed that he could hear Miss Coldfield breathing just beyond the wall beside him," such that the sound of a "scraped match was like an explosion, a pistol; . . . he could not even move for a moment even though something of sanity roared silently inside his skull" (p. 368).

The effect of this casing of silence is difficult to explain. I have described it as one which both intensifies and mutes. On the one hand, it would seem to provide, so to speak, a bare stage upon which sound and action encounter no competition; there are no distractions to blur the focus upon them. In a world quiet enough to make the sound of tearing cigarette paper "an almost audible report," a gunshot or scream would be deafening.[12] Yet the effect is not this simple. For although the silence does make the sounds clear and distinct, the fact that it remains while they are occurring somehow mutes them and makes them puny. The contradictory effect is similar to that produced by

[12] Regarded from another point of view, the audibility of the tearing cigarette paper and of other minute sounds helps to create and emphasize the surrounding silence. If one hears a pin drop one may presume quietness. As often as not, however, Faulkner explicitly suggests the silence. For example, "there was no sound save the clock and the fire" (*SF*, 290), or a bit less obviously, "the voice dies again, beyond the window the steady insects whirr. Then the voice goes on, flat, toneless" (*LIA*, 339).

contradictory phrases like "soundless explosion" and "thunderous silence," in which the suggestions of sound and silence remain in permanent struggling deadlock, at once intensifying each other by contrast and negating one another by contradiction. And although an opposition of sound and silence involves less tension than an opposition of motion and immobility, the effect is also similar to that produced by conditions of "dynamic immobility" and by the various other sorts of permanent struggling deadlock and irreconcilable opposition in Faulkner's writing we shall be looking at.

« 3 »

Quiescence and Turbulence

FAULKNER'S emphases on motion and immobility and sound and silence, while important in themselves, must also be viewed, as suggested earlier, as part of a general antithesis, in which the opposed conditions are a minimum of activity or intensity of any kind and a maximum of activity or intensity, or, more briefly, quiescence and turbulence. This way of looking at and presenting things is so fundamental a part of Faulkner's world and vision that it is almost impossible to remember while reading his works that there could be any other way of seeing or rendering a world. The emphasis upon quiescence and turbulence is so much the form of the vision that we tend not to see it as form.

When we read, for example, about "a stumppocked scene of profound and peaceful desolation . . . gutting slowly . . . beneath the long quiet rains of autumn and the galloping fury of vernal equinoxes" (*LIA*, 4), we are not aware that the words "peaceful," "slowly," "quiet," and "galloping fury" are by no means inevitable, and that the antithesis of "long quiet" and "galloping fury" might even be called gratuitous. Nor are we consciously aware while reading Faulkner how much our experience is a matter of encountering alternations and juxtapositions of quiescent and turbulent conditions and of encountering conditions of tension between quiescence and turbulence. This rather simple and effective level of communication is worth looking at in further detail, for it is a central part of Faulkner's art and vision, which has so far been virtually overlooked. It is, I believe, in great part this level of communication beneath the complexities which makes Faulkner's works powerful and alive.

Faulkner's world has usually been seen as a violent one. Certainly many violent events occur within it. But if by violence is meant an unrestrained explosion of energy or activity or brutality, the word seems terribly inadequate. For one thing, it does not suggest the striking emphasis on things that are quiet, calm, still, and peaceful. This emphasis is not merely a matter of characters like Dilsey, Cash Bundren, Lena Grove, Byron Bunch, Ratliff, Eula Varner, Ike McCaslin, the Jefferson sheriff, and various Indians and farmers whose essential natures and actions are unusually calm and quiet. Nor is it simply a matter of occasional lengthy descriptions of peaceful scenery and peaceful human activities, although these are more common in his works than is sometimes suspected. For there are, scattered throughout the works, numerous passages and phrases which give us glimpses of something fixed and calm beneath or behind whatever furies rage above—glimpses of a mule plodding slowly, farmers squatting or sitting somewhere unhurriedly talking, groups moving decorously along the streets on Sundays, the peaceful sound of bells or birds or crickets, and beneath all the "tranquil earth" itself and the "quiet" biding dust.

Compared, however, with unpeaceful characters and scenes, the peaceful ones do not bulk large. Alone, they would not entitle us to speak of quiescence as an important emphasis or allow us seriously to reject a characterization of Faulkner's world as violent. What does entitle us to do so is the extent to which turbulence is preceded, accompanied, or followed by quiescence, and the place of quiescence in his treatment of human emotion and experience.

I have spoken already of the immobility that often precedes or accompanies motion and of the silence that encases sound.

Far more often than not, when there is a suggestion or act of
turbulence or violence, there is a simultaneous or almost simultaneous suggestion of some kind of quiescence:

In Quentin's imagination, Sutpen abrupts "out of quiet
thunderclap . . . upon a scene peaceful and decorous as a
school prize water color." His band of wild Negroes stand in
"attitudes wild and reposed." Sutpen sits "immobile";

Behind him the wild blacks and the captive architect huddled quietly,
carrying in bloodless paradox the shovels and picks and axes of peaceful conquest. Then in the long unamaze Quentin seemed to watch
them overrun suddenly the hundred square miles of tranquil and astonished earth and drag house and formal gardens violently out of the
soundless Nothing and clap them down like cards upon a table beneath the up-palm immobile and pontific, creating the Sutpen's Hundred. [*AA*, 8–9]

The flood in *The Wild Palms*, when first seen, is "a flat, still
sheet of brown water." The men in the speeding truck watch
it "quietly":

It was perfectly motionless, perfectly flat. It looked, not innocent,
but bland. It looked almost demure. . . . It looked so still that they
did not realize it possessed motion until they came to the first bridge.
. . . Here they both saw and heard movement—the slow profound
eastward and upstream ("It's running backward," one convict said
quietly.) set of the still rigid surface, from beneath which came a
deep faint subaquean rumble which . . . sounded like a subway
train passing far beneath the street and which inferred a terrific and
secret speed. It was as if the water itself were in three strata, separate
and distinct, the bland and unhurried surface bearing a frothy scum
and a miniature flotsam of twigs and screening . . . the rush and
fury of the flood itself, and beneath this in turn the original stream,
trickle, murmuring along in the opposite direction, following undis-
turbed and unaware its appointed course and serving its Lilliputian
end, like a thread of ants beneath the rails on which an express train
passes, they (the ants) as unaware of the power and fury as if it were
a cyclone crossing Saturn. [pp. 62–63]

Throughout the work, what makes the description of the flood so memorable is Faulkner's awareness of the various kinds of calm and stillness which are part of it, just as he is aware of the calmness which alternates with and accompanies the tall convict's fury.

In both the examples just given there is not only an initial suggestion or description of quiescence but some kind of quiescence which remains during the violence, at once heightening and muting it. One can say, I think, that the more violent or turbulent the action or emotion, the more Faulkner insists on its quietness or sets it off by contrast with something quiet. As the dietitian in *Light in August* becomes more and more obsessed with the fear that Joe Christmas will report her promiscuity, she becomes more calm: "On the fourth day she became quite calmly and completely mad" (p. 110). Joanna Burden's calmness also increases with her madness. As she pulls the trigger to shoot Joe, "her eyes did not waver at all. They were as still as the round black ring of the pistol muzzle. But there was no heat in them, no fury. They were calm and still as all pity and all despair and all conviction" (p. 247). In *The Hamlet*, the farmer whose grain Ike Snopes steals, frustrated in his attempts to trace the culprit, finally becomes "calm and contained and rigidly boiling" (p. 222). Throughout the series of beatings McEachern gives Joe Christmas in *Light in August* each is again and again decribed as immobile. The more Joe is beaten the more calm he appears: "He [Joe] was looking straight ahead, with a rapt, calm expression like a monk in a picture. McEachern began to strike methodically, with slow and deliberate force, still without heat or anger. It would have been hard to say which face was the more rapt, more calm, more convinced." [1]

[1] Page 131. See also pp. 134, 140. Joe is almost always peaceful during and after physical punishment. See pp. 189–193, 407. These sorts of reactions might be attributed to the fact that Joe is partially conceived as a Christ figure, but a number of other Faulkner characters react similarly. See, for example, *LIA*, 385–386; *SF*, 180–183; *WP*, 147; *P*, 157; *H*, 142.

Perhaps the most violently and persistently frustrated character in all of Faulkner's works is the tall convict in *The Wild Palms*. The more exasperated he becomes the quieter his words become. When he has reached the point of "terrific and absolutely unbearable exasperation" (p. 271), a point where he has to be tied hand and foot, Faulkner describes the scene as follows:

> "I aint going without my boat," the convict said. He said it calmly and with complete finality, so calm, so final that for almost a minute nobody answered him, they just stood looking quietly down at him as he lay, half-naked, blistered and scarred, helpless and manacled hand and foot, on his back, delivering his ultimatum in a voice peaceful and quiet as that in which you talk to your bedfellow before going to sleep. Then the man in the launch moved; he spat quietly over the side and said in a voice as calm and quiet as the convict's:
> "All right. Bring his boat." [p. 272]

In *The Hamlet* the utterly self-sufficient quiescence and tranquil bemusement of Eula even further torment her already violently stimulated admirers and serve as continual contrast to their turbulence. Labove finally wants above all, to hurt her, to "see blood spring and run, watch that serene face warp to the indelible mark of terror and agony" (p. 135). When finally he assaults her, "the two bodies hurling together violently," "she seemed to be momentarily mesmerized by a complete inert soft surprise, big, immobile" (p. 137). "Then the body gathered itself into furious and silent resistance" (p. 138). Every Sunday "through the long drowsing afternoons" Eula's admirers would sit on the Varner veranda "leashed and savage and loud and wild at the vain galloping seconds while the shadows lengthened and the frogs and whippoorwills began and the fireflies began to blow and drift above the creek." Later they would leave "seething and decorous, to mount the patient mules and ride in furious wordless amity" to a creek ford where they fought "silently and savagely" until they were "for the time being freed even of rage and frustration and desire" (pp. 149–150).

In these examples and generally throughout Faulkner's works the quiescence, peacefulness, or silence which accompanies or sets off the turbulence seems reasonably well justified by the scenes or characters involved; and although it might seem curious that so many characters fight silently or are immobile while furious, we do not feel that the quiescence is suggested simply for effect. At times, however, we can watch the author strain to bring in the suggestion of quiescence which will throw the turbulence or violence into sharper relief. The rape of Temple in *Sanctuary* is an illustration of this. Not only is the encasing silence pounded home to us noisily, but amid Temple's screams we are given the image of the old man "sitting in his chair in the sunlight his hands crossed on top of his stick" (p. 122). Less noticeable, perhaps, but even more expressive of Faulkner's desire for the quiet setting or contrast is this example from *The Sound and the Fury*, which occurs after several paragraphs describing Jason's struggle with the enraged circus cook:

Jason glared wildly about, holding the other. Outside it was now bright and sunny, swift and bright and empty, and he thought of the people soon to be going quietly home to Sunday dinner, decorously festive, and of himself trying to hold the fatal, furious little old man whom he dared not release long enough to turn his back and run. [p. 325]

Apart from the general contrast between the turbulence of Jason's struggle and the quiescence of the Sunday scene he imagines, we may note also the mildly opposing suggestions of quiescence and turbulence in the phrases "swift and bright and empty" and "decorously festive." On occasion Faulkner is willing to let the contrast rest on a single word. Thus, amid

Quentin's struggle with the crazed Julio, someone pulls him "up in time to see another stark naked figure come around the *tranquil* bend in the path" (p. 158, italics mine). What we are presented with in most of these examples, of course, is not so much violence as tension.

The examples in the last few paragraphs illustrate, so to speak, the calms before and during storms. Calms after storms [2] are also common and heavily stressed. After a violent free-for-all in *Sanctuary* involving Goodwin, Van, Popeye, Tommy, and Gowan, Faulkner writes: "Then it was over, gone like a furious gust of black wind, leaving a peaceful vacuum in which they moved quietly about, lifting Gowan out of the weeds with low-spoken, amicable directions to one another" (p. 85). When they have been beaten or hurt, characters often experience a sense of peace. After his fight with Brown, Byron Bunch lies

---

[2] In the following description from *The Wild Palms* of an actual storm, note the effective movement from turbulence to quiescence. Wilbourne is in jail after Charlotte's death, "and all that night a buoy outside the river moaned and bellowed and the palm beyond the window thrashed and clashed and just before dawn, in a driving squall, the tail of the hurricane struck. Not the hurricane; it was galloping off somewhere in the Gulf, just the tail of it, a flick of the mane in passing, driving up the shore ten feet of roiled and yellow tide which did not fall for twenty hours and driving fiercely through the wild frenzied palm which still sounded dry and across the roof of the cell, so that all that second night he could hear the boom of seas against the breakwater in the crashing darkness and the buoy too, gurgling now between bellows; he could even seem to hear the roar of water streaming from it as it surged up again with each choking cry, the rain driving on, into the next dawn but with less fury now, on across the flat land before the east wind. It would be even quieter inland, it would become only a bright silver murmur among the heavy decorous trees, upon the clipped sward; it would be clipped; he could imagine it, it would be a good deal like the park where he had waited, maybe even with children and nurses at times, the best, the very best; there would even be a headstone soon, at just exactly the right time, when restored earth and decorum stipulated, telling nothing; it would be clipped and green and quiet, the body, the shape of it under the drawn sheet, flat and small and moving in the hands of two men as if without weight though it did, nevertheless bearing and quiet beneath the iron weight of earth" (*WP*, 315-316).

quietly among the broken and trampled undergrowth, bleeding quietly. . . . He feels no particular pain now, but better than that, he feels no haste, no urgency, to do anything or go anywhere. He just lies bleeding and quiet, knowing that after a while will be time enough to re-enter the world and time. [p. 385]

After being struck by the skiff, the tall convict in *The Wild Palms* "lay flat on his face, slightly spread-eagled and in an attitude almost peaceful, a kind of abject meditation" (p. 147).

This kind of quiescent state of consciousness almost all Faulkner characters sometimes attain, and it characterizes protracted periods in the lives of a number of them. For at least six characters—Lena Grove, Eula Varner, Charles Bon's mulatto mistress, Houston's wife, Marya in *A Fable*, and Mokketubbe in "Red Leaves"—it is a perpetual condition and an utterly extreme one. At least four other characters—Anse and Cash Bundren, the sheriff of Jefferson, and Judith Sutpen—are more or less characterized by some variety of quiescence or serenity.

For most of Faulkner's characters, however, the quiescent states are no more than interruptions of tension or torment. As Faulkner says of Joanna Burden, who is not permitted even to "be dead in peace and quiet," peace is not that often" (*LIA*, 252). But quiescence does seem to be virtually the only alternative to torment, and the best that most of Faulkner's characters can hope for. They cannot resolve their problems, but they can exist for awhile as Wilbourne does, "in a drowsy and foetuslike state, passive and almost unsentient in the womb of solitude and peace" (*WP*, 110), or as Judith, Clytie, and Rosa do, "in an apathy which was almost peace, like that of the blind unsentient earth itself" (*AA*, 155), or as the reporter in *Pylon* does, in a "state of peaceful physical anaesthesia" (p. 239). The self-driven Sutpen is hardly capable of attaining any real peace or quiescence. Still, after his engagement, "the flesh on his bones had become quieter, as though passive after some actual breasting of atmosphere like in running" (*AA*, 48).

Later in life, puzzled by the failure of his design, his condition, at times, is one of "sober and quiet bemusement" (*AA*, 273).

During the morning of the day he kills Joanna Burden, Joe Christmas experiences an utterly quiet suspended feeling and thinks, "*All I wanted was peace*" (p. 97). Several times during his flight after the murder he experiences similar sensations of peace:

> It is just dawn, daylight: that gray and lonely suspension filled with the peaceful and tentative waking of birds. . . . He breathes deep and slow, feeling with each breath himself diffuse in the neutral grayness, becoming one with loneliness and quiet that has never known fury or despair. "That was all I wanted," he thinks, in a quiet and slow amazement. "That was all, for thirty years." [p. 289]

Quiet is what the tormented Jewel Bundren wants for himself and his mother Addie (*AILD*, 347–348). And for Addie, Jewel's birth provided a kind of peace: "The wild blood boiled away and the sound of it ceased. Then there was only the milk, warm and calm, and I lying calm in the slow silence, getting ready to clean my house" (*AILD*, 467). At the end of *Pylon*, Shumann's father cries out that he has reached a point where "nothing is worth anything but peace, peace, peace, even with bereavement and grief—nothing! nothing!" (p. 306). "All that any man can hope for," says Hightower, "is to be permitted to live quietly among his fellows" (*LIA*, 64).

I do not mean to suggest that these various states of quiescence, peace, placidity, or serenity are identical or that Faulkner sees them as the ideal human condition. As we shall see later, there is considerable evidence that he does not. What I have wished to stress is the extent to which a quiescent, placid, or peaceful state of being is presented as a possible human condition and is contrasted with the turbulent states. Psychologically, as well as meteorologically and behaviorally, there are the "long quiet rains of autumn" as well as the "galloping fury of vernal equinoxes."

O

It might be argued that the final effect of the emphasis on quiescence is to heighten the effect of violence. This is often an immediate effect, to be sure, but paradoxically the quiescence also serves to give the violence an evanescent and at times even a puny quality. The sound and fury expends itself; something or someone quiet and steadfast remains.

The quiescent aspects of Faulkner's world can easily be overstressed, and it must be remembered that quiescence in Faulkner is not necessarily peaceful. I do not mean to suggest that peaceful quietness in his world has the solidity it has in George Eliot's, for example. On the other hand, I believe his world contains more of a picture of, and possibility for, peace and quiet than the worlds, for example, of Dreiser, Farrell, Dos Passos, or Joyce. The affirmation of Molly Bloom is frenetic compared with that of Lena Grove. Of course, Faulkner's world contains more extreme violence than do those of most other major novelists. But just as quiescence can heighten the effect of violence, violence, as violator, can emphasize the existence and importance of peace and quiet.

Before going on I had better make clear that my concern here is not to compare the number of quiescent and turbulent conditions in Faulkner's world with the number of such conditions in other fictional worlds. To do that would be impossible and pointless. I have made a few such comparisons merely to suggest further the inadequacy of considering Faulkner's world primarily as a violent one. My concern is with what is emphasized in a novelist's world. Of moment, then, is the fact that Faulkner is immensely concerned with quiescent and turbulent aspects of life and of the world in general, while other novelists are far more concerned with other aspects of the human and nonhuman condition. It is safe to say, I think, that the emphasis on quiescence and turbulence dominates Faulkner's narrative and description to a greater extent than it does the narration and description of any other major English or American novelists, with the doubtful exceptions of George

Eliot, Hardy, Conrad, and D. H. Lawrence.[3] With other
novelists the question of whether a character, action, or scene is
quiescent or not, is less important than other questions. In many
other fictional worlds it is more important whether a scene or
character is attractive or not. In most it is more important
whether a character is happy or not. To Faulkner this is almost
completely irrelevant. In Faulkner's world we may not know
how a character looks or what he is wearing or what he is

[3] There are a considerable number of passages in the works of each of
these novelists where the emphasis upon quiescence and turbulence is as
strong as in any passages in Faulkner. A considerable amount of comparison, however, has made me feel reasonably certain that in none of
these novelists' works is the emphasis as persistent as in Faulkner or ex-
hibited in the presentation of such varied aspects and levels of experience.
I feel least confident about the comparison with Conrad, in whose descriptions of action and scene the emphasis is persistent and pronounced.
On the other hand, when one compares any of Conrad's extended descriptions of storms at sea with Faulkner's presentation of the tall convict's experiences in the Mississippi flood in *The Wild Palms*, or compares
Conrad's treatment of the death of Kurtz in "Heart of Darkness," in
which the emphasis is perhaps greatest, with Faulkner's presentation of
the deaths of Sutpen or Joe Christmas, it seems clear that Faulkner's concern with quiescence and turbulence is far more fundamental and significant. Here is Conrad's presentation of Kurtz' death:

"Anything approaching the change that came over his features I have
never seen before, and hope never to see again. Oh, I wasn't touched. I
was fascinated. It was as though a veil had been rent. I saw on that ivory
face the expression of somber pride, of ruthless power, of craven terror—
of an intense and hopeless despair. Did he live his life again in every detail
of desire, temptation, and surrender during that supreme moment of
complete knowledge? He cried in a whisper at some image, at some
vision—he cried out twice, a cry that was no more than a breath. 'The
horror! The horror!'

"I blew the candle out and left the cabin. The pilgrims were dining in
the messroom, and I took my place opposite the manager, who lifted his
eyes to give me a questioning glance which I successfully ignored. He
leaned back, serene, with that peculiar smile of his sealing the unexpressed
depths of his meanness. A continuous shower of small flies streamed upon
the lamp, upon the cloth, upon our hands and faces. Suddenly the manager's boy put his insolent black head in the doorway, and said in a tone
of scathing contempt—

" 'Mistah Kurtz—he dead.'

"All the pilgrims rushed out to see. I remained, and went on with my thinking, but we will almost always know whether his body is quiescent or active and whether his general psychological condition is placid or turbulent. At times, we know nothing more than this about him. Faulkner characters almost never smile, laugh, or frown. Their faces are mobile, or they are still, sometimes quietly so, sometimes tensely, the stillness a rigid cover for exasperation or fury.

Whoever the character, whatever the event or object, whether he is describing a life history, panorama, flood, fight, conversation, facial expression, tone of voice, or state of consciousness, Faulkner is more likely to note and emphasize its degree of turbulence and quiescence than he is any of its other characteristics. Even the action of spitting may be described as slow

dinner. I believe I was considered brutally callous. However, I did not eat much. There was a lamp in there—light, don't you know—and outside it was so beastly, beastly dark" (Joseph Conrad, "Heart of Darkness," *Youth and Two Other Stories* [New York: Doubleday, Page, 1912], pp. 160–170).

Compare Faulkner: "But the Player was not done yet. When the others reached the kitchen they saw the table flung aside now and Grimm stooping over the body. When they approached to see what he was about, they saw that the man was not dead yet, and when they saw what Grimm was doing one of the men gave a choked cry and stumbled back into the wall and began to vomit. Then Grimm too sprang back, flinging behind him the bloody butcher knife. 'Now you'll let white women alone, even in hell,' he said. But the man on the floor had not moved. He just lay there, with his eyes open and empty of everything save consciousness, and with something, a shadow, about his mouth. For a long moment he looked up at them with peaceful and unfathomable and unbearable eyes. Then his face, body, all, seemed to collapse, to fall in upon itself, and from out the slashed garments about his hips and loins the pent black blood seemed to rush like a released breath. It seemed to rush out of his pale body like the rush of sparks from a rising rocket; upon that black blast the man seemed to rise soaring into their memories forever and ever. They are not to lose it, in whatever peaceful valleys, beside whatever placid and reassuring streams of old age, in the mirroring faces of whatever children they will contemplate old disasters and newer hopes. It will be there, musing, quiet, steadfast, not fading and not particularly threatful, but of itself alone serene, of itself alone triumphant. Again from the town, deadened a little by the walls, the scream of the siren mounted toward its unbelievable crescendo, passing out of the realm of hearing" (*LIA*, 406–407).

or quiet, and the tone of the bell on a fire truck as serene. Such unlikely entities as sunlight and the board fronts of oil towns are described as savage.

Above all, as we have seen, he is likely to place the two conditions in antithesis or to suggest them simultaneously. This is true of his treatment of scenes and objects. It is even more true of his treatment of characters; even the most violent usually seethe behind an immobile or calm exterior, or their fury escapes accompanied by some kind of control.

In Faulkner's world the posture of the agonized and damned is not a frenzied one. They do not writhe in flames. Like Dante's worst sinners, the most tormented of Faulkner's characters are often frozen in their rage. Or they pass to a stage beyond that, in which they are "calm and contained and rigidly boiling," and even beyond that to a calm and quiet madness.

The flood and the maelstrom are frequent in image and fact, but there is usually a dam which holds for a long while, or which is strained to the breaking point but never gives way.

These conditions of simultaneous quiescence and turbulence, of course, are conditions of tension, as are those presented by Faulkner's juxtapositions and simultaneous suggestions of motion and immobility, relative velocities, and sound and silence. In general, the persistence and intensity of Faulkner's emphasis upon states of tension is such that tension comes to be the dominant, even the normal, condition in his world. Primarily these states of tension are achieved by various forms of antithesis, simultaneous suggestion, and irresolution, by Faulkner's overwhelming tendency to place entities of all kinds in opposition. We have seen something of this tendency already, and I shall have more to say about it in the section called "The Polar Imagination." But first it would be well to look at some of the other ways in which Faulkner creates and emphasizes conditions of tension, ways which tell us more about how he conceives of those conditions and about the extent of his fascination with them.

« 4 »

Tension

MOST novelists and most people seem to visualize a stable norm of moderate physical and emotional activity from which both quiescence and turbulence are deviations. Faulkner, on the other hand, seems to see and present as norm an unstable condition, a disequilibrium of quiescence and turbulence. From this disequilibrium, extreme quiescence and extreme turbulence are not so much deviations as releases; they, rather than moderate activity, seem the stable condition.

This idea is developed further in the next section, where it is shown that Faulkner's thought and writing, in general, are characterized by an emphasis on polar conditions and a relative absence of stable mean positions. Here I wish only to illustrate his particularly persistent tendency to present and emphasize certain kinds of unstable or unresolved conditions. These conditions are of several varieties and resist neat classification. In all of them, however, there is potential or imminent activity: something might happen or is about to happen. In most of them there is the suggestion of a force or impulse under restraint. Faulkner often thinks of this force or impulse as something (usually air, fluid, or muscular energy) which is gathered and which may be released. What is most striking, however, as we shall see, is the extent to which impulse or tension is not released, to which conflict remains unresolved. This condition of

53

unreleased tension, of temporarily or permanently frustrated impulse, seems to fascinate Faulkner and is perhaps the most characteristic state of being presented in his works.

The sense of potential or imminent activity may be carefully and lengthily built up, as in *Intruder in the Dust*, where Faulkner devotes several pages to the condition of the square in Jefferson on the Sunday night that everyone expects will end with the lynching of Lucas Beauchamp. That condition is "an emptiness you could call emptiness provided you called vacant and empty the silent and lifeless terrain in front of a mobilised army or peaceful the vestibule to a powder magazine or quiet the spillway under the locks of a dam" (p. 213).

On the other hand, the emphasis on the imminent event may be no more than the bald statement that something is going to happen. Near the end of *Pylon* the reporter says "quietly, with tragic and passive clairvoyance, . . . 'Something is going to happen to me. I have got myself stretched out too far and too thin and something is going to bust' " (p. 300). In *Sanctuary*, Temple "could hear silence in a thick rustling as he [Popeye] moved toward her through it, thrusting it aside, and she began to say Something is going to happen to me" (p. 122). Before he enters Joanna Burden's house for the last time Joe Christmas sits for an hour against a tree.

He just sat there, not moving, until after a while he heard the clock two miles away strike twelve. Then he rose and moved toward the house. He didn't go fast. He didn't think even then *Something is going to happen. Something is going to happen to me.* [p. 103]

The potential events in these last three illustrations are physical and emotional collapse, rape, and murder. If the emphasis on the imminent and potential were confined primarily to these sorts of violent and significant events, we might assume that we had to do merely with devices designed to arouse suspense, devices common throughout fiction. Certainly the effect of this emphasis is in large measure suspense, and certainly Faulkner employs more than his share of such devices. His whole method of delayed disclosure, in large constructions and small, can be considered in part as a suspense-producing device, and his works abound with hints as unsubtle and unabashed as the ones illustrated above. Note that in the illustration above from *Light in August*, Faulkner does not even bother to hide the device: Joe does *not* yet think *"Something is going to happen to me."* Note also that actually this comment announces two imminent events: a mental one and one whose nature is unknown.[1]

It will be clear, however, that the emphasis on potential and imminent events is a far more fundamental matter. Much of *The Wild Palms* is a narration of the struggles of a convict caught in a Mississippi flood in a small boat. It is difficult to conceive of a more unstable condition or one more infuriating for the convict, who has no desire to escape prison and wants only to get back to it. This is not sufficient for Faulkner, however. Into the boat he places a woman in an advanced stage of pregnancy. The "pregnant moment," a figurative condition which most novelists use sparingly, becomes here a literal one, and the moment is stretched into days. It is as though Faulkner were trying to see how much tension he could build up in his reader and chief character before they would explode.

In the story "Death Drag," an aviator is described as having "the most tragic face we had ever seen; an expression of outraged and convinced and indomitable despair." But this is not enough; Faulkner goes on to suggest an even greater degree of tension, adding, "like that of a man carrying through choice a bomb which, at a certain hour each day, may or may not explode" (CS, 187). The potential activity of his plane is suggested by terms we are already familiar with. "It reared on its muddy wheels, the propeller motionless, rigid, with a quality immobile and poised and dynamic" (CS, 188–189). Even trees

---

[1] For other examples of especially brash creation of tension and suspense, see *AA*, 377 and *GDM*, 37. See also Faulkner's treatment of the poker game between Hubert and Uncle Buddy (*GDM*, 27–29).

can exhibit this tense and pregnant condition: "motionless . . .
ruffled out to the last twig, swollen, increased as though quick
with young" (*AILD*, 392).

Perhaps the most convincing testimony to Faulkner's preoccupation with the pregnant moment is the frequency with
which he notes the imminence of relatively insignificant or un-
dramatic events: a smile, a simple movement, a thought. In
Light in August, for example, the literally pregnant Lena Grove
enters the Armstid kitchen "pausing at the door with less than
a pause, her face already fixed in an expression immanent [2] with
smiling, with speech, prepared speech" (p. 19). Even in this
very insignificant situation the impulse is not released, for the
passage continues, "but she said nothing; the pause was less than
a pause" (p. 20). She enters the sawmill in Jefferson, where she
hopes to find Lucas, "her face already shaped with serene
anticipatory smiling, her mouth already shaped upon a name"
(p. 43). Again her impulse is frustrated, for the man whose
back she sees is not Lucas. The book ends with Lena sitting in
the truck of a furniture dealer, who narrates that he

". . . looked back and saw her face. And it was like it was already
fixed and waiting to be surprised, and that she knew that when the
surprise come, she was going to enjoy it. [This time the impulse is not
thwarted.] And it did come and it did suit her. Because she said,

"'My, my. A body does get around. Here we aint been coming
from Alabama but two months, and now it's already Tennessee.'"

Again and again we are told that someone did not move *yet*,
or think, know, feel, or believe something *yet*, often in cases
where the foreshadowed event is of no major consequence. For
example, "Hightower does not yet think *love*." [3] On occasion,
we have a double "not yet" construction: "'I ought to eat,' he

---

[2] Even if we grant the propriety of Faulkner's use of "immanent"
rather than "imminent," the context clearly emphasizes the *imminence*
of the actions.

[3] *LIA*, 71. For other examples, see 105, 155, 193, 210; *AA*, 140; *WP*,
111; *GDM*, 321; *CS*, 783.

thought. 'I ought to,' not moving yet as though he hung static in a promise made to someone which he did not believe even yet that he was going to break" (*P*, 140).

Faulkner obviously relishes and frequently emphasizes the "tip of tongue" state of mind in which some kind of knowledge or realization is or seems imminent. In *Absalom, Absalom!* Shreve imagines Bon as

maybe leaning there in that solitude between panting smoke and engines and almost touching the answer, aware of the jigsaw puzzle picture integers of it waiting, almost lurking, just beyond his reach, inextricable, jumbled, and unrecognizable yet on the point of falling into pattern which would reveal to him at once, like a flash of light, the meaning of his whole life, past. [p. 313]

In *The Wild Palms*, Wilbourne's recognition that he prefers grief to nothing comes slowly. On page 312 we read:

"I wish I could stop [thinking of Charlotte]. I wish I could. No I dont. Maybe that's it. Maybe that's the reason—" Maybe that was; that was the first time he almost touched it. But not yet: and that was all right too; it would return; he would find it, hold it, when the time was ready.

On page 316 we watch him groping again: "That was the second time he almost got it. But it escaped him again. But he was not trying yet; it was still all right, he was not worried; it would return when the time was ready and even stand still to his hand." On page 323 we watch the idea finally taking shape, and on page 324 it finally "did stand to his hand, incontrovertible and plain, serene."

Very often characters generate tension in themselves and the reader by anticipating or waiting for their own reactions. In *The Unvanquished*, for example, Bayard says he does not look at his father's body "yet because I knew that when I did I would begin to pant" (p. 270). A few moments later he reports, "and then I knew that in a minute I would begin to pant" (p. 272). He then reports, "I knew soon that I would begin to

pant. I could feel it beginning like you feel regurgitation beginning" (p. 276). A page later we read: "Then she was gone
too and now it could begin. I knew that in a minute I would
look at him and it would begin and I did look at him, feeling
the long-held breath, the hiatus before it started" (p. 277).
After eating almost a whole tube of tooth paste, the five-year-
old Joe Christmas

seemed to be turned in upon himself, watching himself sweating,
watching himself smear another worm of paste into his mouth which
his stomach did not want. Sure enough, it refused to go down. Motionless now, utterly contemplative, he seemed to stoop above himself
like a chemist in his laboratory, waiting. [*LIA*, 106]

What follows in the story is in a number of ways characteristic of Faulkner's treatment of tension. There is a gathering, and then a temporary release of tension through regurgitation:

He didn't have to wait long. At once the paste which he had already
swallowed lifted inside him, trying to get back out. . . . He squatted,
pinkfoamed, listening to his insides, waiting with astonished fatalism
for what was about to happen to him. Then it happened. [p. 107]

For the moment at least there is the peace of "complete and
passive surrender." But almost immediately we are exposed to
a new set of tensions. The dietitian, whose tooth paste Joe ate,
believes he has seen and will report her illicit love affair. He,
on the other hand, believes he is to be punished for eating and
vomiting the tooth paste. Both suffer terrible suspense.

She believed that he not only intended to tell, but that he deferred
doing it deliberately in order to make her suffer more. It never occurred to her that he believed that he was the one who had been taken
in sin and was being tortured with punishment deferred and that he
was putting himself in her way in order to get it over with, get his
whipping and strike the balance and write it off.

By the second day she was well nigh desperate. . . . She lay most
of the night now tense, teeth and hands clenched, panting with fury
and terror and worst of all, regret. [pp. 107–108]

Joe is not physically tense yet. His face is "perfectly empty of everything except waiting." But when she approaches him on the third day, his body, too, begins to gather muscular tension. "The child waited, still, motionless. Slowly and gradually the muscles of his backside were becoming flat and rigid and tense as boards" (p. 108). He watches the clenched hand in her pocket, expecting her to strike him, to end his suspense. Finally, "he could feel her, hear her, her long shuddering breath. *Now it's coming* he thought in a flashing instant" (p. 109). But it doesn't come. There is no real release for either one of them, for she does not punish him. "That was the third day. On the fourth day she became quite calmly and completely mad" (p. 110).

These are a few examples of Faulkner's preoccupation with various kinds of potential or imminent events. The degree of suspense varies greatly, but in each case the description depicts or induces some kind of expectation, an expectation frequently disappointed. Joe does not get punished. Lena does not speak her words. The lynching does not take place.

Put a little differently, Faulkner has presented varied conditions which are tense and unstable because some element in them remains to be realized. Some kind of potential for change has been strongly suggested. In some instances the potential was inherent in the condition itself—in the advanced pregnancy of the woman with the convict, for example, or in the clenched fists of the dietitian or in the tenseness of the muscles of Joe's backside. In other cases the potential was suggested or emphasized rhetorically—by a bomb metaphor, by words like "poised" and "dynamic," or by the simple phrase "not yet." In some of the illustrations the potential event whose occurrence would relieve the tension is violent, in some a peaceful falling into place. In some of the illustrations the tension is the property of a situation, in some the property of a character. In each instance, however, and in countless others in Faulkner's works, the emphasis is upon the condition of tension.

The tooth paste incident between Joe Christmas and the dietitian illustrates an especially persistent and powerful pattern in Faulkner's presentation of events, a pattern in which there is the suggestion of gathered energy or power held under restraint which could or must give way. When it does give way, there is the sense of something being released. This pattern of gathering, containment, and release of tension is often communicated explicitly as well as by diction and imagery. It usually involves visceral or kinesthetic images and conceptions.

We are often made aware of the gathering itself.[4] In *The Wild Palms*, when Rittenmeyer, Charlotte's husband, enters the courtroom in which Wilbourne is being tried for the murder of Charlotte, Wilbourne hears "the caught breath." Then Rittenmeyer indicates that he has come not to kill Wilbourne but to make a plea for him. In the passage which follows observe not only Wilbourne's explicit conception but the way in which Faulkner builds up tension by slowing down the action and delaying the release. Observe also the tensions that come from the antitheses of immobility and motion and quiescence and turbulence.

"I wish to make a plea," he said. For a moment the judge did not move, staring at Rittenmeyer, the gavel still clutched in his fist like a saber, then he leaned slowly forward, staring at Rittenmeyer: and Wilbourne heard it begin, the long in-sucking, the gathering of amazement and incredulity.

"You what?" the judge said. "A what? A plea? For this man? This man who wilfully and deliberately performed an operation on your wife which he knew might cause her death and which did?" And now it did roar, in waves, renewed; . . . a vortex of fury and turmoil about the calm immobile outrageous face above the smooth beautifully cut coat. [p. 320]

As in the illustration above, the gathering is often an insuck or a caught or held breath; the release, an exhalation. The re-

---

[4] For other examples of the "gathering" of energy or power, see *S*, 347; *LIA*, 429; *AA*, 321; *P*, 108; *U*, 276; *H*, 254, 256, 312; *GDM*, 184; *ID*, 136.

lease may be violent as in the illustration above, or it may be quiet. In *Absalom, Absalom!* for example, when Sutpen enters the house Bon "would let his held breath go quiet and easy, a profound exhalation, his heart quiet too." [5] Again and again, at times with astounding repetitiveness, Faulkner describes characters as panting or as experiencing a sensation of suffocation: "and then Boon's chest began to heave as though there were not enough air in all the woods, in all the wilderness, for all of them, for him and anyone else, even for him alone." [6] Faulkner also extends and capitalizes in numerous ways upon the effect of the idea of gathered, held, and released breath. As the door of the jail opens in *Intruder in the Dust*, "there seemed to rush out and down . . . the stale breath of all human degradation and shame" (p. 56). The foul air in the tree trunk in which Mink Snopes has hidden Houston's body "seemed to burst [out] with an audible sound" (*H*, 291). Many of Faulkner's images of things being blown or sucked away or out, and the blasts of air, and long sighing sounds may also be regarded as extended visceral images.[7] In the following example describing the death of Joe Christmas we see again the building of tension and the sense of release accomplished by the "long moment . . . then" combination, as well as the sense of gathered tension and release conveyed by the imagery:

For a long moment he looked up at them with peaceful and unfathomable and unbearable eyes. Then his face, body, all, seemed to collapse, to fall in upon itself, and from out the slashed garments about his hips and loins the pent black blood seemed to rush like a released breath. It seemed to rush out of his pale body like the rush

---

[5] *AA*, 333. For other "exhalations" see *SF*, 309, 310; *LIA*, 10–11; *S*, 346, 347; *P*, 163.

[6] *GDM*, 253. See also, pp. 140, 141, 142, 209, 212, 225, 247, 249, 250, 254. For other examples of a strikingly persistent emphasis upon these sensations, see *CS*, 326, 327, 328, 330, 331, 332, 336, 339, 340, 341; *AA*, 365, 371, 372, 378; *U*, 270, 272, 276, 277, 278, 287; *H*, 276, 277, 279, 284, 287, 288, 289, 290–291; *CS*, 798.

[7] See, for example, *LIA*, 188–189, 386, 431; *S*, 85, 348; *P*, 208.

of sparks from a rising rocket; upon that black blast the man seemed to rise soaring into their memories forever and ever. [*LIA*, 407]

Similar in conception and effect are Faulkner's frequent dam images:

It was as though, instead of putting an inked cross at the foot of a sheet of paper, she had lighted the train of a mine set beneath a dam, a dyke, a barrier already straining, bulging, bellying, not only towering over the land but leaning, looming, imminent with collapse, so that it only required the single light touch of the pen in that illiterate hand, and the wagon did not vanish slowly and terrifically from the scene to the terrific sound of its ungreased wheels, but was swept, hurled, flung not only out of Yoknapatawpha County and Mississippi but the United States too. [*RN*, 221–222]

Here the accumulated pressure is tremendous and the release, of course, violent. In the following image the pressure on the confining body is not emphasized so much, but the power of the force when it is released implies an earlier tension:

It is as though the moving wall of dingy cars were a dyke beyond which the world, time, hope unbelievable and certainty incontrovertible, waited, giving him yet a little more of peace. Anyway, when the last car passes, moving fast now, the world rushes down on him like a flood, a tidal wave. [*LIA*, 386–387]

This next is a much more delicate treatment, but even here Faulkner first builds his dam by postponing the action and heightens the sense of release with a "then."

He stopped. For a moment he didn't answer. Then he said peacefully, in a peaceful rushing burst, as when a boy's miniature dam in a little brook gives way: "All right. Yes. But how?" [8]

In these descriptions and suggestions of gathering, tension, and release and in numerous others, Faulkner employs visceral images related to our respiratory and circulatory systems, or he emphasizes the respiratory sensations and tensions of characters.

[8] *GDM*, 206. For other dam images or suggestions, see *LIA*, 431; *AA*, 301–302; *WP*, 306; *GDM*, 254.

On many other occasions he communicates the pattern of gathering, tension, and release, by literal or figurative references to the digestive system, especially to the process of regurgitation. We have already seen Joe Christmas watch the gathering and expulsion of the tooth paste he had eaten. In *Pylon* we watch and feel the drunken reporter gag for three pages until he and we are finally given release:

The hot corrupted coffee gathering inside him like a big heavy bird beginning to fly as he plunged out the door and struck a lamppost and clinging to it surrendered, as life, sense, all, seemed to burst out of his mouth as though his entire body were trying in one fierce orgasm to turn itself wrongsideout. [pp. 109–110]

In the following description observe that on the explicit level, at least, the visceral sensation is not used to define the tension and release of the combat experience, but the reverse. Observe also the emphasis upon the moment of maximum tension which immediately precedes the release.

Beneath the alcohol I could feel that hard, hot ball beginning in my stomach, like in combat, like when you know something is about to happen; that instant [note again the momentary stoppage] when you think Now. Now I can dump everything overboard and just be. Now. Now. It is quite pleasant. [*CS*, 421]

Sometimes Faulkner combines the visceral and kinesthetic. Here there is the suggestion of a gathering and tension in some cavity of the body and a partial release through muscular action. "He [Mink Snopes] began to struggle, with a cold condensed fury which did not seem quite able or perhaps ready to emerge yet from his body. Then he lashed suddenly out, still not at her but to break her grip. But she held him" (*H*, 275).

In the following description, the mild Byron Bunch is for the first time experiencing the kind of tension which is the normal state of many Faulkner characters. There are suggestions of respiratory strain, of pressure against a barrier, and of both latent and imminent explosiveness. And again there is an immense and unabashed emphasis upon the moment of maximum tension just prior to release, a release which is not provided by either rhetoric or story until much later.

He began to breathe deep. He could feel himself breathing deep, as if each time his insides were afraid that next breath they would not be able to give far enough and that something terrible would happen, and that all the time he could look down at himself breathing, at his chest, and see no movement at all, like when dynamite first begins, gathers itself for the now Now NOW, the shape of the outside of the stick does not change. [p. 365]

Lying in the barrel of a plane the reporter in *Pylon* feels nothing "but terrific motion—not speed and not progress—just blind, furious motion like a sealed force trying to explode the monocoque barrel in which he lay" (pp. 216–217).

Most frequently the force which is gathered, held in check, and sometimes released is muscle or nerve tension. Again and again Faulkner suggests a gathering or containment of muscular tension and focuses upon moments when this tension is at its maximum. Again and again we encounter immobile figures tremendous with effort, or in mounting muscular hiatus, or in only slightly less bursting conditions of rigid, furious, or tense immobility. Typical is the "poised and swooping immobility" (p. 77) of the reporter in *Pylon* and the condition of Jiggs who "squatted beneath the engine with the spraddled tenseness of an umbrellarib" (p. 131) and who, while standing weakly immobile, "gave that illusion of tautly sprung steel set delicately on a hair trigger" (p. 146). One further example will suffice. It is a case study in the use of construction, diction, and imagery to suggest (and induce) tension and release. Observe especially the number of moments of tense or charged immobility.

Jewel whistles again; the horse comes dropping down the slope, stiff-legged, his ears cocking and flicking, his mis-matched eyes rolling, and fetches up twenty feet away, broadside on, watching Jewel over his shoulder in an attitude kittenish and alert.

"Come here, sir," Jewel says. He moves. Moving that quick his coat, bunching, tongues swirling like so many flames. With tossing mane and tail and rolling eye the horse makes another short curveting rush and stops again, feet bunched, watching Jewel. Jewel walks steadily toward him, his hands at his sides. Save for Jewel's legs they are like two figures carved for a tableau savage in the sun.

When Jewel can almost touch him, the horse stands on his hind legs and slashes down at Jewel. Then Jewel is enclosed by a glittering maze of hooves as by an illusion of wings; among them, beneath the upreared chest, he moves with the flashing limberness of a snake.

For an instant before the jerk comes on to his arms he sees his whole body earth-free, horizontal, whipping snake-limber, until he finds the horse's nostrils and touches earth again. Then they are rigid, motionless, terrific, the horse back-thrust on stiffened, quivering legs, with lowered head; Jewel with dug heels, shutting off the horse's wind with one hand, with the other patting the horse's neck in short strokes myriad and caressing, cursing the horse with obscene ferocity.

They stand in rigid terrific hiatus, the horse trembling and groaning. Then Jewel is on the horse's back. He flows upward in a stooping swirl like the lash of a whip, his body in mid-air shaped to the horse. For another moment the horse stands spraddled, with lowered head, before it bursts into motion. They descend the hill in a series of spine-jolting jumps, Jewel high, leech-like on the withers, to the fence where the horse bunches to a scuttering halt again. [*AILD*, 345–346]

As a kind of summary, let me condense from the description in *Light in August* of Hightower's last moments. Here Faulkner emphasizes and juxtaposes motion and immobility and quiescence and turbulence, and brings together various images and suggestions of gathering, tension, and release. These powerfully communicate the minister's state of mind and emotion as for the first time he faces the evil in himself.

Thinking goes quietly, tranquilly, flowing on. . . . Thinking begins to slow now. It slows like a wheel beginning to run in sand, the axle, the vehicle, the power which propels it not yet aware. . . .

The wheel of thinking slows; the axle knows it now but the vehicle itself is still unaware. . . . He stops [thinking] suddenly. Motionless, unbreathing, there comes upon him a consternation which is about to be actual horror. He is aware of the sand now; with the realization of it he feels within himself a gathering as though for some tremendous effort. . . . As he sits in the window, leaning forward above his motionless hands, sweat begins to pour from him, springing out like blood, and pouring. Out of the instant [of recognition of his own guilt] the sandclutched wheel of thinking turns on with the slow implacability of a medieval torture instrument, beneath the wrenched and broken sockets of his spirit, his life. . . . The wheel, released, seems to rush on with a long sighing sound. He sits motionless in its aftermath, in his cooling sweat, while the sweat pours and pours. The wheel whirls on. It is going fast and smooth now. . . . Then it seems to him that some ultimate dammed flood within him breaks and rushes away. He seems to watch it, feeling himself losing contact with earth, lighter and lighter, emptying, floating. . . . The wheel turns on. It spins now, fading, without progress, as though turned by that final flood which had rushed out of him, leaving his body empty and lighter than a forgotten leaf and even more trivial than flotsam lying spent and still upon the window ledge. [pp. 426–431]

These various patterns and effects of tension and release are a persistent element in Faulkner's works and an important part of his vision. But what is most remarkable about his presentation and world is the emphasis upon tension itself and the amount of tension not released—the frequency with which, so to speak, the terrific muscular hiatuses are not followed by bursts of motion, with which the "straining, bulging, bellying" barriers "leaning, looming, imminent with collapse" do not give way, with which the explosions do not take place. The conditions that seem most fascinating to Faulkner and are most often called to our attention are those in which impulse pushes against some kind of restraint, in which forces remain in deadlock, unresolved. Most of the slow or arrested moments before release are such conditions, and they add up to a great many hours of tenseness for characters and readers. But even these comprise only a small part of this emphasis.

Very frequently, Faulkner simply announces the condition. Joe Christmas works "with a kind of baleful and restrained steadiness" (*LIA*, 29). He glares "from face to face with a sort of outraged yet still patient exasperation" (p. 188). Hightower's wife brushes aside a remark of his with "passionate and leashed humorlessness" (p. 422). Clytie thrusts food at Bon's son with "restrained savageness" (*AA*, 195). The jumper in *Pylon* is "tense, furious, restrained" (p. 121). Roth Edmonds in *Go Down, Moses* speaks with "harsh, restrained, furious impatience." [9] Often, Faulkner suggests the restraint by the word "contained" or by describing violent actions as "steady," "deliberate," "measured," or "methodical": McEachern whips Christmas "methodically, with slow and deliberate force." [10] Often he suggests it by emphasizing the stiffness or rigidity of a character's bearing. His treatment of Jewel in *As I Lay Dying* and Ab Snopes in "Barn Burning" are especially good examples of this.

The primary way in which Faulkner suggests this condition of unreleased tension will be further examined in the next section, but it has already been abundantly illustrated in the discussion of Faulkner's simultaneous assertions of various sorts of quiescence and turbulence. The states of rigid or furious or tense immobility, of calm, rapt, or static fury, quiet rage, or silent savageness, of furious electric immobile urgency, of calm, contained, rigid, boiling, of patient and seething fury—all suggest forces pushing against and being blocked by some kind of restraint. Other combinations of epithets suggesting this condition are "savage steadiness," "unflagging savageness," "quiet and desperate amazement," quiet or grave or peaceful astonishment, "musing and respectful consternation," "terrific and aimless and restive idleness," and "serene suspicion."

[9] Page 355. For other examples, see *CS*, 339; *ID*, 103; *H*, 149, 332.
[10] *LIA*, 131. For other examples, see pp. 35, 90.

Faulkner's pet word "outrage," although it does not suggest leashed forces directly, does suggest the existence of a barrier which is being violated, or a struggle between an active and a passive force. The frequent epithet "terrific" is usually more than a simple intensifier. Most often it seems to suggest leashed or unexpended rather than released power. We find it again and again in conjunction with immobility or with descriptions of motion in which a differential between apparent and real velocity has been suggested: an engine "has an effect of terrific nomotion. Yet it does move, creeping terrifically up and over the crest of the grade." [11] The sense of leashed power comes about because there is, in effect, a "drag" or brake on momentum. If the drag were removed, the engine would burst forward. Somewhat similar is the condition of the reader who has received simultaneous suggestions of motion and no motion, of force and barrier.

The conditions just described are effective because force remains undissipated; the power loses little or none of its potential. The condition remains one of suspense and tension. Faulkner's world, then, is much more aptly described as tense or explosive than as violent. Far more striking than the amount of force released is that which remains in check.

So far we have looked primarily at Faulkner's emphasis upon moments or hours or at most days of tension, and I have indicated that these play a large part in the lives of Faulkner's characters. For many of these characters, however, such tension is not merely an intermittent or occasional thing but a general quality of their experience and life predicament. What is most remarkable about many of the beings, even the most violent, who inhabit Faulkner's world is not the violent acts they commit or are exposed to, but the incredible states of tension or torment in which they exist, and which some of them seem determined to maintain and even heighten. They are not so much doomed as frustrated or exasperated almost beyond bearing.

[11] *LIA*, 386. See also pp. 7, 176, 182, 183; *AILD*, 443; *P*, 61, 217.

In *The Sound and the Fury*, for example, neither Benjy nor Quentin is ever able to escape or to diminish for more than a moment or two, the torment caused him by Caddy's promiscuity and its consequences. And both are peculiarly impotent to do anything about either her behavior or their own suffering. Benjy's idiocy prevents him from comprehending or accepting that Caddy will never return, and he goes on year after year waiting expectantly at the gate for her return and bellowing in anguish at each reminder of her absence. And sometimes there is not only anguish but unbearable frustration, as in the scene where he escapes from the yard and grabs a little girl and can neither speak nor cry nor satisfy either his physical or emotional needs:

I was trying to say, and I caught her, trying to say, and she screamed and I was trying to say and trying and the bright shapes began to stop and I tried to get out. I tried to get it off of my face, but the bright shapes were going again . . . and I tried to cry. But when I breathed in, I couldn't breathe out again to cry, and I tried to keep from falling off the hill and I fell off the hill into the bright, whirling shapes. [p. 72]

Quentin suffers a double torment since Caddy's behavior clashes not only with his ideal of virginity but with his own incestuous desires for her. He is driven at once toward killing her and possessing her and is capable of neither. Not only is he incapable of reconciling himself to her marriage months after it has taken place but his torment seems to continue at maximum intensity. He does not even yearn for release but rather for a sort of clean and perpetual torment in which he and Caddy will be in Hell *"amid the pointing and the horror walled by the clean flame"* (p. 136). And if Mr. Compson is correct, Quentin's suicide is not an attempt to escape his torment but to preserve it, for he fears that time might ease the pain. In his Appendix to the book Faulkner writes that Quentin "loved and lived in a deliberate and almost perverted anticipation of death as a lover loves and deliberately refrains from the waiting willing friendly tender incredible body of his beloved" (p. 9).

Jason Compson sees life almost entirely as a conspiracy designed to frustrate him, and he exists in an almost perpetual state of outrage. When his niece steals his money, he experiences a "red unbearable fury which on that night and at intervals recurring with little or no diminishment for the next five years, made him seriously believe would at some unwarned instant destroy him" (p. 20). Like other Faulkner characters Jason often seems "to get an actual pleasure out of his outrage and impotence" (p. 319). Caddy is frustrated in her attempts to see and provide for her illegitimate daughter, Quentin, to the point where she resembles "some kind of a toy that's wound up too tight and about to burst all to pieces" (p. 227).

The usual condition of Jewel Bundren in *As I Lay Dying* is one of smouldering fury. His occasional eruptions bring him no release. The lives of Addie, Darl, Dewey Dell, and Vardaman are largely characterized by varying kinds of tension and self-torment which they do not know how to escape. Darl views the inner being even of the placid Cash as a thing of tension and terror. He and Cash "look at one another with long probing looks, looks that plunge unimpeded through one another's eyes and into the ultimate secret place where for an instant Cash and Darl crouch flagrant and unabashed in all the old terror and the old foreboding, alert and secret and without shame" (p. 439). In *Light in August*, Joe Christmas is in large measure conceived as a tension between white and black blood and between conflicting needs to hurt others and to be hurt himself. His usual state is one of restrained fury. His astonishment at his occasional moments of peace is a measure of his usual state of torment. He gains no release through his violent actions, for as Faulkner emphasizes, his enemy in his own breast. Joanna Burden is obviously a desperately divided and frustrated woman, and the frustration is responsible for the wildness of her behavior. Hightower, too, is a divided soul whose life is marked

by debilitating internal conflict. Like Joe's, his death is conceived as a release of pent-up substance. Even Byron Bunch
goes through a minor ordeal of tension and frustration at the
hands of his beloved Lena.

In *Sanctuary* all the characters suffer some major frustration,
and most of them go through periods of intense mental and
emotional torment. Even the cold and seemingly emotionless
Popeye is clearly tormented by his sexual impotence, and most
of his violent acts are closely related to this central frustration.
But in this work, fear and terror rather than tension seem
dominant. In *Absalom, Absalom!* Rosa Coldfield exists in a
state of "impotent yet indomitable frustration" and gains no
relief from her endless flood of language. She can "neither forgive nor revenge herself" upon the dead Sutpen. In a letter to
his son about her death, Mr. Compson goes so far as to suggest
that her torment is so necessary to her that it would be un-
fortunate if it had to end with her death (pp. 174, 377). Sutpen,
who above all wants a son, and yet refuses to recognize one son
and thus loses another, and who is killed largely because of his
bitterness at having failed to produce a third, is perhaps the
most tragically frustrated of Faulkner's characters. Not only
is he utterly defeated in his effort to achieve his "design" but
he is never able to comprehend why he failed or to accept his
defeat. Henry Sutpen and Charles Bon so continually behave
in precisely the ways that will maintain and intensify their
already severe mental and emotional tension that one can only
assume that they somehow relish the spectacle of their torment.
Of Henry, Shreve says,

Jesus, think of the load he had to carry, born of two Methodists
(or of one long invincible line of Methodists) and raised in pro-
vincial north Mississippi, faced with incest, incest of all things that
might have been reserved for him, that all his heredity and training
had to rebel against on principle, and in a situation where he knew
that neither incest nor training was going to help him solve it. [p.
340]

And there is even one more turn of the screw reserved for him, for he will learn that his friend Bon, who loves his sister, is not only his and her half-brother but also part Negro, and that the marriage would therefore involve miscegenation as well as incest. Moreover he learns this only after four years of suspense as to what Bon will decide about the marriage and as to what he himself will decide and only after having wrestled with himself to the point where he has learned to bear the idea of incest. Finally, unable to bear the idea of miscegenation, he must kill Bon, who is not only his brother but his closest friend. Bon must suffer not only the frustration of his desire for Judith but he is denied the thing he wants even more than he wants Judith and for which he has waited and waited for four years—some word of recognition from Sutpen, his father.

Judith Sutpen's surface calm is never broken, even when her beloved is killed by her brother. We may guess at her interior, however, from the letter she leaves to posterity, in which she describes living as a struggle against restraining forces, "like trying to, having to, move your arms and legs with strings only the same strings are hitched to all the other arms and legs and the others are all trying and . . . the strings are all in one another's way" (p. 127).

In Faulkner's other novels most of the main characters experience similar tensions, torment and frustration which they seem incapable of relieving or diminishing. Especially noteworthy are the reporter in *Pylon* and the tall convict in *The Wild Palms*. The former is another of those who behaves in just the ways most likely to heighten and prolong his torment and whose fate is utter frustration and defeat. Alcohol, no sleep, unrequited love, and a sense of guilt bring him to a point where he feels he has got himself "stretched out too far and too thin and something is going to bust" (p. 300). As far as we can tell, it doesn't bust. No character in fiction is more exasperated and frustrated and unable to release his fury than the tall convict, who not only is faced with a Mississippi flood but is forced to share his little boat with, and be responsible for, a pregnant woman, or as she seems to him, an "inert monstrous sentient womb" (p. 163). Already "toyed with twice by that risible and concentrated power of water, once more than should have fallen to the lot of any one man, any one lifetime" (p. 250), he still has something else in store for him.

At first he refused to believe it, not that he felt that now he had served out and discharged his apprenticeship to mischance, had with the birth of the child reached and crossed the crest of his Golgotha and would now be, possibly not permitted so much as ignored, to descend the opposite slope free-wheeling. That was not his feeling at all. What he declined to accept was the fact that a power, a force such as that which had been consistent enough to concentrate upon him with deadly undeviation for weeks, should with all the wealth of cosmic violence and disaster to draw from, have been so barren of invention and imagination, so lacking in pride of artistry and craftsmanship, as to repeat itself twice. Once he had accepted, twice he even forgave, but three times he simply declined to believe, particularly when he was at last persuaded to realize that this third time was to be instigated not by the blind potency of volume and motion but by human direction and hands: that now the cosmic joker, foiled twice, had stooped in its vindictive concentration to the employing of dynamite. [pp. 264–265]

In addition, there are a host of minor characters, like Mrs. Armstid and Doc Hines in *Light in August,* the jumper in *Pylon,* Ab Snopes in "Barn Burning," and Ginsfarb in "Death Drag," whose characteristic condition is one of seething or restrained or latent fury. And there are those brought to the breaking point by frustration, like Mink Snopes, Houston, and Eula's admirers in *The Hamlet;* like Boon in "The Bear" and the dietitian in *Light in August;* and like Brown in the last-named work, who reaches a point where his "rage and impotence are now almost ecstatic. He seems to muse now upon a sort of timeless and beautiful infallibility in his unpredictable frustrations" (p. 381).

But even this rage and impotence must have been mild compared with that of Crawford Gowrie in *Intruder in the Dust*. First he is forced to watch Jake Montgomery dig up the body of the man he has murdered: "—watching there in the woods behind the fence seeing himself not merely betrayed out of the blackmail but all the agony and suspense to go through again not to mention the physical labor" (p. 230). Then, after killing Montgomery, putting him in the grave, and filling it again,

"—and here it is again, the desperate the dreadful urgency, the loneliness the pariah-hood having not only the horror and repudiation of all man against him but having to struggle with the sheer inertia of earth and the terrible heedless rush of time but even beating all that coalition at last, the grave decent again even to the displaced flowers and the evidence of his original crime at last disposed and secure . . . then to straighten up at last and for the first time draw a full breath since the moment when Jake had approached him . . . and then to hear whatever it was that sent him plunging back up the hill then crawling creeping to lie once more panting but this time not merely in rage and terror but in almost incredulous disbelief that a single man could be subject to this much bad luck, watching you three not only undo his work for the second time but double it now since you not only exposed Jake Montgomery but you refilled the grave and even put the flowers back." [pp. 230–231]

Not only this, but the cause of all his "agony and frustration and outrage and grief and shame and irreparable loss . . . not even a white man but a nigger" (p. 232).

In Faulkner's world, then, conditions in general and the psychological conditions of characters are persistently defined in terms of quiescence, turbulence, and tension. Turbulence and violence are generally conceived of as releases or attempted releases of tension. But, although Faulkner's presentation is to a large extent governed by the notion of tension and release, he seems most fascinated by temporarily or permanently unreleased tension, by frustrated impulse. It is these unresolved and unstable conditions that are most emphasized and that seem the normal ones in his world. In their mildest form these are simply conditions in which there is some element of suspense because of a potential or imminent event. At their most severe they are highly explosive states in which some kind of barrier or container is strained to the breaking point. This is a fairly common condition among Faulkner characters, and one which—if we were to judge from their avoidance of behavior that would give them release—they seem to want. We might wonder whether their creator, perhaps, also relishes their condition unduly. It does not necessarily follow that a writer who enjoys the linguistic tension and frustration of the oxymoron also enjoys human tension and frustration. On the other hand, fictional characters are largely constructed from, and, in one sense, are no more than, figures of speech.

It is no coincidence, I think, that virtually all of Faulkner's experiments with form and style—his rapidly shifting points of view, his disordered time sequences, his unsyntactical marathon sentences, his oxymorons, his whole method, as Conrad Aiken puts it, "of *deliberately withheld meaning*, of progressive and partial and delayed disclosure"—have one effect in common: tension and frustration in the reader. Not only is the reader uneasy about what is going to happen; he is also disturbed and tense because he is not sure of the meaning of what is happening and often is not even sure what is happening. As Joseph Warren Beach says:

Half the time we are swimming under water, holding our breath and straining our eyes to read off the meaning of submarine phenomena, unable to tell fact from figure, to fix the reference of pronouns, or distinguish between guess and certainty. From time to time we come to the surface, gasping, to breathe the air of concrete fact and recorded truth, only to go floundering again the next moment through crashing waves of doubt and speculation.[12]

[12] Quoted in *William Faulkner: Two Decades of Criticism*, ed. F. J. Hoffman and O. W. Vickery (East Lansing: Michigan State College Press, 1950), p. 29.

This is to say nothing of the tension induced by Faulkner's visceral and kinesthetic imagery and his persistent use of opposition. Our tense condition very much resembles the characteristic state of Faulkner's characters, a state we also share through empathy. No more than they are we permitted to achieve final resolution or release.

The patterns of rhetoric and perception we have been looking at all strikingly reveal Faulkner's tendency to present experience in antithetic terms and clearly indicate what might well be called a polar imagination. But let me stress again that this should not be allowed to obscure the importance of these patterns in their own right. They must not be viewed simply as illustrations of the polar imagination. Of significance is not only that Faulkner juxtaposes motion and immobility or quiescence and turbulence, or that he emphasizes the conflicting forces which produce tension, but also that he chooses these particular aspects of experience to emphasize and that he emphasizes them as much as he does. His concern with these rather simple and elemental kinds of experience may not be so obvious or exciting as many other aspects of his presentation, but as much as anything else, I believe, it helps to provide the shape and impact of his fictional world.

PART II

The Polar Imagination

« 5 »

The Attraction of Extremes

THE extent to which Faulkner creates, emphasizes, and perpetuates conditions of tension is remarkable, and I have gone so far as to maintain that tension comes to seem the usual or dominant condition in his fictional world and in the characters who inhabit it, and in his readers as they experience it. I have suggested also that the emphasis on tension is not simply a matter of rhetoric or of conscious artistic intent, but part of a fundamental mode of thought and perception which lies behind and influences both rhetoric and intent. It is only a part, however, and perhaps as much a by-product as a part.

This underlying mode of perception I have labeled "the polar imagination." I have no psychological warrant for the term, nor is it an entirely adequate one. I use it to describe what must be a deep-seated tendency in Faulkner to view and interpret experience in extreme terms and to see life as composed essentially of pairs of warring entities. Nothing less than a basic habit or bent of mind could account for the extent and variety of antithesis we find in his writing or for the degree to which he presents a world of extremes.

I do not think I exaggerate by saying that there is scarcely a major character in Faulkner's novels save Byron Bunch and V. K. Ratliff who does not represent some extreme or exhibit extreme behavior of some variety. It is a tribute to Faulkner's skill that we are so little disturbed by this as we read and that his fictional world comes to seem as plausible as it does. One tends to forget, for example, in *The Sound and the Fury*, how utterly monstrous the Compson family is: the father, a failure at almost everything, hopelessly immersed in cynicism, the past, and the bottle; the mother, an extreme hypochondriac, capable of little more than self-pity; the children, an idiot, a severe neurotic who commits suicide, an utterly lost and tormented girl who abandons her own daughter, and a ruthlessly inhuman materialist with deep feelings of persecution. Nor are we as aware as we might be through much of *Light in August* that the cast includes a murderer, a suicide, a man who runs out on his pregnant sweetheart, a man and woman each divided and tormented almost to the point of schizophrenia, a fanatically bigoted zealot, and a madman who has, in effect, murdered his own daughter. Or perhaps it is merely familiarity that blurs our awareness of these extremities, for many of the early critics of Faulkner were able to see nothing but the abnormalities, and the casual reader is still shocked by them. Or perhaps we have been too busy explicating to see the characters clearly.

The remarkable thing about this push toward extremities is the variety of areas in which it operates. If a character is loquacious, he tends like Darl, Rosa Coldfield, Gavin Stevens, or the reporter in *Pylon* not merely to flood but to drown himself and his hearers with language. If he is laconic like Jewel Bundren or Flem Snopes, he scarcely speaks at all. If he is thin like the reporter in *Pylon*, he is incredibly thin, so thin that when he sits down it is with "a loose dry scarecrowlike clatter as though of his own skeleton and the wooden chair's in contact" (p. 43). If he is proud and irascible like Lucas Beauchamp, he is so proud and irascible that he infuriates almost everyone he encounters. Eula Varner is not merely sexually provocative, she torments all men virtually beyond endurance. The polar imagination, I suspect, finds the notion of marrying this fertility "goddess" to the impotent Flem Snopes attractive in much the same way it finds attractive the notion of having the apparently cold and puritanical Joanna Burden engage in sexual excesses that shock even Joe Christmas, or finds attractive the idea of making Joe Christmas at once a killer and a Christ symbol, or finds attractive the verbal extremity, tension, and opposition of phrases like "stern fury" or "chained irrevocably . . . not by love but by implacable constancy and invincible repudiation" (*H*, 237).

In the preceding section we saw numerous examples of extremities of tension or torment, conditions in which the patience or sanity of a character was strained almost to the breaking point. And in a number of the illustrations it was as though even the extremes were insufficient, as though Faulkner were seeking somehow to go even beyond the extreme, to give the screw a turn or even several turns beyond the final turn. Thus Chick Mallison is tormented to "rage and fury beyond even his own concept of his capacity" (*ID*, 81). Thus Crawford Gowrie and the tall convict experience a succession of misfortunes which drive them beyond rage or terror to states of "incredulous disbelief" that they could be subject to so much bad luck. The description of Gowrie's torment already quoted (*ID*, 230–232) contains what is surely one of the most visible and unabashed rhetorical tightenings of the screw in literature.

The word "outrage," one of Faulkner's favorites, suggests, in itself, the violation of some extreme limit, and is another indication of his straining toward and beyond extremities. But here again Faulkner sometimes presses even farther. Thus when Clytie stops Rosa Coldfield from running up to Judith, Rosa describes the impact as "too soon and too quick to be mere amazement and outrage" and then realizes "it was not outrage that I waited for, out of which I had instinctively cried; it was not terror: it was some cumulative over-reach of despair itself" (*AA*, 139–140).

In more humorous fashion, Jason Compson seems often to exist in a fatalistic state somewhere beyond outrage and despair.

The last straw has long since been laid upon him and he not only expects additional ones but is surprised whenever they do not turn out to be whole bales. Perhaps the most delightful example of this occurs during his first chase of Quentin and the man in the red tie. Already suffering from an unbearable headache which has been made worse by bumpy roads, he must walk across a plowed field,

the only one I had seen since I left town, with every step like somebody was walking along behind me, hitting me on the head with a club. I kept thinking that when I got across the field at least I'd have something level to walk on, that wouldn't jolt me every step, but when I got into the woods it was full of underbrush and I had to twist around through it, and then I came to a ditch full of briers. I went along it for awhile, but it got thicker and thicker, and all the time Earl probably telephoning home about where I was and getting Mother all upset again.

When I finally got through I had had to wind around so much that I had to stop and figure out just where the car would be. I knew they wouldn't be far from it, just under the closest bush, so I turned and worked back toward the road. Then I couldn't tell just how far I was, so I'd have to stop and listen, and then with my legs not using so much blood, it all would go into my head like it would explode any minute, and the sun getting down just to where it could shine straight into my eyes and my ears ringing so I couldn't hear anything. I went on, trying to move quiet, then I heard a dog or something and I knew that when he scented me he'd have to come helling up, then it would be all off.

I had gotten beggar lice and twigs and stuff all over me, inside my clothes and shoes and all, and then I happened to look around and I had my hand right on a bunch of poison oak. The only thing I couldn't understand was why it was just poison oak and not a snake or something. So I didn't even bother to move it. I just stood there until the dog went away. Then I went on. [*SF*, 257–258]

Faulkner's experiments with form and style strikingly reveal this same tendency to strain toward and even beyond extremities, to press against customary limits and barriers. More persistently even than Joyce or Virginia Woolf, and in more varied ways, he has sought new and unconventional structures. In *The Wild Palms* he juxtaposes by alternation the chapters of two independent narratives; in *Requiem for a Nun* he alternates historical narrative and the acts of a play. In *As I Lay Dying* he experiments with kaleidoscopically rapid shifts in tone and point of view, and in the same work and elsewhere with the points of view of the mentally deficient and deranged. And he has gone farther than most moderns in his experiments with stream of consciousness and fluid chronology.

Stylistically, of course, his most obvious and dramatic straining has been at the limits of the sentence—the limits of both length and syntax. Few would deny that in this he has frequently pushed far beyond the limits. The "Jail" section of *Requiem for a Nun*, which runs for fifty pages without a period, is not strictly speaking a single sentence, and it is easier to follow than some of his one- or two-page sentences, but the very attempt to create such an entity suggests the strength of his desire to press beyond conventional boundaries. His frequently inflated rhetoric and his tendency to use hyperbole of all sorts are further stylistic movements toward extremity.

But for all its importance and obvious force, Faulkner's tendency toward extremity, in itself, is perhaps the least interesting aspect of what I have called his polar imagination. Most interesting is the extent to which he seems to view and present life in antithetic terms and the extent to which he seems fascinated by that especially tense sort of antithesis in which the opposed entities remain in a state of deadlock where they can neither be separated nor reconciled. The most extreme and dramatic indication of this fascination is the number and variety of his self-contradictory or oxymoronic constructions. We have already seen many of these in his simultaneous suggestions of motion and immobility, sound and silence, and quiescence and turbulence, and we have seen some characters who are in a sense living oxymorons. But even these give little idea of the

astonishing number and variety of characters and events described in oxymoronic or near oxymoronic terms in every
Faulkner novel. Here is a small sampling of only the most
compact oxymorons from two of Faulkner's novels, which may
give some idea of the pervasiveness of the phenomenon and the
variety of contexts in which it occurs.

In *Light in August,* Doc Hines is "paradoxically rapt and
alert at the same time" (p. 323) and has the ability "to flux
instantaneously between complete attention that does not seem
to hear, and that comalike bemusement in which the stare of
his apparently inverted eye is as uncomfortable as though he
held them [his companions] with his hand" (p. 334). His
wife's face is at the same time "peaceful and terrible" and her
attitude is "at once like a rock and like a crouching beast" (p.
348). The face of Hightower, with whom the Hineses are talking is "at once gaunt and flabby" (p. 77). He is capable of thinking "not quizzical, not humorous; not unquizzical and not hu-
morless too" (p. 419). The Sunday morning service in the church
in which he once preached has "a stern and formal fury" (p.
321). He hears singing from the church, "a sound at once
austere and rich, abject and proud" (p. 65). He thinks of his
father as being "two separate and complete people" (p. 415).
The father is further described as "a minister without a church
and a soldier without an enemy" (p. 415). The slave of his father
has a face "both irascible and calm" (p. 416). Hightower thinks
his "only salvation must be to return to the place to die where
my life had already ceased before it began" (p. 418). When he
resigns his pulpit "the town was sorry with being glad" (p. 60).

Joe Christmas' feet are capable of moving at "deliberate random" (p. 291). He can "hear without hearing them wails of terror and distress quieter than sighs all about him" (p. 293). He
knows that he should flee from Joanna Burden, but remains,

watching the two creatures that struggled in the one body like two
moongleamed shapes struggling drowning in alternate throes upon
the surface of a thick black pool beneath the last moon. Now it

would be that still, cold, contained figure of the first phase who, even though lost and damned, remained somehow impervious and impregnable; then it would be the other, the second one, who in furious denial of that impregnability strove to drown in the black abyss of its own creating that physical purity which had been preserved too long now even to be lost. Now and then they would come to the black surface, locked like sisters. [p. 228]

Joanna's father and grandfather fight with "a kind of deadly play and smiling seriousness" (p. 215). Lena Grove gives Armstid, Winterbottom, and Armstid's wagon a glance which is at once "innocent and profound" (p. 7). Later she and the wagon come slowly together "without any semblance of progress" (p. 10). She passes fields and woods "at once static and fluid" (p. 24). Her seducer, Lucas Burch, has a tone and manner "that carried within itself its own confounding and mendacity" (p. 32).

. Joe Christmas is a tormented mixture of white and black blood, at once a killer and Christ symbol. Joanna Burden is a Northerner who lives all her life in the South, a puritan who gives herself to violent sexual excess. Hightower cannot separate or reconcile religion, galloping cavalry, and his dead grandfather. Like his father, he is a minister without a church. Lena Grove is a mother without a husband.

In *The Hamlet*, Will Varner is "at once active and lazy" (p. 6). His son Jody wears a costume that is "at once ceremonial and negligee" (p. 11). Tull has a "gentle, almost sad face until you unravelled what were actually two separate expressions —a temporary one of static peace and quiet overlaying a constant one of definite even though faint harriedness" (p. 10). Armstid's eyes are "at once vague and intense" (p. 331). After his illness Ratliff emanates "a sort of delicate robustness" (p. 78). Ab Snopes's homestead is a "cluttered desolation" (p. 54). Eula Varner exists in a "teeming vacuum" (p. 107). At the age of eleven, sitting on the schoolhouse steps eating a cold potato, she "postulated that ungirdled quality of the very goddesses in . . . Homer and Thucydides: of being at once corrupt and immaculate, at once virgins and the mothers of warriors and of grown men" (p. 128). She is "at once supremely unchaste and inviolable" (p. 131). Her admirers depart "seething and decorous" and ride in "furious wordless amity" (p. 150). Houston and the girl he is to marry are "chained irrevocably . . . not by love but by implacable constancy and invincible repudiation" (p. 237). Up to a point their struggle, "for all its deadly seriousness . . . had retained something of childhood, something both illogical and consistent, both reasonable and bizarre" (p. 239). Houston can never escape her face, "tranquil, terrifying" (p. 240). After being shot by Mink Snopes he looks "up out of the red roar, into the face [of Mink] which with his own was wedded and twinned forever now by the explosion of that ten-gauge shell—the dead who would carry the living into the ground with him; the living who must bear about the repudiating earth with him forever, the deathless slain" (p. 249).

I have given this much space to the oxymoron not only to give dramatic illustration of the polar imagination at work, but because that curious figure, more than anything else, can help to illuminate Faulkner's work in general. Not only does its abundance indicate a great deal about Faulkner's general intentions and effects, but the figure, itself, in miniature form contains or suggests many of the most important qualities of his art and vision.

Like Faulkner's writing in general, the oxymoron involves sharp polarity, extreme tension, a high degree of conceptual and stylistic antithesis, and the simultaneous suggestion of disparate or opposed elements. Moreover, the figure tends to hold these elements in suspension rather than to fuse them. Both terms of an oxymoron are in a sense true. One's recognition that the contradiction is apparent rather than real does not eliminate the tension between the terms, for the conflicting elements remain. Neither negates the other. The oxymoron, on the one hand, achieves a kind of order, definiteness, and coherence by virtue of the clear and sharp antithesis it involves. On the other, it moves toward disorder and incoherence by virtue of its qualities of irresolution and self-contradiction. Its validity is usually intuitive and emotional rather than logical or intellectual. It does not so much explore or analyze a condition as render it forcefully. Traditionally it has often been used to reflect desperately divided states of mind. I shall expand upon most of these qualities later. For the moment let me point out some other ways in which Faulkner's writing is governed by the polar imagination and its penchant for antithesis.

« 6 »

Conceptual Antithesis

ALL authors, and all human beings for that matter, tend very much to conceptualize life in broad polar or antithetic terms: black-white, right-wrong, heaven-hell, flesh-spirit, true-false, and the like. And I suppose that the major themes of any novel could be expressed antithetically. But even in this respect Faulkner goes beyond most; his works are unusual in the number, variety, and intensity even of major conceptual or thematic antitheses.

The most striking and persistent of these major conceptual antitheses is, of course, that of white and black. It is so obvious a part of his work that illustration is hardly necessary. Let me stress, however, that this antithesis involves much more than the mere presence of whites and Negroes, that as individuals and groups, as physical bodies and "ideas," they are again and again dramatically and conceptually sharply juxtaposed.[1] In addition, and perhaps most striking, there are the juxtapositions of white and black within single families and single individuals, to which I will confine the illustrations here.

Light in August, Absalom, Absalom! Go Down, Moses, and

[1] For a few especially vivid juxtapositions of white and Negro figures or of concepts of white and black, see *SF*, 105–107, 315–316; *LIA*, 99–102, 196–197, 221–222; *AA*, 139–140, 205–207, 377–378; *U*, 116–118; GDM, 53–57, 115–118, 262–295; *ID*, 15–27, 58–65, 153–156, 203–204, 215–217; *RN*, 270–284.

Intruder in the Dust are in varying degrees concerned with the problem of miscegenation. Miscegenation could be conceived of and dramatized as a fusion of races or bloods, and the emphasis could be placed upon that fusion and upon the idea of the half-caste. As presented by Faulkner, however, the bloods do not fuse; they remain independent and antithetic. This conception is most pronounced in *Light in August*. Joe Christmas is not a mulatto. He is white and Negro. The white and black bloods run separately in his veins.

The black blood drove him first to the Negro cabin. And then the white blood drove him out of there, as it was the black blood which snatched up the pistol and the white blood which would not let him fire it. And it was the white blood which sent him to the minister. . . . Then I believe that the white blood deserted him for the moment . . . allowing the black to rise in its final moment and make him turn upon that on which he had postulated his hope of salvation. It was the black blood which swept him by his own desire beyond the aid of any man, swept him up into that ecstasy out of a black jungle where life has already ceased before the heart stops and death is desire and fulfillment. And then the black blood failed him again, as it must have in crises all his life. He did not kill the minister. He merely struck him with the pistol and ran on and crouched behind that table and defied the black blood for the last time, as he had been defying it for thirty years. He crouched behind that overturned table and let them shoot him to death, with that loaded and unfired pistol in his hand.[2]

The antithesis is apparent even in Joe's clothing, which, Faulkner frequently reminds us, consists of dark and white.

Often in close connection with the antithesis of white and

[2] *LIA*, 393–394. Compare the description of the relationship between the white and black blood in Lucas Beauchamp (*GDM*, 104). In the quotation above the fact that white and black become in part symbolic of good and evil, of restraint and energy, and perhaps of Christianity and paganism does not deny my point but rather strengthens it. One may question the ability of that single antithesis to carry so much symbolic weight.

black, as might be expected, there is the antithesis of North and South:

The North: not north but North, outland and circumscribing and not even a geographical place but an emotional idea, a condition of which he had fed from his mother's milk to be ever and constant on the alert not at all to fear and not actually anymore to hate but just—a little wearily sometimes and sometimes even with tongue in cheek—to defy.[3]

The passage continues with the boy's vision of the gap between the North and South growing ever greater. Observe the initial stress on the identity of the groups before the emphasis upon the gap.

There looked down on him and his countless row on row of faces which resembled his face and spoke the same language he spoke and at times even answered to the same names he bore yet between whom and him and his there was no longer any real kinship and soon there would not even be any contact since the very mutual words they used would no longer have the same significance and soon after that even this would be gone because they would be too far asunder even to hear one another. [*ID*, 152–153]

Gavin Stevens continues the boy's thoughts about the antithesis. As we shall see again in a variety of instances, when the gap has been fully established, there is the attempt to cross it or to suggest the possibility or existence of fusion:

"That's why we must resist the North: not just to preserve ourselves nor even the two of us as one to remain one nation because that will be the inescapable byproduct of what we will preserve." [*ID*, 154]

So naturally congenial to Faulkner's polar imagination are these white-Negro North-South tensions and oppositions that one feels

[3] *ID*, 152. For further examples, see the continuation of this passage, pp. 153–156; also *LIA*, 408–426; *AA*, 287, 346–347; and *GDM*, 283–287. In *The Unvanquished*, the Civil War and post–Civil War North-South conflicts are a dominant motif throughout.

that if they had not existed he would have had to invent them. For they are not only clear and sharp antitheses but conditions in which the opposed entities seem at once antagonistic and yet curiously inseparable and interdependent.

The relationship between the Southern past and present has much this same quality; and while the O'Donnell, Cowley, Warren line of criticism has probably overstressed the extent and consistency of this antithesis in Faulkner, it unquestionably plays an enormous part in his thought and work. It is most dramatically asserted in a story like "A Rose for Emily" or in passages like the much-quoted comment about the men of the past in *Absalom, Absalom!* who were

"people too as we are, and victims too as we are, but victims of a different circumstance, simpler and therefore, integer for integer, larger, more heroic and the figures therefore more heroic too, not dwarfed and involved but distinct, uncomplex who had the gift of loving once or dying once instead of being diffused and scattered creatures drawn blindly limb from limb from a grab bag and assembled." [p. 89]

"The Jail" sequence in *Requiem for a Nun* is almost entirely constructed of juxtapositions of past and present such as the following:

There were new people in the town now, strangers, outlanders, living in new minute glass-walled houses set as neat and orderly and antiseptic as cribs in a nursery ward, in new subdivisions named Fairfield or Longwood or Halcyon Acres which had once been the lawn or back yard or kitchen garden of the old residences (the old obsolete columned houses still standing among them like old horses surged suddenly out of slumber in the middle of a flock of sheep). [p. 249]

But, in addition, scattered throughout his writing are countless brief comparisons and juxtapositions which remind us of the gap between the two eras and indicate that Faulkner is continually aware of it.

Besides the major antithesis of two eras there is, of course, the continual juxtaposition of past and present events, which is one of Faulkner's most persistent and widely noted structural devices. And while the events juxtaposed are not necessarily contrasting ones, the result of the persistent juxtaposition is in part a sense of separateness between moments in time. We watch, so to speak, the clock jump back and forth between moments rather than move imperceptibly from one to another. It is true that Faulkner is very much concerned with the idea of the past fusing with the present either in someone's consciousness or in a realm outside time, but his method is such that the past exists largely as moments or flashes with gaps in between and with gaps between them and the present.[4] Again we encounter the simultaneous suggestion of gap and fusion, a particularly striking explicit illustration of which is provided at the end of "The Jail" section of *Requiem for a Nun:*

You know again now that there is no time: no space: no distance; . . . there is the clear undistanced voice as though out of the delicate antenna-skeins of radio, further than empress's throne, than splendid insatiation, even than matriarch's peaceful rocking chair, across the vast instantaneous intervention, from the long long time ago: *"Listen, stranger; this was myself: this was I."* [pp. 261–262]

[4] Lowrey, Swiggart, and others argue that Faulkner's form and content, both, emphasize a view of time as continuous and whole. Such an emphasis may, at times, be Faulkner's intent, but I would insist that his method does as much to fragment time as to fuse it. Sartre, as Bowling points out, pays insufficient attention to Dilsey's view of time, but this does not negate his description of Faulkner's effects. Sutherland suggests that Faulkner's "real basis of composition is an absolute past, not a consecutive history. It is a flat simultaneous past over which the 'order of the heart' can move as it pleases. . . . Faulkner's past feels like the paintings of Pompeii, which are all as if painted the very day they were buried in ashes, an inordinately rich and fluid sensuality arrested and separated from us both by a terrible hardness of surface and a definite catastrophe. I think this hard and immobile past, separate both from us and from the continuity of history, is the only kind of past that really convinces us" (Donald Sutherland, "Time on Our Hands," *Yale French Studies*, no. 10 [1953], 7).

Worth noting here also is Faulkner's characteristic effort to stress the contradictory aspects of his statement. We have first the immense emphasis on the unity of past and present, provided by the parallel and repetitive "no time: no space: no distance," followed by the equally persuasive emphasis on the gap between the two, provided by the "further than . . . than . . . even" construction, the phrase "vast intervention," and the repetition of "long."

This dual emphasis helps us to understand why some critics like Lowrey and Swiggart insist that Faulkner sees and presents time as continuous and whole, while others like Sartre and Sutherland insist that his presentation makes time discontinuous and seals off the past from the present. For, clearly, Faulkner wants to do both these things, to emphasize both the pastness of the past and its presentness. His frequent reminder that characters out of the past, like the Sutpens, are ghosts works in both these directions, for the word ghost emphasizes that the character is dead and in a different realm and at the same time suggests that he hovers about the present.

Much has been written and will undoubtedly continue to be written about Faulkner's treatment of the relationship between man and nature.[5] But, whatever the ethical and economic intricacies suggested in *Go Down, Moses*, the overwhelmingly dominant relationship between man and nature, dramatized and made explicit in his works, is one of sharp antithesis. I am thinking not only of such obvious examples as the titanic struggles between man and nature presented in *As I Lay Dying* and *The Wild Palms* or of the frequent images in *Go Down, Moses* and

[5] Robert Penn Warren's discussion is particularly interesting ("William Faulkner," in *Two Decades of Criticism*, pp. 88–92). See also Irving Howe, *William Faulkner: A Critical Study* (New York: Random House, 1951), pp. 94–97; and H. M. Campbell and R. F. Foster, *William Faulkner: A Critical Appraisal* (Norman: University of Oklahoma Press, 1951), pp. 140–158. Vincent F. Hopper sees the "natural" pole of this antithesis as including the natural functions of the body ("Faulkner's Paradise Lost," *Virginia Quarterly Review*, XXIII [1947], 406–408).

elsewhere of man punily scratching at the wilderness or pushing it back or destroying it or fouling it.[6] Nor am I thinking only of the not-yet-explored emphasis upon nature as the devourer and obliterator of man and his works.[7] The antithesis often remains even in the scenes in *Go Down, Moses* where Ike McCaslin and others are most a part of the wilderness, for Faulkner frequently juxtaposes the little figures and the immense, separate, "inattentive," and "looming" surroundings.[8] Ike, himself, continually emphasizes the antithesis and separateness of the two, and near the end of his life cries out passionately: "No wonder the ruined woods I used to know dont cry for retribution! . . . The people who have destroyed it will accomplish its revenge" (p. 364). If, as Faulkner sometimes suggests, we are to think of the wilderness as Ike's mother, mistress, and wife, the respective sizes and one-sided affection of the parties is deeply disturbing. Ike's meeting with the snake (p. 329) can hardly be described as a maternal or marital embrace. It is, like many conditions in Faulkner's world, an uneasy armistice.

The persistence and strength of this antithesis[9] becomes clearest, perhaps, when we read the one section of Faulkner's works in which a type of fusion is achieved: the description in *The Hamlet* of the idiot Ike's idyll with the cow (pp. 204–213). But, interestingly, as we shall see also in his "celebrations" of fecundity, he shifts here to a style and tone that is largely a

---

[6] See *GDM*, 177, 257–258, 318–321, 340–343, 353–354; *S*, 1 ff.; *RN*, 39.

[7] See, for example, *H*, 3–4, 22, 207; *GDM*, 205. Consider the floods in *As I Lay Dying* and *The Wild Palms*.

[8] For example, pp. 202 and 208.

[9] Let me stress, however, that although the antithesis between man and nature is persistent, the nature of the juxtaposed elements and the relationship between them is by no means consistent. Compare, for example, the relationship between man and the flood in *The Wild Palms* with that between man and the wilderness in *Go Down, Moses*. Or compare the attitude toward the encroachment upon the wilderness generally prevalent in *Go Down, Moses* with that expressed in *Requiem for a Nun*: "the broad rich fecund burgeoning fields, pushing thrusting each year further and further back the wilderness and its denizens" (p. 39).

parody of a pastoral and romantic view of life. And the "man," after all, who is involved in the fusion, is an idiot. Then, too, the fusion, itself, in one important respect, is a highly unnatural one.

Somewhat related to the antithesis of man and nature are the oppositions between the natural and the mechanical and the human and the machine. These play an important part in *Sartoris* and *Pylon* and are present in most of the later works.[10] In *Requiem for a Nun*, Faulkner visualizes a day "when all America, after cutting down all the trees and leveling the hills and mountains with bulldozers, would have to move underground to make room for, get out of the way of, the motor cars" (p. 248). In *A Fable* he develops this idea into a powerful three-page satiric sketch (pp. 352–354). *Pylon* is in large measure the story of men who *seem* to straddle the gap between the human and mechanical. On the one hand, Faulkner does present them as having lost much of their humanity and at times suggests that they have lost it entirely. "They aint human," the reporter keeps telling himself. "Burn them like this one tonight and they dont even holler in the fire; crash and it aint even blood when you haul him out: it's cylinder oil the same as in the crankcase." [11]

But the terrible irony is that they are human: capable of nobility and sacrifice, subject to grief, pain, and death. Watch Faulkner emphasize both the human and the mechanical a moment before Shumann's plane explodes. The reporter is holding Shumann's son on his shoulder.

"That's it," he thought quietly, with that faint quiet grimace almost like smiling, "they aint human. It aint adultery; you can't anymore imagine two of them making love than you can two of them aeroplanes back in the corner of the hangar, coupled." With one hand he supported the boy on his shoulder, feeling through the harsh

[10] See, for example, *GDM*, 318–321, 354; *ID*, 235–239; *RN*, 245–246, 248; *F*, 252–254.
[11] Page 45. See also pp. 48, 62, 63, 231.

khaki the young brief living flesh. "Yair; cut him and it's cylinder oil; dissect him and it aint bones: it's little rockerarms and connecting rods." [p. 231]

He then buys the boy candy and ice cream cones. The first thing we are told after the description of the explosion is that Shumann had the humanity to use the last of his control to avoid cracking up the other planes and to plunge into a lake rather than into the "close-peopled land." The chapter ends with Laverne's grief-stricken cry to the reporter, who was responsible for getting Shumann the dangerous plane: "God damn you to hell! Get away from me!" [12]

A number of critics have seen the antithesis of primitivism and various forms of corruption or modernism as a predominant element in Faulkner's works, and some have gone so far as to try to divide almost all his characters according to a primitive non-primitive dichotomy.[13] It is clear that the problem of Faulkner's primitivism is a complex one and also that any such general division of characters is too mechanical. And while Faulkner undoubtedly considers certain "primitive" characters superior to certain nonprimitive ones, to see him as making a simple choice between the two poles is seriously to oversimplify his vision. On the other hand, there can be no question about the fact that Faulkner does tend to an unusual degree to focus upon and

[12] Page 235. For further evidence of the humanity of the fliers see the conversation between the jumper and the reporter, pp. 257–261. The book is by no means as simple or clear, however, as this brief analysis might suggest, for there are numerous other themes, and even the man-machine theme is complicated by the fact that the fliers are given a kind of purposefulness and heroism which is contrasted with both the general confusion of the moiling crowd and the callousness of various groundlings who either exploit or mock them. At the same time, Faulkner sometimes suggests that the fliers have been dehumanized to the point where a human who tries to establish contact with them will be hurt.

[13] See Campbell and Foster, *William Faulkner*, ch. vii, especially pp. 143–144. See also pp. 48–49, and Melvin Backman, "Sickness and Primitivism: A Dominant Pattern in William Faulkner's Work," *Accent*, XVI (1954), 61–73.

contrast extremes of intellectualism and nonintellectualism and of simplicity and corruption.

In *The Sound and the Fury* there are the contrasts between the idiot Benjy, on the one hand, and the highly intellectual and philosophic Quentin and his father, on the other, and between the nagging ratiocinations of Quentin, Quentin's father, and Jason and the simple sanity of Dilsey's mind. In *As I Lay Dying* the virtually inchoate and inarticulate Jewel is placed in persistent antithesis with the highly articulate Darl, who suffers from an overrefined perceptive apparatus. In *Sanctuary* the feeble-minded Tommy, whose naturalness is emphasized by his bare feet, feeling for nature, and simple human friendliness, is in sharp contrast with his murderer Popeye, whose life and qualities are in antithesis to almost every sense of the word natural. In contrast to almost all the other characters, whose vocabularies, intellectual capacities, and interests are rudimentary, is the highly intellectual and articulate Benbow. In *Light in August*, Lena Grove has an animallike simplicity and trust in instinct, her environment, and providence, while Joanna Burden is, above all, one who has repressed her natural desires and spends much of her energy trying to change the world. There are no direct antitheses of the sort I have been describing in *Absalom, Absalom!* with the possible exception of that between Judith and Clytie, who are virtually inarticulate, and Rosa, who is a fountain of words. But again we encounter in the work an idiot, who communicates primarily by "howling," and characters like Rosa, Quentin, Shreve, and Quentin's father, who have an excessive tendency to verbalize experience. The fliers in *Pylon* are marked by their rudimentary verbal processes; the reporter is characterized by his inability to keep quiet and by his verbal elaborations. In *The Hamlet*, as in *The Sound and the Fury*, we again have an idiot, who may be contrasted with an utterly practical and "rational" being, Flem. Those who seriously insist upon Faulkner's primitivism should note, however, that although Ike is natural in his idiocy and kinship with nature, that kinship is in one important respect an unnatural and perverted one. In *Requiem for a Nun* the sophisticated and "civilized" Temple is contrasted with the simple and inarticulate Negro woman, Nancy.

The antithesis of the fecund and sterile is a frequent though not consistent element in a number of Faulkner's works. It is especially prominent in *Light in August, The Wild Palms,* and *The Hamlet* and plays a part in *The Sound and the Fury, Sanctuary,* and *Absalom, Absalom!* In *Light in August* the pregnant Lena Grove, who successfully delivers a child after bouncing around in wagons for two months, stands in sharp contrast to Joanna Burden, who can only pretend she is pregnant, and to Hightower and Christmas as well, who produce nothing. In *The Wild Palms* the nameless "sentient womb" in the boat with the tall convict produces her child adrift in a Mississippi flood, while Charlotte dies in the attempt to abort hers. In *The Hamlet* the explicit fertility symbol Eula is wedded to the presumably impotent Flem Snopes. The Negroes in *The Sound and the Fury* go on procreating, while the whites die out. In *Sanctuary,* Ruby and her child are sharply contrasted with the hipless Temple, whose peculiarly unnatural rape, as Wyndham Lewis suggests, is peculiarly fitting for her.[14] The impotence of Popeye is placed in sharp contrast with the virility of Red.[15]

[14] Wyndham Lewis, "Moralist with a Corn Cob," *Life and Letters,* X (1934), 312–328. For a discussion of this theme in *The Hamlet,* see Russell Roth, "The Centaur and the Pear," *Western Review,* XVI (1952), 199–205. It is interesting that the most sex-absorbed or lascivious of Faulkner's women—Temple, Joanna Burden, and Charlotte—are symbols of sterility. His fertility symbols—Lena, Eula, and the woman in the convict's boat—are apparently not much concerned with sex.

[15] Any attempt seriously to regard this antithesis as a controlling theme, however, leads to severe difficulties. In the first place Faulkner treats his most fertile characters—Lena, Eula, and the woman in the boat—much less seriously than he does his sterile figures and on occasion seems to mock them. In *The Wild Palms,* Charlotte does die from an abortion, but, on the other hand, she already has two children from her lawful husband. Flem Snopes may be sterile, but so presumably is the sympa-

The antithesis of words and action, as Olga Vickery has pointed out,[16] is an important conception in a number of novels. The gap between the two is expressed with peculiar force by Addie Bundren in *As I Lay Dying:*

I would think how words go straight up in a thin line, quick and harmless, and how terribly doing goes along the earth, clinging to it, so that after a while the two lines are too far apart for the same person to straddle from one to the other. [p. 465]

Other more or less extensive conceptual or thematic antitheses which have been observed in Faulkner's works are those of rigidity and pliability of belief or spirit,[17] self-love and outgoing love,[18] freedom and society,[19] and soul and body.[20] His works have also, of course, been discussed in relation to such universal antitheses as good and evil, order and disorder, life and death, sin and redemption, and man and destiny.

Still other conceptual antitheses which are given frequent explicit expression in Faulkner's works remain to be noted or explored. There are, for example, the antitheses of oblivion and consciousness and of oblivion and memory, expressed most forcibly, perhaps, by Wilbourne at the end of *The Wild Palms*, as he thinks of the dead Charlotte.

---

thetic Ratliff, and the rest of the Snopeses breed like fruit flies. The near-robot fliers of *Pylon* have a child, while Ike McCaslin, the character most closely identified with nature, is childless. In his later writings Faulkner explicitly celebrates the idea that man will endure. But the birth rate in his world in relation to the amount of sterility and death hardly justifies his optimism.

[16] Olga Vickery, "*As I Lay Dying*," in *Two Decades*, pp. 189–205; Olga Vickery, "Gavin Stevens: From Rhetoric to Dialectic," *Faulkner Studies*, II (1953), 1–4.

[17] See W. V. O'Connor, *The Tangled Fire of William Faulkner* (Minneapolis: University of Minnesota Press, 1954). Note, for example, the comparisons in *Light in August* of McEachern and his wife, of Lena and Mrs. Armstid, and of Christmas and Brown.

[18] Thompson, "Mirror Analogues," pp. 83–106.

[19] Howe, *William Faulkner*, pp. 100, 177–179.

[20] Hopper, "Faulkner's Paradise Lost," p. 406.

When she became not then half of memory became not and if I become not then all of remembering will cease to be.—Yes, he thought, *between grief and nothing I will take grief.*[21]

These antitheses are reflections of a general concern with the concepts of timelessness and transience, immutability and change, whose importance in Faulkner's vision has yet to be recognized.[22] Other antitheses which need further study are those of reality and dream,[23] fact and truth,[24] mind and body,[25] and heart and brain.[26] All of these antitheses find a degree of "expression" in one of Rosa Coldfield's outpourings. The passage may also serve as an illustration of Faulkner's use of stylistic and structural antithesis, and of the astonishing complexity and confusion that can be compounded out of an accumulation of antitheses.

Living is one constant and perpetual instant when the arras-veil before what-is-to-be hangs docile and even glad to the lightest naked thrust if we had dared, were brave enough (not wise enough: no wisdom needed here) to make the rending gash. Or perhaps it is no lack of courage either: not cowardice which will not face that sick-

---

[21] Page 324. This antithesis is identically phrased in *A Fable*, p. 399: "Between grief and nothing only the coward takes nothing." For other especially sharp expressions of the antithesis of oblivion and memory see *AA*, 127–129; *U*, 112; *GDM*, 186, 326. Most often Faulkner or his characters conceive of memory as the only immortality and see memory as dependent upon flesh. On occasion, however, there is the assertion that spirit can exist apart from flesh. The judge in "Beyond," whose son has died, decides finally that " 'to lie beside him will be sufficient for me. There will be a wall of dust between us: that is true, and he is already dust these twenty years. But some day I shall be dust too. And—' he spoke now firmly, quietly, with a kind of triumph: 'who is he who will affirm that there must be a web of flesh and bone to hold the shape of love' " (*CS*, 796)?

[22] Consider, for example, the explicit concern with immortality and transience in Faulkner's Foreword to *The Faulkner Reader* (New York: Random House, 1954), pp. ix–xi, and in his Nobel Prize speech and the implicit concern suggested by his word "endure." Or, consider simply the emphasis on death throughout the works.

[23] *AA*, 140–143; *RN*, 261.   [24] *AA*, 140–143; *RN*, 261.

[25] *AA*, 139, 349.   [26] *GDM*, 260.

ness somewhere at the prime foundation of this factual scheme from which the prisoner soul, miasmal-distillant, wroils ever upward sunward, tugs its tenuous prisoner arteries and veins and prisoning in its turn that spark, that dream which, as the globy and complete instant of its freedom mirrors and repeats (repeats? creates, reduces to a fragile evanescent iridescent sphere) all of space and time and massy earth, relicts the seething and anonymous miasmal mass which in all the years of time has taught itself no boon of death but only how to recreate, renew; and dies, is gone, vanished: nothing— but is that true wisdom which can comprehend that there is a might-have-been, which is more true than truth, from which the dreamer, waking, says not "Did I but dream?" but rather says, indicts high heaven's very self with: "Why did I wake since waking I shall never sleep again?"

. . . That is the substance of remembering—sense, sight, smell: the muscles with which we see and hear and feel—not mind, not thought: there is no such thing as memory: the brain recalls just what the muscles grope for: no more, no less: and its resultant sum is usually incorrect and false and worthy only of the name of dream. [*AA*, 142–143]

One further conceptual antithesis which has been frequently noted,[27] but whose implications with respect to Faulkner's approach to literature and language need further study, is that between reality and language. Interestingly, this antithesis receives its most extreme expression in *The Unvanquished*, in which Faulkner's language is most clearly designed to "communicate." Bayard has just been passionately embraced by Drusilla:

I thought then of the woman of thirty, the symbol of the ancient and eternal Snake and of the men who have written of her, and I realised then the immitigable chasm between all life and all print. [p. 262]

These thematic or more or less extensive conceptual antitheses further illustrate Faulkner's tendency to perceive and present

[27] See, for example, Warren Beck, "William Faulkner's Style," in *Two Decades*, p. 163.

life in polar terms. As dramatized in his works, they also illustrate some of the same qualities of simultaneous opposition and union which characterize the oxymoron. Just as Faulkner unites but does not reconcile motion and immobility in "dynamic immobilities," sound and silence in "soundless explosions," and the substantial and insubstantial in solid ghosts and weightless objects, so he often "unites" these thematic poles into conditions in which they can neither be separated nor reconciled.

White and black are brought together in the bodies of single individuals like Joe Christmas, Charles Bon, Clytie, and Lucas Beauchamp, or in single families like the Sutpens and McCaslins, in which they can neither be fused nor separated, reconciled nor ignored. Or white and black are tied by wedlock or sex as in the cases of Etienne Bon and his wife, Christmas and Joanna Burden, and numerous other more casual white-black sexual encounters. North and South are brought together in a single temperament and life condition like that of Joanna Burden, or in a single room like that of Quentin and Shreve at Harvard, or in a marriage like that of Fonsiba and the scholarly Northern Negro.

The past and present are brought together and pull apart within single minds such as those of Benjy, Quentin, Hightower, and Rosa Coldfield, who are incapable either of accepting and integrating the past with the present or of letting go of it. Faulkner's structural techniques also bring past and present into juxtaposition but do not fuse them. When man and nature are brought together in *The Wild Palms*, the tall convict can neither get along with the river nor escape from it. Faulkner suggests that the human condition, in general, is analogous to the predicament of the convict. The latter, who has just watched the birth of a baby, thinks to himself:

And this is all. This is what severed me violently from all I ever knew and did not wish to leave and cast me upon a medium I was born to fear, to fetch up at last in a place I never saw before and where I do not even know where I am. [p. 231]

Man and nature, Faulkner sometimes suggests, are most nearly united in the hunt and through death.[28] But the first is a conflict or battle as much as a union, and the latter is only a fusion if we accept other paradoxes: the knoll in which Sam Fathers is buried is "no abode of the dead because there was no death, not Lion and not Sam: not held fast in earth but free in earth and not in earth but of earth, myriad yet undiffused of every myriad part . . . and, being myriad, one." [29]

The fliers in *Pylon* are half men and half machines. Their tragedy is that they can neither ignore their human needs nor satisfy them, can live neither with the machines nor without them. The machine-cut Popeye is tormented by natural desires which he has no way of satisfying naturally. In their search for freedom, the lovers, Charlotte and Wilbourne, can neither accept nor escape society.

Many of Faulkner's characters can neither escape nor reconcile themselves to the fact that they inhabit a world of time and change, and they seek desperately "to make that scratch, that undying mark on the blank face of oblivion to which we are all doomed" (*AA*, 129), to cross the chasm between the immortal and the mortal, life and death. Those, like Sutpen, and Emily in "A Rose for Emily," who try to erect a bridge of substance or flesh live to see their bridges crumble into dust. Those like Judith Sutpen, Wilbourne, and Faulkner, whose bridge is mind and memory, cannot escape the fact that they, too, are building with potential dust:

—not mind, not thought: there is no such thing as memory: the brain recalls just what the muscles grope for: no more, no less. [*AA*, 143]

So it is the old meat after all, no matter how old. Because if memory exists outside of the flesh it wont be memory because it wont know what it remembers. [WP, 324]

[28] See *GDM*, 328–329.

[29] *GDM*, 328–329. But this passage is not typical. Faulkner rarely conceives of death in this way.

The artist, who would bridge the gap with words,[30] faces the "immitigable chasm between all life and all print" (*U*, 262), between "words" and "doing," which move "too far apart for the same person to straddle from one to the other" (*AILD*, 465).

Let me emphasize that these thematic and extended conceptual antitheses are not simply implicit in Faulkner's works, not mere contrasts which the critic may make in interpreting the works, for, as we have seen, the polar entities are often juxtaposed in the works both dramatically and explicitly. It should be emphasized, also, that Faulkner's conceptual antitheses are by no means limited to those mentioned. The following illustrations may give some idea of the variety of these and of the extent to which this kind of conceptualization may dominate thought. These illustrations are from *As I Lay Dying*, which is probably the work of Faulkner *least* dominated by antitheses. It also was written before formal rhetorical antithesis had become a major ingredient of his style. Yet note even here the high degree of rhetorical as well as conceptual opposition.

Dr. Peabody thinks:

I can remember how when I was young I believed death to be a phenomenon of the body; now I know it to be merely a function of the mind. . . . The nihilists say it is the end; the fundamentalists, the beginning; when in reality it is no more than a single tenant or family moving out of a tenement or a town. [p. 368]

[30] In his Foreword to *The Faulkner Reader*, Faulkner writes that the artist seeks to "uplift man's heart . . . because in that way he can say No to death. He is saying No to death for himself by means of the hearts which he has hoped to uplift, or even by means of the mere base glands which he has disturbed to that extent where they can say No to death on their own account by knowing, realizing, having been told and believing it. . . . So he who, from the isolation of cold and impersonal print, can engender this excitement, himself partakes of the immortality he has engendered. Some day he will be no more, which will not matter then, because isolated and itself invulnerable in the cold print remains that which is capable of engendering still the old deathless excitement in hearts and glands whose owners and custodians are generations from even the air he breathed and anguished in" (pp. x–xi).

The child Vardaman can produce the phrases: "all one yet neither; all either yet none" (p. 379). Dewey Dell thinks:

I said You don't know what worry is. I don't know what it is. I don't know whether I am worrying or not. Whether I can or not. I don't know whether I can cry or not. I don't know whether I have tried to or not. [p. 384]

Darl muses, and again we observe the phenomenon of confusion resulting from an accumulation of antitheses:

In a strange room you must empty yourself for sleep. And before you are emptied for sleep, what are you. And when you are emptied for sleep, you are not. And when you are filled with sleep, you never were. I don't know what I am. I don't know if I am or not. Jewel knows he is, because he does not know that he does not know whether he is or not. He cannot empty himself for sleep because he is not what he is and he is what he is not. Beyond the unlamped wall I can hear the rain shaping the wagon that is ours, the load that is no longer theirs that felled and sawed it nor yet theirs that bought it and which is not ours either, lie on our wagon though it does, since only the rain and wind shape it only to Jewel and me, that are not asleep. And since sleep is is-not and rain and wind are *was*, it is not. Yet the wagon *is*, because when the wagon is *was*, Addie Bundren will not be. And Jewel *is*, so Addie Bundren must be. And then I must be, or I could not empty myself for sleep in a strange room. And so if I am not emptied yet, I am *is*.[31]

Cash is thinking about the fact that he beveled the edges of Addie's coffin. His thoughts are numbered by Faulkner to suggest the orderly quality of his mind.

4. In a house people are upright two-thirds of the time. So the seams and joints are made up-and-down. Because the stress is up-and-down.
5. In a bed where people lie down all the time, the joints and seams are made sideways, because the stress is sideways. [p. 397]

We have already encountered Addie's sharp opposition between "words" and "doing." She observes also that "people to whom

[31] Page 396. Note the pseudo logic in this passage, a phenomenon common in Faulkner's writing.

sin is just a matter of words, to them salvation is just words too" (p. 468). Anse, like Cash, and like Addie in her contrast between words and doing, uses a vertical horizontal antithesis to rationalize his laziness:

When He aims for something to be always a-moving, He makes it long ways, like a road or a horse or a wagon, but when He aims for something to stay put, He makes it up-and-down ways, like a tree or a man. [p. 362]

I must emphasize finally that, while Faulkner's thought and writing are dominated by thematic and conceptual antitheses of all sorts, they are not governed throughout by any particular antitheses, with the possible exception of that between white and black. To attempt, as some critics have done, to interpret his vision or even individual novels in terms of any single thematic antithesis is to give his work a simplicity and order it does not possess. Faulkner is not that consistent or systematic. Different antitheses operate at different times, or several operate simultaneously and more or less independently. What we have in Faulkner's writing is not so much variations on a theme as a multiplicity of themes. This idea will be expanded later. For the moment I wish only to explore further the enormous role of the polar imagination.

« 7 »

Character Antithesis

CHARACTER antithesis, like conceptual antithesis, is an important element in almost all fiction and in the interpretation of fiction. But again, it will be clear, I think, that the extent, variety, and intensity of such antitheses in Faulkner's works is unusual and, in some respects, unique.

As they are finally developed by all literary means, most of Faulkner's characters can be described as neither flat nor round. On the one hand, as was pointed out earlier, almost all of them represent some kind of extreme, or exhibit extreme qualities or behaviors of some variety; and to the extent that the characters are extremes they often seem to contrast with one another even when there is no direct opposition of characteristics or behavior. For example, when one visualizes Rosa Coldfield and Quentin together, or Christmas and Hightower, or Charles Mallison and Lucas Beauchamp, the figures stand in almost as sharp relief as if they were directly or completely contrasting characters, such as Tom Jones and Blifil in *Tom Jones* or Becky and Amelia in *Vanity Fair*. On the other hand, Faulkner's characters, although extremes, are not simply types. They escape this, in part through their very extremity, which places them at or beyond the edges of the groups they might have represented, in part because of the intensity and sometimes fullness with which Faulkner renders their individual experiences and consciousnesses, and primarily, perhaps, because they face in various directions depending upon whom they are compared with. Benjy, for example, is an idiot. In contrast with the intellectual Quentin, it is the rudimentary and sensory aspect of his perceptions that may seem most important. In constant with the "practical" and callous Jason, his innocence seems most significant. Quentin and Jason are both extremes but appear in decidedly different lights depending upon whether they are compared with each other or with Benjy or Dilsey.

In other words, most of Faulkner's characters, although extreme, are not "fixed." Their dominant characteristics are not fixed nor are their relationships with other characters. Nor are most of them fixed on a moral scale. Quentin and Benjy may be viewed along with Jason as awful illustrations of the decay of the Compson family and as standing in pitiful contrast to Dilsey. Contrasted with Jason, however, Benjy and Quentin are good. Considered in isolation, Quentin may with some justice and explicit support from Faulkner be viewed as a Hamlet figure. Viewed in antithesis to Brown, Joe Christmas has the virtues of strength and will. In contrast to Byron Bunch, he is an epitome of arrogance and malevolence. Hightower and Joanna Burden are both generous in ways that Lena Grove is not; yet they both are in a sense murderers. Lena is soft and gentle in contrast to Mrs. Armstid; in contrast to Byron or Hightower, she is hard and inflexible. Like many other elements in Faulkner's works, when viewed in total context, his characters seem to exist in a loose suspension rather than in fixed relationships to one another.

On the other hand, an enormous part is played in Faulkner's works by oppositions between individuals, individuals and animals, individuals and groups, and individuals and societal and natural forces. In addition, Faulkner again and again places individuals in striking antithesis by rhetorical means. To give an adequate idea of the phenomenal extent to which these human oppositions fill and shape the novels would require almost complete retelling of them, for not only are most of them built around one or more extended major oppositions, but their moment-to-moment progress is largely a series of briefer minor clashes. Let me note briefly in a few of the novels only the most protracted, violent, or dramatic of these oppositions, considered, for the moment, apart from their rhetorical presentation.

The Sound and the Fury is about a family torn by dissensions. There are protracted general oppositions between Mrs. Compson and the rest of the family, between Jason and the rest of the family, and between Jason and the world in general. Jason's extended struggles with Caddy, with his niece Quentin, and with Dilsey play an especially significant part in the novel. Among his many briefer conflicts, his verbal clash with the sheriff and his physical clashes with the circus cook, Luster, and Benjy deserve mention. Quentin, who sees himself at war with the world and time, clashes physically with Dalton Ames, Gerald, and Julio and, like one or more characters in every Faulkner novel, has a conflict with the law.

The Bundrens in *As I Lay Dying* are engaged in an extended struggle with natural forces—flood, fire, and the decomposition of flesh. As a result of the latter they come into continual conflict with various individuals, communities, and the law. The family itself is torn by the perpetual and profound antipathy between Jewel and Darl and by lesser antipathies between Darl and Dewey Dell and Jewel and Anse. Jewel, who seethes with a general hostility toward the world, clashes physically with Gillespie and Darl, and is physically restrained from a battle with a stranger in Jefferson. His extended and important relationship with his horse is one of simultaneous love and violent physical opposition. Further oppositions exist between Addie and Cora, Addie and Anse, and Vardaman and Peabody. Whitfield, in his own estimation, at any rate, wrestles with Satan.

Life for Joe Christmas of *Light in August* is primarily a series of oppositions, most of which involve physical violence. We watch in considerable detail his more or less protracted struggles with the dietitian, McEachern, Mrs. McEachern, Brown, Joanna Burden, the sheriff's posse, and Grimm. He has sharp brief clashes with Bobbie, Max, Hightower, Halliday, Doc Hines, a Negro minister and three members of his congregation, and various other assorted whites and Negroes, males and females. Like numerous other Faulkner characters, he also struggles with an animal, a horse. The friends Byron Bunch and Hightower become engaged in an important contest of will, and Bunch tangles physically with Brown. There are further direct oppositions between McEachern and his wife, McEachern and Bobbie, Hightower and Grimm, Brown and the sheriff, Brown and the workers at the sawmill plant, the sheriff and a nameless Negro, and Doc Hines and his wife, his daughter, the dietitian, and Christmas. Beyond these are the extended oppositions between the town and Hightower and the town and Joanna Burden and between black and white within both the corporate and individual body.

Absalom, Absalom! is in large measure dominated by a group of extended and implacable conflicts: between Rosa and Sutpen, Rosa and Clytie, Sutpen and Charles Bon, Henry and Charles, and Charles' mother and Sutpen. Less-extended battles of some consequence occur between Sutpen and Henry, Sutpen and Wash Jones, Sutpen and assorted wild Negroes, Wash and a posse, and Charles and a lawyer. All but three of the oppositions so far named involve a physical clash. Beyond these are the more general conflicts between Sutpen and the town and Sutpen and time.

This same pattern continues throughout Faulkner's works, and to go on listing even the major oppositions in detail would be tedious and unnecessary. Apart from the more or less extended major or violent clashes of the sort just listed, there are also countless minor clashes between individuals. One can go so far as to say that the characteristic relationship depicted between individuals in Faulkner's world is one of opposition or conflict. In *The Sound and the Fury*, for example, apart from the oppositions already mentioned, there are continual minor conflicts between Luster and Benjy, Dilsey and Mrs. Compson, and Dilsey and her children, and further conflicts between Mr. and Mrs. Compson, between Mrs. Compson and Uncle Maury, and between Dilsey and Quentin. Apart from Quentin's physical fights with Julio, Dalton, and Gerald, there are his clashes with Caddy and with the boys at the swimming hole, his attempts to get rid of the little Italian girl, and various assorted conflicts with his classmates at Harvard. Except for his mistress, Jason comes into some kind of conflict with every one of the several dozen individuals he encounters in the novel.

Continual conflict might be expected in such predatory wastelands as those presented in *Sanctuary* and *Pylon* or when we are following such generally hostile characters as Jason, Jewel Bundren, Popeye, Joe Christmas, Doc Hines, or the groom in *A Fable,* or such aggressively proud ones as Colonel Sartoris, Sutpen, or Lucas Beauchamp. But consider even the "idyllic" opening and closing chapters of *Light in August.* In the opening chapter Armstid and Winterbottom are bargaining over a cultivator. Lena and Mrs. Armstid for several pages (15–18) engage in a verbal duel and Faulkner repeatedly emphasizes the antithesis between them:

They look at one another, suddenly naked, watching one another: the young woman in the chair, with her neat hair and her inert hands upon her lap, and the older one beside the stove, turning, motionless too, with a savage screw of gray hair at the base of her skull. [pp. 15–16]

In the final chapter the surface relationship between the furniture dealer and his wife is one of conflict, bickering, and teasing, and Lena is calmly driving Byron into a state of desperate frustration.

Or consider the relationships depicted between husbands and wives in Faulkner's works. With few exceptions these can be described only as ones of mutual frustration or conflict. Mr.

and Mrs. Compson seem to have virtually separated; Addie
Bundren despises her husband and commits adultery; Ruby and
Lee Goodwin are in perpetual conflict in the scenes when we observe them; Benbow has left his wife; Hightower's wife is
frustrated to the point where she commits adultery and finally
suicide; Mr. and Mrs. McEachern are unalterably opposed in
temperament and aims; Sutpen and Ellen are grossly incom-
patible; Charlotte Rittenmeyer runs away from her husband
with another man; Laverne's few expressions of love for Shumann take the form of blows or curses; between Mink Snopes
and his wife the opposition is desperate and often violent; between Flem and Eula there is no observable affection or communication of any kind; Armstid and his wife clash violently
over the spotted horses; Houston and his wife apparently lived
together happily for a while, although their earlier relationship
was one of violent struggle, but she is killed after six months
of marriage; Lucas Beauchamp and Mollie are usually engaged
in a battle of wills; and even Ike McCaslin and his wife, on
the one occasion we observe them, are involved in an intense
conflict. Between Temple and Gowan Stevens there is a terrifying chasm of guilt and resentment.[1] At the same time,
however, cutting through or across many of these marital oppositions, binding together the conflicting entities, is a strong
fidelity.

What is most significant about Faulkner's presentation of
character conflict is not simply the frequency or intensity of it.
Many novelists establish intense and protracted conflicts. What

[1] Howe observes that "seldom in Faulkner's work is there a mature
recognition of the happier possibilities in the relations between men and
women, the possibilities, I might specify, of fulfilled love" (*William
Faulkner*, p. 97). See also his somewhat oversimplified but probably valid
observations about Faulkner's generally biased attitude toward women
(pp. 97–99). See also Hopper's remarks on Faulkner's "puritanism" and
Swiftian fascination and repulsion by natural functions ("Faulkner's
Paradise Lost," pp. 407–408). Of course, in view of the amount of general
conflict between all sorts of individuals in Faulkner's world, the prevalence of marital difficulties needs no special explanation.

distinguishes Faulkner is that conflict plays such a large part in almost every human relationship that he depicts, even those in which the characters are not essentially antagonistic or are on the same side in a larger conflict. In *The Sound and the Fury*, for example, we expect Jason and Caddy to clash, but Quentin and Caddy are also usually shown in some kind of conflict. Or again, we expect opposition between Mrs. Compson and Dilsey, but the relations between Mrs. Compson and Uncle Maury and between Dilsey and her children and between Dilsey and the Compson children also involve a good deal of conflict and bickering. Even where characters are drawn together by a deep bond of sympathy, as for example Gavin Stevens and Charles Mallison, Charles Bon and Henry Sutpen, Wilbourne and Charlotte, and Byron Bunch and Hightower, much of their relationship is a matter of conflict or opposition. The same can be said about the relationships between Ike and the bear in *Go Down, Moses* or Jewel and his horse in *As I Lay Dying*.

We have seen earlier that many of Faulkner's individual characters are presented as battlegrounds of opposing forces. His world, in general, is to a very large extent a battleground of individuals struggling with one another or with some other adversary. Some of these struggles result in victory of a sort for one of the antagonists, but the overwhelming emphasis is upon the struggles themselves, upon the opposing forces in a protracted balance, deadlock, or tension. The quality is often very much like that suggested by Faulkner's images of gathered forces, as in the description of Goodwin and Ruby standing in "a mounting terrific muscular hiatus" (*S*, 114) or as in the description of Jewel and his horse: "rigid, motionless, terrific, the horse back-thrust on stiffened, quivering legs, with lowered head; Jewel with dug heels . . . in rigid terrific hiatus" (*AILD*, 346). I am not thinking only of the quality of such dramatic single encounters as those between Rosa and Clytie in *Absalom, Absalom!* (pp. 137–140), between Jason and the circus cook in *The Sound and the Fury* (p. 325), or between Hubert and

Uncle Buddy over the poker table in *Go Down, Moses* (pp. 27–29). I am thinking also of the quality of implacable opposition of such extended conflicts as those between Jason and Dilsey, Darl and Jewel, Christmas and McEachern, Christmas and Joanna Burden, Rosa and Sutpen, Charles Bon and Henry Sutpen, the tall convict and the river, Charlotte Rittenmeyer and convention, Ratliff and Flem Snopes, Mink Snopes and Houston's dog, Frenchman's bend and the spotted horses, Boon and the bear, Uncle Buddy and Tomey's Turl, and Lucas Beauchamp and all men. The conflicts between Faulkner's characters are almost never resolved except by death. The oppositions between most of the pairs named in this discussion are as irreconcilable as the terms of any oxymoron.

Up to this point I have spoken of these character antitheses independently of their rhetorical and descriptive presentation, for I wished to suggest the extent to which Faulkner's works are dominated by conflict, which would have been impossible had I attempted to illustrate. It is largely the manner of presentation of these conflicts, however, and the rhetorical creation of opposition which gives Faulkner's character antitheses their particular strength and quality, that quality of simultaneous opposition and connection possessed in its most extreme form by the oxymoron.

There are novelists—Fielding and Thackeray, for example—who more frequently than Faulkner conceive of their characters as complete antitheses to one another, but I am reasonably certain that no major English or American novelist even closely approaches Faulkner in the frequency and obviousness with which rhetorical devices and description are used to place characters in some kind of antithesis [2] or to heighten the sense of

[2] In making this statement I am thinking of Faulkner's works in general. A few of his novels—*The Sound and the Fury*, *As I Lay Dying*, and *The Wild Palms*—do not contain a notable amount of such antithesis. In each of these cases, however, the larger structural units juxtapose the qualities, perceptions, and experiences of contrasting or partly contrasting characters.

opposition between them. By no means are all his antitheses as elaborate and highly stylized as the following, but it epitomizes the kind of effect Faulkner continually seems to be seeking and the lengths he is willing to go to achieve it:

"the one saying to Henry *I have waited long enough* and Henry saying to the other *Do you renounce then?* . . . and the other saying, *I do not renounce* . . . the one calm and undeviating, perhaps unresisting even, the fatalist to the last; the other remorseless with implacable and unalterable grief and despair——" (It seemed to Quentin that he could actually see them, facing one another at the gate. . . . They faced one another on the two gaunt horses, two men, young, not yet in the world, not yet breathed over long enough to be old but with old eyes, with unkempt hair and faces gaunt and weathered as if east [*sic*] by some spartan and even niggard hand from bronze, in worn and patched gray weathered now to the color of dead leaves, the one with the tarnished braid of an officer, the other plain of cuff, the pistol lying yet across the saddle bow unaimed, the two faces calm, the voices not even raised: *Dont you pass the shadow of this post, this branch, Charles;* and *I am going to pass it, Henry*). [*AA*, 132–133]

Apart from the thrice repeated "the one . . . the other" construction and the parallelism of the "fighting words," we may note that Faulkner also heightens the sense of opposition by stressing various similarities or identities between the men and by emphasizing their face-to-face position.

Again and again Faulkner places antagonists in this kind of tense face-to-face position. In *Light in August*, for example, in the course of three pages (142–144) we read that Joe and McEachern "faced one another." "For a while longer they faced one another. Perhaps they were looking at one another." "Again they stood face to face." "Facing him, the two of them almost toe to toe, he struck at Joe with his fist." "They faced one another." Later, the faces of Joe and Joanna are described as "not a foot apart: the one cold, dead white, fanatical, mad; the other parchment colored, the lip lifted into the shape of a soundless and rigid snarl" (p. 242). Likewise Christmas and Grimm "looked at one another almost face to face. . . . For an instant they glared at one another, the one stopped in the act of crouching from the leap, the other in midstride of running" (p. 404). Note that here Faulkner is not content with the arrested motion or tableau effect produced by the formal "the one . . . the other" construction or even by the "instant" of glaring; he insists upon the literal "stopped in the act."

Very often he gains additional tension by having his antagonists face one another across some physical barrier, as in the opening scene in *Sanctuary*. There, in the course of two pages (pp. 2–3) we read that Benbow sees Popeye "facing him across the spring," that Popeye appeared to contemplate Benbow "across the spring," that "across the spring they looked at one another," and that Popeye squatted, "facing the man across the spring. . . . They squatted so, facing one another across the spring, for two hours." [3]

Henry and Judith Sutpen face each other "across the wedding dress which she was not to use . . . the two of them slashing at one another with twelve or fourteen words" (p. 174). In an earlier description of the same event Faulkner again simultaneously suggests both identity and conflict by emphasizing the similarity of the two figures immediately before describing the opposition:

the two of them, brother and sister, curiously alike as if the difference in sex had merely sharpened the common blood to a terrific, an almost unbearable, similarity, speaking to one another in short brief staccato sentences like slaps, as if they stood breast to breast striking one another in turn neither making any attempt to guard against the blows.
Now you cant marry him.
Why cant I marry him?
Because he's dead.

[3] See also Temple's confrontation with a rat (pp. 111–112).

Dead?

Yes. I killed him. [p. 172]

Observe that the intensity and directness of the opposition suggested by the description is not quite in accord with the dialogue.[4] Note also that it is a "difference" which sharpens the
blood to a "similarity." The similarity is further described as
"terrific" and "unbearable," which suggests difference and conflict.

In *Go Down, Moses*, Hubert faces Uncle Buck and then
Uncle Buddy across a poker table (pp. 25–29); McCaslin and
Boon "faced one another across Lion's grave" (p. 253); Lucas
Beauchamp and Zack Edmonds face each other across a bed.
Again, at the height of the conflict Faulkner reminds us of the
"oneness" of the antagonists:

> Then Lucas was beside the bed. He didn't remember moving at
> all. He was kneeling, their hands gripped, facing across the bed and
> the pistol the man whom he had known from infancy, with whom
> he had lived until they were both grown almost as brothers lived.
> They had fished and hunted together, they had learned to swim in
> the same water, they had eaten at the same table in the white boy's
> kitchen and in the cabin of the negro's mother; they had slept under
> the same blanket before a fire in the woods. [p. 55]

As the struggle continues, Faulkner describes Edmonds as
staring at the "frantic face opposite his," reminds us of the "bed
between them," reports that Lucas "faced the white man" (p.
56). Finally,

> The white man sprang, hurling himself across the bed, grasping at
> the pistol and the hand which held it. Lucas sprang too; they met
> over the center of the bed.[5]

Lucas pulls the trigger, but the gun misfires, allowing the conflict to continue throughout not only the life of Zack but that

---

[4] Compare the dialogue of Quentin and Henry Sutpen, p. 373.

[5] Page 57. In the same work see also the oppositions between Lucas and
Roth Edmonds (pp. 97–98) and Boon and McCaslin (pp. 252–254).

of his son, whose twenty years of running the Edmonds' estate "seemed to him one long and unbroken course of outrageous trouble and conflict, not with the land or weather (or even lately, with the federal government) but with the old negro" (p. 116).

Throughout much of their reconstruction of the Sutpen story in *Absalom, Absalom!* Shreve and Quentin sit "opposite" (p. 255) each other, "facing" (pp. 293, 346) each other across a table. They are several times described as looking at, staring at, or glaring at one another (pp. 293, 299, 303, 324, 359). Even at the point where Faulkner suggests their oneness of mind and the fact that it did not matter which of them was talking, he writes that "they stared—glared—at one another" (p. 303), an example of a hardly justifiable attempt simultaneously to reap the effects of opposition and fusion.[6] Similarly (although with more justice in view of the conflict existing between Charles and Henry), at the very moment he emphasizes their empathic fusion with Charles and Henry, he places them in an especially striking and paradoxical antithesis:

—the two the four the two facing one another in the tomblike room: Shreve, the Canadian, the child of blizzards and of cold in a bathrobe with an overcoat above it, the collar turned up about his ears; Quentin, the Southerner, the morose and delicate offspring of rain and steamy heat in the thin suitable clothing which he had brought from Mississippi, his overcoat . . . lying on the floor where he had not even bothered to raise it. [p. 346]

In addition, Faulkner arranges parts of their narration as question-answer sequences[7] and frequently emphasizes the conflict between the two over how fast or slowly or clearly the story is moving. "Just get on with it," Shreve keeps urging near the beginning of the narrative.[8] But soon he is desperately cry-

[6] Compare the sense of opposition and attachment communicated on p. 299.

[7] Pages 176–181, 215–216, 322–325.   [8] Pages 258, 260, 261.

ing, "Wait . . . for Christ's sake wait." [9] On the final page of the book we find Shreve asking:

"And so do you know what I think?" Now he did expect an answer, and now he got one:
"No," Quentin said.
"Do you want to know what I think?"
"No," Quentin said.
"Then I'll tell you. . . . Now I want you to tell me just one thing more. Why do you hate the South?"
"I dont hate it," Quentin said. [p. 378]

These are a few instances of Faulkner's methods of dramatizing or heightening the sense of opposition between antagonistic characters. Perhaps even more revealing of the strength of his tendency to see most relationships in polar terms is his use of the same techniques to juxtapose characters who are not essentially antagonistic. Thus, Joe Christmas and Bobbie became acquainted across a restaurant counter:

Facing one another across the dark, stained, greasecrusted and frictionsmooth counter, they must have looked a little like they were praying: the youth countryfaced, in clean and Spartan clothing, with an awkwardness which invested him with a quality unworldly and innocent; and the woman opposite him, downcast, still, waiting, who because of her smallness partook likewise of that quality of his, of something beyond flesh. [LIA, 156–157]

In passing note also the oppositions between, and also within, the words "greasecrusted" and "frictionsmooth."

Similarly, Faulkner uses both physical and rhetorical opposition to describe Jason and Mrs. Compson, between whom there is relatively little conflict. They sit

across the table from one another, in identical attitudes; the one cold and shrewd, with close-thatched brown hair curled into two stubborn hooks, one on either side of his forehead like a bartender in caricature, and hazel eyes with black-ringed irises like marbles, the

[9] Pages 286, 289, 292, 321.

other cold and querulous, with perfectly white hair and eyes
pouched and baffled and so dark as to appear to be all pupil or all
iris. [p. 295]

Here again there is the simultaneous suggestion of oneness and
opposition. One might expect the assertion of identity to be followed by a rhetoric emphasizing that identity. Instead, Faulkner uses a "the one . . . the other" construction and a series of
parallelisms that emphasize the differences between them.

Probably his most common way of providing a slight suggestion of opposition is to have his characters glare, stare, or
simply watch one another, as Temple Drake and Gavin Stevens
do throughout much of *Requiem for a Nun*. For example:
"(she stands, tense, rigid, facing him, staring at him). . . . She
stares at him; another moment. Then he rises, still watching her;
she stares steadily and implacably back" (p. 93).

At times, we can even watch Faulkner plant these suggestions
at the very moment he denies them. He tells us in *Intruder in the
Dust*, for example, that Gowrie "glared back up at the sheriff"
and follows with the statement that Gowrie "was not trembling,
not eager, baffled, amazed, not anything." [10] A page later the
sheriff has just asked Gavin Stevens a question.

They looked, stared at one another, or that is his uncle stared—
the too-thin bony eager face, the bright intent rapid eyes, and opposite the sheriff's vast sleepy face, the eyes not staring, apparently
not even looking, blinking almost drowsily, the two of them cutting
without speech across all that too. [p. 169]

Here Faulkner first gains the effect of antithesis suggested by
"stared at one another." Having secured this effect, he vaguely
denies it with "or that is his uncle stared," which then permits
him to place in sharp antithesis the qualities of the faces and

[10] Page 168. *Pylon* is especially full of "glaring" which seems hardly
justified. The reporter "glare[s] down" at Jiggs with "a curious glazed
expression" and then a few lines later with "that curious dazed look."
Then he "glare[s]" at all the fliers with his "dazed, strained and urgent
face" (pp. 78–79). See also *GDM*, 359.

eyes of the two men. He ends with a phrase, "cutting . . . across all that," which suggests both opposition and union.

Faulkner's characters, then, as presented both by story and rhetoric, exist to a very large extent in antithesis or opposition to one another. At the same time we frequently find in both story and rhetoric an emphasis upon that which binds the opposed characters. They are, in effect, often simultaneously pulling apart and being pulled together, in much the same way, for example, as the black and white blood in the body of Joe Christmas, or as the forces within a man who is behaving with "calm fury" or "moving sitting still," or as the terms of any oxymoron. Jewel and Darl, who hate one another, are bound by their common mother and common task. The tall convict is immersed in the chaos and substance he most abhors. The relationships between Quentin and Caddy, Henry Sutpen and Charles Bon, Joe Christmas and Joanna Burden, Laverne and Shumann, Lucas and Chick, the corporal and the old general, and numerous other pairs are strongly suggested by the description of the relationship between Jewel and his horse, the two, sometimes fused, sometimes standing "rigid, motionless, terrific, the horse back-thrust on stiffened, quivering legs, with lowered head; Jewel with dug heels, shutting off the horse's wind with one hand, with the other patting the horse's neck in short strokes myriad and caressing, cursing the horse with obscene ferocity" (*AILD*, 346), a relationship finally compressed into Jewel's words to the horse, the oxymoron with which Faulkner ends this description: "You sweet son of a bitch" (p. 346).

« 8 »

Stylistic Antithesis

IT may seem anticlimactic to come from these major conceptual and character antitheses to antitheses which might seem merely matters of sentence structure. But beginning with *Light in August* and becoming more and more common in the works that follow are certain stylistic forms of antithesis which are also a significant aspect of Faulkner's tendency to view and present things in polar terms and to yoke together opposing elements.

The most common of these antitheses is the negative-positive one, most often conveyed by a "not . . . but" construction. In *Light in August* these are usually fairly casual and do not often involve an opposition of directly polar terms.[1] Typical examples are the description of McEachern as speaking with "the voice of a man who demanded that he be listened to not so much with attention but in silence" (p. 124) and the description of Lena crying "not loud and not hard, but with a patient and hopeless abjectness" (p. 362). In later works they may be as formal as the statement in *Intruder in the Dust* that "the vast millrace of time roared not toward midnight but dragging midnight with it, not to hurl midnight into wreckage but to hurl the wreckage of midnight down upon them" (p. 79). They may become as complicated and extended as Rosa Coldfield's:

---

[1] Exceedingly frequent, however, is the negatively phrased statement, which, I shall suggest later, has a similar effect.

122

and I (I was fourteen)—I will not insist on bloom, at whom no man had yet to look—nor would ever—twice, as not as child but less than even child; as not more child than woman but even as less than any female flesh. Nor do I say leaf. . . . But root and urge I do insist and claim . . . lay not dead but merely slept forgot. [*AA*, 144]

In *Absalom, Absalom! Intruder in the Dust, A Fable,* and the narrative sections of *Requiem for a Nun,* we not infrequently find pages with three or more "not . . . but" or "not only . . . but" constructions.[2] At least two pages in *Requiem for a Nun* (pp. 214, 227) contain five.

"Neither . . . nor" antitheses, some examples of which will appear below, are also fairly common throughout the works, and so are those which present a contrast between past and present or present and future. Concise examples of the last two sorts are the descriptions in *Go Down, Moses* of Boon's face as "no longer wild . . . but quite calm" (p. 241) and in *Light in August* of "the loose abandon of her [Miss Burden's] hair, not yet wild."[3] Any cataloguing of the various forms of stylistic antithesis to be found in Faulkner's works, however, is impossible here, and unnecessary, since we have already in other parts of this study observed a great many examples and since any random examination of pages in Faulkner will supply abundant illustrations.

Of especial interest, however, is Faulkner's use of what I will call "gratuitous" antithesis; that is, his suggestion of opposition or of polar or near-polar states when they are not the property of the object or event being described, a phenomenon we have already observed in some of his character antitheses. In *The Hamlet,* for example, when Faulkner writes that Eula Varner experiences "neither fright nor even outrage but merely surprise

---

[2] For example, *RN,* 218, 225, 228, 229, 230, 255. See also the Appendix to *SF,* 5, 10.

[3] Page 210. The antithesis of different times is usually not a formal one nor composed of such small units. For other concise examples, however, see *LIA,* 48, 155; *WP,* 111; *GDM,* 321; *ID,* 54; *CS,* 783.

and annoyance" (p. 138) and that she is "breathing deep but not panting" (p. 138) or when he describes Ike McCaslin in *Go Down, Moses* as lying "wakeful and peaceful . . . peaceful, without regret or fretting" (p. 343), he is suggesting polar conditions and presenting oppositions which for the moment, at least, are nonexistent. The suggestion, of course, is a negative one, but surely there is positive effect. The words "neither," "nor," "not," and "without," deny but do not obliterate the suggestions of the terms which follow them.[4] We can also say that the more or less mean conditions described in the examples above, and also in those which follow immediately, are made somewhat unstable by the polar suggestions. In the examples just given, polar conditions are merely possible or potential. In the description of Lena's hair as "not yet wild" the polar condition is imminent. Let me give a few more examples. Joe Christmas in *Light in August* has been knocked to the floor: "There was nothing in his eyes at all, no pain, no surprise" (p. 190). In the story "Beyond," a face is described as "quiet and quite intelligent, with a faint and long constant overtone of quizzical bemusement not yet tinctured with surprised speculation, not yet puzzled, not yet wary" (*CS*, 783). Rosa Coldfield's negative assertions of polar conditions surely have great positive force in this instance:

I know only that my entire being seemed to run at blind full tilt into something monstrous and immobile, with a shocking impact too soon and too quick to be mere amazement and outrage; . . . the shock which was not yet outrage because it would be terror soon. . . .

[4] Compare King Lear's words to Goneril:

> "thou art a boil,
> A plague-sore, an embossed carbuncle,
> In my corrupted blood. But I'll not chide thee;
> Let shame come when it will, I do not call it.
> I do not bid the thunder-bearer shoot,
> Nor tell tales of thee to high-judging Jove."
> (II, iv, ll. 226–231)

Or consider the effect of Joseph McCarthy's "I will not say he is a Communist."

Then suddenly it was not outrage that I waited for; . . . it was not terror: it was some cumulative over-reach of despair itself. [*AA*, 139–140]

Note the positive suggestion of the word "sigh" in the following description from *Light in August:* "She expels her breath. It is not a sigh so much as a peaceful expiration, as though of peaceful astonishment" (pp. 10–11). Or consider the positive effect of the negative suggestions in the description in *Go Down, Moses* of Sam Fathers as "flabby-looking though he actually was not" (p. 166). The positive influence here is such that the effect is not distant from that of the oxymoron "at once gaunt and flabby" which is used in *Light in August* to describe Hightower's face.

Although, strictly speaking, we cannot speak of Faulkner's frequent simple negative statements such as "he did not move," or "he was not surprised," or "there was no sound," or "without substance"[5] as antitheses, they are similar to the kinds of anti-theses we have been considering in that they do make a negative suggestion which opposes, directly opposes, the positive one. Compare, for example, the statement "he did not move" with "he remained still." We can also say that the negative polar suggestion is gratuitous since it is not a property of the action or condition described. We may note also that the simple negative is the next-to-the-most concise way in which polar opposites can be sug-gested and fused. The most concise way is in words like "mo-tionless," "immobile," "soundless," and "substanceless," which are favorites of Faulkner's, words which simultaneously suggest and deny a polar opposition. Is it utterly fanciful to think of such statements and words as being somewhat like the "tone" of Lucas Burch in *Light in August* "that carried within itself its own confounding and mendacity" (p. 32) or like Sam Fathers, "himself his own battleground, the scene of his own vanquish-ment and the mausoleum of his defeat" (*GDM*, 168)?

In a large number of Faulkner's gratuitous negative statements

[5] A glance at a few pages of any Faulkner novel will provide examples. In *Light in August* they are especially common.

the actually existing conditions are defined as nameless deviations from, or absences of, polar or near-polar conditions or qualities. In *As I Lay Dying*, for example, Addie looks at Anse "without reproach, without anything" (p. 371). Laverne in *Pylon* is "not tall and not thin" (p. 24). Boon, in *Go Down, Moses*, has "little hard shoe-button eyes without depth or meanness or generosity or viciousness or gentleness or anything else" (p. 227). In the same work the eyes of Fonsiba watch McCaslin "without alarm, without recognition, without hope" (p. 280).

Another form of gratuitous polar suggestion, quite common in *Light in August* and present in most of Faulkner's works, defines conditions as nameless positions between poles. In *As I Lay Dying*, Addie Bundren looks at Cash "neither with censure nor approbation" (p. 372). Compare "looks impassively" or "noncomittally." In *Light in August*, voices, expressions, or eyes are several times described as "neither cold nor warm" (pp. 16, 71, 74). The voice of a Negro "was not threatful. Neither was it servile" (p. 102). The harness strap with which McEachern beats Joe is "neither new nor old" (p. 130). Both his and Joe's feelings are then negatively defined: He strikes "without heat or anger" (p. 131). Joe is "neither outraged nor surprised" (p. 147) by the punishment and injustice. The jumper in *Pylon* picks up the boy "not gentle and not rough" (p. 82). The reporter is described as "moving for a while yet in the twilight between the delusion of drunkenness and the delusion of sobriety" (p. 134). Faulkner seeks a similar rather delicate balance between polar ideas when he writes that Joe Christmas "no longer deliberately avoided looking at her house; neither did he deliberately look at it" (p. 209). In at least one sentence in *Light in August* we find one condition defined as the absence of near polar qualities and another condition described as existing between two poles:

Yet his voice held again that ambiguous quality, that quality hearty and completely empty and completely without pleasure or mirth . . . which in the past had caused Joe to look at Max with something between puzzlement and anger. [p. 185]

In the examples in the last two paragraphs and in many others, comparatively nonpolar conditions are defined as deviations from poles or extremes, either as mid-points between them or absences of them. The author is obviously sharply aware of the poles, and we are not allowed to forget them. Again, the suggestions of the poles make the mean or neutral conditions unstable, particularly since they apparently have no existence except as deviations from polar conditions. The definitions seem to say, in effect, "Isn't it strange that the condition is not a polar one?" They also suggest that the neutral conditions may not last long. The neutral condition becomes not so much an equilibrium or place of rest as an uneasy condition tending to move toward one pole or another. At first glance the phrase "not gentle and not rough" might seem the antithesis of the oxymoron "gentle roughness." In effect, however, they are not far apart.

« 9 »

The Space Between

IN miniature Faulkner's various stylistic antitheses and gratuitous polar suggestions reflect the same polar mode of perception and thought that is indicated by his treatment of themes and characters, and they help to induce the feeling that we are encountering a world which is in large measure a construct of pairs of entities of all kinds in opposition or tension.

On many levels Faulkner's world lacks substantial centers or middles. If a facial expression is "neither warm nor cold," it has no name. If a character is not some kind of extreme, he is, like Byron Bunch of *Light in August*, seen as "nondescript" (p. 42), "the kind of fellow you wouldn't see the first glance if he was alone by himself in the bottom of an empty concrete swimming pool" (p. 434). Instead of middles or meeting points between things there very often seem to be gaps or chasms between them, which can sometimes be crossed but not easily closed or eliminated. This is true of many of Faulkner's rhetorical structures and also of many of his conceptual structures. Between white and Negro, North and South, past and present, man and nature, the human and mechanical, words and action, reality and dream, the mortal and immortal, life and print, there are chasms, rarely crossed without pain or disaster. Between characters and groups of characters there are also terrible gaps, across which they stand in temporary armistice or stare and glare at one another or which they cross momentarily with blows or equally furious caresses or passion. They may desperately and violently seek to cross the chasm, to fuse somehow the separate beings, as does Joanna Burden, or as does Addie Bundren, who day after day has to look at her pupils "each with his and her secret and selfish thought, and blood strange to each other blood and strange to mine" and who tries to make contact with them through pain:

I would look forward to the times when they faulted, so I could whip them. When the switch fell I could feel it upon my flesh; when it welted and ridged it was my blood that ran, and I would think with each blow of the switch: Now you are aware of me! Now I am something in your secret and selfish life, who have marked your blood with my own for ever and ever. [*AILD*, 461–462]

They may, like Benjy, Quentin, Rosa Coldfield, Wilbourne, the reporter, and Houston, simply grieve because no crossing or fusion is possible. Yet, in a sense, the suffering is peculiarly acute because they are bound to one another by blood, marriage, fidelity, love, or hate and cannot simply turn their backs and walk away.

Most striking, perhaps, are the gaps within characters. Parts of them move while other parts of them remain immobile. Forces within them seek to explode while other forces within them hold the explosive ones in check. There are often gaps in their appearances or qualities. They may be at once flabby and gaunt, active and lazy, chaste and unchaste. Their faces may contain two separate expressions: peace and terror, irascibility and calmness, quietness and harriedness. Or they may divide more totally into two selves like Quentin—in *The Sound and the Fury* separated into body and shadow which he cannot reconcile; in *Absalom, Absalom!*:

two separate Quentins . . . the Quentin Compson preparing for Harvard in the South . . . and the Quentin Compson who was still too young to deserve yet to be a ghost, but nevertheless having to be one for all that . . . the two separate Quentins now talking to one another in the long silence of notpeople, in notlanguage.[1]

Or they may divide in two like Joanna Burden, "two creatures that struggled in the one body . . . struggling drowning in alternate throes" (*LIA*, 228). Or they are divided into ever bound and separate bloods: white and black, as Joe Christmas, Charles and Etienne Bon, Lucas Beauchamp and others, or, like Sam Fathers, Indian, black, and white, "the blood of the warriors and chiefs," and "not only the blood of slaves but even a little of the very blood which had enslaved it; himself his own battle-ground, the scene of his own vanquishment and the mausoleum of his defeat" (*GDM*, 168).

Even when there is no battle between the different bloods, as in the case of Lucas Beauchamp, they do not fuse but merely stalemate each other:

> Yet it was not that Lucas made capital of his white or even his McCaslin blood, but the contrary. It was as if he were not only impervious to that blood, he was indifferent to it. He didn't even need to strive with it. He didn't even have to bother to defy it. He resisted it simply by being the composite of the two races which had made him, simply by possessing it. Instead of being at once the battleground and victim of the two strains, he was a vessel, durable, ancestryless, nonconductive, in which the toxin and its anti stalemated one another, seetheless, unrumored in the outside air.[2]

On one occasion in Faulkner we encounter an individual with a literal gap where his middle ought to be. Houston, in *The Hamlet*, has been shot in the stomach and lies on the ground waiting for the pain to begin. The description which follows vividly suggests the kinds of relationships which exist between

---

[1] Page 9. But compare p. 12, where Quentin is described as a "common-wealth."

[2] *GDM*, 104. Observe the negative suggestions of opposition and the suggestions of opposition provided by "resisted," "toxin and its anti," and "stalemated."

and within a great many entities in Faulkner's world. It suggests, also, the desperate need and desire for fusion that is inevitable in a polarized world and the impossibility of fusion once the polarization has taken place.

If I don't get the hurting started quick, I am going to die. He willed to start it, and for an instant he could not understand why it did not start. Then he saw the blank gap, the chasm somewhere between vision and where his feet should have been, and he lay on his back watching the ravelled and shattered ends of sentience and will projecting into the gap, hair-light and worm-blind and groping to meet and fuse again, and he lay there trying to will the sentience to meet and fuse. Then he saw the pain blast like lightning across the gap. [p. 249]

But there is no fusion, and a moment later Houston dies. Only thus are most of the gaps between and within the inhabitants of Faulkner's world finally closed.[3] For the living there is no closure

[3] This statement is no mere rhetorical flourish. I cannot think of a single one of Faulkner's more violent, tormented, or divided characters, with the exception of Nancy Mannigoe and the possible exception of Addie Bundren, who achieves a real reconciliation with any of his adversaries or any measure of self-integration or self-understanding except by death. The fulfillments and releases of tension within Joe Christmas and Hightower take place as they are dying. Quentin, McEachern, Joanna Burden, Popeye, Rosa Coldfield, Sutpen, Henry Sutpen, Charles Bon, Charlotte Rittenmeyer, Shumann, and Houston die without any apparent catharsis. Characters like Jason Compson, Jewel Bundren, and the jumper in *Pylon* presumably go on seething forever, just as the mad Henry Armstid goes on digging, with "spent and unflagging fury" (*H*, 418).
    On at least one occasion Faulkner suggests that a character's torment is so necessary to her that it would be unfortunate if it had to end with her death. Quentin's father is writing to him about Rosa Coldfield's death:
    "And if there can be either access of comfort or cessation of pain in the ultimate escape from a stubborn and amazed outrage which over a period of forty-three years has been companionship and bread and fire and all, I do not know that either—[203-page ellipsis]or perhaps there is. Surely it can harm no one to believe that perhaps she has escaped not at all the privilege of being outraged and amazed and of not forgiving but on the contrary has herself gained that place or bourne where the objects of the outrage and of the commiseration also are no longer ghosts but are

in Faulkner's world. The conflicts and tensions within and between them remain unresolved. Much the same is true for Faulkner's readers.

---

actual people to be actual recipients of the hatred and the pity" (*AA*,
174, 377).

PART III

The Quest For Failure

« 10 »

Some Insoluble Suspensions

WE have seen that Faulkner conceptualizes and renders a great variety of experience in polar terms and also that he seems especially fascinated by relationships in which opposed forces or entities remain in conflict, relationships in which there is no resolution or release of tension. It seemed to make little difference what sort of materials he was dealing with—trains, buggies, animals, people, physical appearances, actions, psychological conditions, relationships between people, ideas, rhetorical entities. In all he tended to establish relationships of tension and unresolved conflict. Very often he seemed to seek the extreme form of tension and irreconcilability possessed by the oxymoron, that is, to present relationships in which no complete resolution was possible, in which irresolution, so to speak, was a crucial and ineradicable ingredient. I wish now to show that certain kinds of irresolution lie at the very heart of Faulkner's work.

It has generally been recognized that the purpose of some of Faulkner's stylistic and structural experiments is to keep his material in a state of flux or suspension. But it has also generally been thought and argued or assumed that these suspensions are finally resolved, that by the ends of the novels the jigsaw-puzzle integers do fall into place. Conrad Aiken writes that Faulkner's whole method is a

135

persistent offering of obstacles, a calculated system of screens and obtrusions, of confusions and ambiguous interpolations and delays, with one express purpose; and that purpose is simply to keep the form—and the idea—fluid and unfinished, still in motion, as it were, and unknown, until the dropping into place of the very last syllable.[1]

Aiken's use of the words "obstacles" and "screens" implies that the meanings of the novels are simply hidden, rather than ambiguous. His "until" and "dropping into place" imply that some final resolution or crystallization takes place. William Van O'Connor writes that Faulkner's experiments involve forcing the reader

to stay with page-long sentences until he has their content not as statement but as a state of mind, and forcing him to hold in mind detailed phrases, bits of information or tentative statements until they are *related meaningfully in a full, homogeneous context*.[2] [Italics mine.]

As we shall see, however, the "last syllables" of Faulkner's novels, as much as any other part of them, seem designed to prevent resolution, to leave the reader with conflicting thoughts and feelings. Not only do the "endings" fail to resolve most of the tensions generated by the novels but they often provide new ones. Above all, they leave unresolved the question of the meaningfulness or significance of the events and experiences which have made up the novel, the question whether the events we have witnessed are part of a tragic design or merely some grim and pointless cosmic joke.

A good deal of evidence has been shown which does suggest a strong desire on Faulkner's part to leave a variety of matters at least temporarily unresolved, and we have seen something of the extent to which he makes use of the oxymoron. Any oxymoron tends to hold elements in suspension rather than to fuse them; any oxymoron to some degree defies our customary intellectual

[1] "William Faulkner: The Novel as Form," in *Two Decades*, p. 142.
[2] "The State of Faulkner Criticism," *Sewanee Review*, LX (1952), 180–181.

desire for logical resolution, for, even when we see beyond the contradiction, it still leaves us with the conflicting assertions. But what is perhaps even more significant, is the fact that many, probably most, of Faulkner's oxymorons (e.g., "vague and intense") leave us with especially insoluble suspensions. They involve so complete or balanced a contradiction that they not only oppose our desire for resolution but remain in opposition to it; no amount of thought and analysis can move us beyond the suspension of opposed elements. In the traditional oxymoron, such as "cruel kindness" or "living death," at least a partial resolution is usually possible because one of the opposing elements is given subordinate emphasis either by context or by logical or grammatical subordination. Faulkner, on the other hand, seems especially fond of juxtaposing contradictory terms of equal rank and emphasis, and very often further blocks resolution by the prefatory phrase "at once" (e.g., "at once corrupt and immaculate"). That he may be indifferent to the effects even when his oxymorons do involve logical or grammatical subordination is suggested by his apparently synonymous use of "implacable weariness" and "weary implacability" (*H*, 254–255). The essential purpose and effect of most of Faulkner's oxymorons, I believe, is not to force the reader to grasp a reality or unity beneath an apparent contradiction but to leave him with the tension of the contradiction itself. We are to feel and to continue to feel, for example, that the struggle between Houston and his wife had in it "something both illogical and consistent, both reasonable and bizarre" (*H*, 239).

It is necessary to stress this in order to show as conclusively as possible that Faulkner frequently seems willing and even anxious to leave his reader with suspensions which are not resolvable in rational terms. This is not to say that he always does so, nor does it prove that his novels as wholes are similarly unresolvable, but it does suggest that his novels may be more ambiguous and more resistant to rational analysis than has often been supposed. This possibility is strengthened by the many other aspects of his presentation which resist rational analysis and leave us with an unresolved suspension of varied or opposed suggestions.

A large number of Faulkner's extended metaphors, for example, have these qualities. This partial description of the sermon of the visiting preacher in *The Sound and the Fury* is characteristic.

> He tramped steadily back and forth . . . hunched, his hands clasped behind him. He was like a worn small rock whelmed by the successive waves of his voice. With his body he seemed to feed the voice that, succubus like, had fleshed its teeth in him. And the congregation seemed to watch with its own eyes while the voice consumed him, until he was nothing and they were nothing and there was not even a voice but instead their hearts were speaking to one another in chanting measures beyond the need for words, so that when he came to rest against the reading desk, his monkey face lifted and his whole attitude that of a serene, tortured crucifix that transcended its shabbiness and insignificance and made it of no moment, a long moaning expulsion of breath rose from them, and a woman's single soprano: "Yes, Jesus!" [p. 310]

In context the passage has considerable emotional force and conveys a sense of the minister's power and effect on the congregation. On the other hand, it is full of opposed and varied suggestions which resist rational integration. We shift from naturalistic description to a simile in which the preacher is likened to a rock and his voice to waves. The voice then acquires teeth, and "succubus like" (i.e., like an *evil* spirit!) consumes him. Is the ugliness of the image intentional, we wonder. Does Faulkner perhaps add teeth because they are in antithesis to the "suck" suggestion of "succubus"? The minister and the congregation become "nothing" but still have hearts. There is no voice, but the hearts "speak" to one another, although without words. We are then reminded of the naturalistic monkey face immediately before the preacher's body (which was a "rock," fleshly food, "nothing," and a speaking "heart") becomes suggestive of a crucifix, at once "serene" and "tortured," "that transcended its [the attitude's? the crucifix's?] shabbiness and insignificance." Upon close examination even the general nature of the experience of the congregation is perplexing, because there is the implication of a peaceful speaking of hearts and then of release of tension. Faulkner's mixed metaphors of this sort are not occasional accidents, for in general he makes no effort to keep them consistent and often makes use of the most "mixed" for his most important communications. And as in the oxymoron, the irresolvable elements are not accidental but seem an integral part of structure. Comparable to these mixed metaphors in effect are Faulkner's frequent synesthetic images, which may be considered psychological oxymorons. Typical examples are "dark cool breeze" (*SF*, 149), "visibility roaring soundless down about him" (*H*, 195), and "walked out of their talking" (*LIA*, 9).

Less obvious, perhaps, but equally common are the conflicting suggestions which often occur in Faulkner's extended presentations of characters and events. A relatively compact illustration is the episode in *Light in August* in which McEachern attacks Joe Christmas in the dance hall. Before this episode, what has been emphasized, above all, about McEachern is his absolute sense of self-righteousness and the calm, heavy, methodical quality of all of his actions, even his violent ones. When he realizes that Joe has climbed out of his room and gone off to what he is sure is lechery, he saddles "his big, old, strong white horse" and goes down the road at a "slow and ponderous gallop" (p. 176). So far he is still very much in character. Faulkner then inserts a suggestion of speed by means of metaphor: "the two of them, man and beast, leaning a little stiffly forward as though in some juggernautish simulation of terrific speed though the actual speed itself was absent, as if in that cold and implacable and undeviating conviction of both omnipotence and clairvoyance of which they both partook known destination and speed were not necessary" (pp. 176–177). When McEachern reaches the dance hall, however, Faulkner has him move with actual speed. He dismounts "almost before the horse had stopped. He did not even tether it. He got down, and in the carpet slippers and the dangling braces and his round head and his short, blunt, outraged beard ran toward the open door" (p. 177). In the next paragraph Faulkner goes on to describe him as thrusting through the dancers, and running toward Joe and the waitress, and then thundering, "Away, Jezebel! . . . Away, harlot!" (p. 178).

McEachern's disarray and uncontrolled running and thunderous shouting provide an emotional climax of strong impact and intensity; but they may come as rather a shock to the understanding of the reader in view of Faulkner's earlier characterizations of the man as utterly deliberate and controlled.[3] The next paragraph reads:

Perhaps it did not seem to him that he had been moving fast nor that his voice was loud. Very likely he seemed to himself to be standing just and rocklike and with neither haste nor anger while on all sides the sluttishness of weak human men seethed in a long sigh of terror about the actual representative of the wrathful and retributive Throne. Perhaps they were not even his hands which struck at the face of the youth whom he had nurtured and sheltered and clothed from a child, and perhaps when the face ducked the blow and came up again it was not the face of that child. But he could not have been surprised at that, since it was not that child's face which he was concerned with: it was the face of Satan, which he knew as well. And when, staring at the face, he walked steadily toward it with his hand still raised, very likely he walked toward it in the furious and dreamlike exaltation of a martyr who has already been absolved, into the descending chair which Joe swung at his head, and into nothingness. [p. 178]

We begin with what appears not to be the real version of what happened but the way it appeared to McEachern. But the passage slips gradually toward what is presumably a statement of what did happen, and the final picture we have is of the McEachern we knew earlier, who, staring at Joe-Satan, walks

[3] See pp. 124–134.

"steadily" toward the raised chair "in the furious and dreamlike exaltation of a martyr." In a generally emotive way we are satisfied by the suggestiveness and over-all movement of this passage. If we stop to reflect, however, we wonder how the event did happen, which image of McEachern to accept: the one of a ponderous and deliberate man whose conviction is such that speed is not necessary; the one suggested by the hanging braces, carpet slippers, the running and thundering rage; or the one of a convinced and peaceful and yet somehow furious martyr? We wonder what McEachern is like. We wonder, also, whether McEachern has been killed. The final description of him offers no resolution: "He looked quite peaceful now. He appeared to sleep: bluntheaded, indomitable even in repose, even the blood on his forehead peaceful and quiet" (p. 178). This final statement is typical of many of Faulkner's endings to situations and even to whole works. It is effective emotionally and dramatically but does not resolve questions which the earlier presentation has raised for the understanding. There is a suggestion of resolution, in this case supplied by the emphasis upon peace and quiescence. At the same time, however, there remain tensions and opposing suggestions, here provided by the unquiet words "bluntheaded," "indomitable," and "blood."

One of the most striking and widely commented upon aspects of Faulkner's writing is his use of marathon sentences the structure and syntax of which are often perplexing or obscure. Here is a fragment of a sentence from *Go Down, Moses*, a sentence which runs for over a page and a half. Among sentences and fragments of this type, it is one of the least complex. Contextually, the sentence and fragment would seem to be important, for they presumably communicate a significant part of Ike McCaslin's education and experience.

. . . a boy who wished to learn humility and pride in order to become skillful and worthy in the woods but found himself becoming so skillful so fast that he feared he would never become worthy because he had not learned humility and pride though he had tried, until one day an old man who could not have defined either led him as though by the hand to where an old bear and a little mongrel dog showed him that, by possessing one thing other, he would possess them both; and a little dog, nameless and mongrel and many-fathered, grown yet weighing less than six pounds, who couldn't be dangerous because there was nothing anywhere much smaller, not fierce because that would have been called just noise, not humble because it was already too near the ground to genuflect, and not proud because it would not have been close enough for anyone to discern what was casting that shadow and which didn't even know it was not going to heaven since they had already decided it had no immortal soul, so that all it could be was brave even though they would probably call that too just noise. [pp. 295–296]

We may note first, that all but one of the clauses beginning "because," "since," or "so that," are deliberate *non sequitur*'s. Moreover, the final statement about the dog's bravery is not consistent with the statement about his fierceness. In one instance the existence of a quality depends upon what people call it; in the other it does not. At the same time, in opposition to the illogicality, there is a promise of clarity, order, and logicality, a promise Faulkner frequently seems to make. The description of the dog pretends to be a definition (presumably of "the one thing other") arrived at through careful exclusion and negation. Further promise of clarity and simplicity is made by the cause and effect terminology, antithesis, persistent parallelism, and general division of things into simple pairs. There is also the promise communicated by the suggestion that the mongrel dog showed Ike that "*one* thing" (italics mine) would solve his problem of gaining humility and pride.

The passage quoted is characteristic of many of Faulkner's other structures, also, in its shifts in tone. The context of the description of the dog is serious. Presumably our understanding of the nature of the dog is essential to our understanding of the nature of pride and humility and to our understanding of Ike.

The surrounding passages are serious. The description of the dog's qualities, however, is largely playful.

As in many other passages close scrutiny leads only to further difficulties. There is first the hurdle of the oxymoron "humility and pride." We are then told that the possession of one thing "other" would enable Ike to possess both qualities. If the one thing other is "bravery" (we cannot be sure), we may wonder why Faulkner communicates it so ambiguously, and we may wonder about the relationship between bravery, humility, and pride. Our understanding of that relationship is not aided by the fact that the dog, who has the bravery, is described specifically as neither humble nor proud. When we read further, we are led to Keats' "Ode on a Grecian Urn" and to the statement: *"Truth is one. It doesn't change. It covers all things which touch the heart—honor and pride and pity and justice and courage and love"* (p. 297)—a statement which McCaslin indicates ought to clarify things for Ike. Even if one is not troubled by the meanings of the words "covers" and "touch" and does not wonder whether such qualities as hatred and greed "touch" the heart, one must certainly wonder why humility is missing from the list. A few lines later Faulkner drops this subject and moves to a "discussion" of the curse on the land.

Again Faulkner's presentation has left us with tensions and questions we cannot resolve. I have dwelt upon the difficulties structures of this sort pose for the understanding and have emphasized their resistance to analysis, because I wish to make clear that they may be organized not merely so as to make intellectual resolution difficult but so as to discourage it and make it impossible, just as synesthetic images make precise sense localization impossible and many of Faulkner's oxymorons make logical resolution impossible. The difficulties in the way of understanding are often not resolvable nor meant to be.

The preceding illustrations show some of the ways by which Faulkner keeps his readers from fitting things together. Instead of moving toward synthesis and resolution, his presentation often provides a suspension of varied or opposed suggestions. Two specific devices which further contribute to this suggestive suspension warrant mention.

The first is the frequent use of "perhaps" and "maybe" and other inconclusive or conjectural terms or phrases in describing motivations, thoughts, and events. The second is that which Warren Beck has labeled "the statement of alternative suggestions," [4] as illustrated in the passage: "The woman had never seen him but once, but perhaps she remembered him, or perhaps his appearance now was enough." [5] Sometimes the juxtaposed alternatives are so important and so divergent that a choice would be of immense philosophic and practical significance, as in *Go Down, Moses* where McCaslin says that the Bible was written to be read "by the heart, not by the wise of the earth because *maybe they dont need it or maybe the wise no longer have any heart*" (p. 260, italics mine). On occasion the alternatives are diametrically opposed:

It was as if only half of her had been born, that mentality and body had somehow become either completely separated or hopelessly involved; that either only one of them had ever emerged, or that one had emerged, itself not accompanied by, but rather pregnant with, the other. [*H*, 109]

Note the complete opposition of the alternatives "completely separated" and "hopelessly involved." If we substitute "at once . . . and" where Faulkner has used "either . . . or," the result is an oxymoron. Even as worded in the text, however, the passage is, in effect, an oxymoron, because no real choice is offered. As is true for almost all of Faulkner's "alternative" suggestions —and his work is largely composed of them—we are to keep in mind both alternatives; no choice or resolution is possible.

---

[4] "William Faulkner's Style," in *Two Decades*, p. 159.

[5] *LIA*, 177. Note that the phrasing "had never seen him but once" communicates almost a double suggestion. Compare "had seen him but once," or "had seen him once only."

« I I »

The Major Fiction

FAULKNER'S novels, of course, are far more complex than the structures we have been looking at, and I certainly do not wish to suggest that the kinds of qualities I have been illustrating fully explain or describe them. They do, however, resemble these structures much more closely than has generally been recognized. They have certain kinds of unity and resolution, of course, but in many ways they remain insoluble. Apart from the evidence we have already seen which suggests this possibility, and apart from internal evidence to be considered later, there is other evidence that Faulkner might regard too much coherence as something to be avoided.

In an interview in 1955 Faulkner is quoted as saying:

I was asked the question who were the five best contemporary writers and how did I rate them. And I said Wolfe, Hemingway, Dos Passos, Caldwell and myself. I rated Wolfe first, myself second. I put Hemingway last. I said we were all failures. All of us had failed to match the dream of perfection and I rated the authors on the basis of their splendid failure to do the impossible. I believed Wolfe tried to do the greatest of the impossible, that he tried to reduce all human experience to literature. And I thought after Wolfe I had tried the most. I rated Hemingway last because he stayed within what he knew. He did it fine, but he didn't try for the impossible.

Faulkner adds:

145

I rated those authors by the way in which they failed to match the dream of perfection. . . . This had nothing to do with the value of the work, the impact or perfection of its own kind that it had. I was talking only about the magnificence of the failure, the attempt to do the impossible within human experience.[1]

There are ambiguities in Faulkner's statement, but it strongly suggests that he would consider full coherence a sign that not enough had been tried. It suggests, also, that he might well wish to avoid such coherence. That is, not only does he place a higher value [2] upon the effort to do the *impossible* than upon accepting human and artistic limitations, but he also seems to measure the effort by the extent of the failure. It can be argued, of course, that Faulkner's emphasis on the word "failure" is merely a matter of rhetoric and that he is rating the writers only by their quest of perfection and is voicing only the conventional ideal that a man's reach should exceed his grasp. Yet there is much in the statement, and in others I shall comment upon later, and much about his works to indicate that his attitude is more complex than that, and that in an important sense his own quest is a quest for "failure."

[1] "A Walk With Faulkner," *New York Times Book Review*, Jan. 30, 1955, p. 4.

[2] It is true that Faulkner has said that his rating "had nothing to do with the value of the work." The whole tenor of the statement, however, indicates that he does attach high value to the quest for the impossible and to the magnificent failure. His very choice to rate the authors in those terms affirms the value of those terms. One might argue that, by saying his rating had nothing to do with value, Faulkner intends only to qualify the preceding part of his statement, but, in fact, the comment about value contradicts his preceding rhetoric and content, both, and involves an unwillingness to commit himself fully to the meanings of that rhetoric and content or to the consequences of his choice to rate the authors in the terms he did. Similar sorts of self-contradiction are present in Faulkner's introduction to the Modern Library edition of *Sanctuary*, in his Foreword to *The Faulkner Reader*, and, a bit less obviously, in his Nobel Prize speech and various other public utterances. That this is true suggests that his literary use of ambiguity may be a matter of temperament as well as of conscious artistic intent.

It is no accident that every one of Faulkner's experiments with form and style—his rapidly shifting points of view, his use of more or less incoherent narrators such as Benjy, Quentin, Darl, Rosa Coldfield, and Gavin Stevens, his disordered time sequences, his juxtapositions of largely independent stories, his unsyntactical marathon sentences, his whole method, as Conrad Aiken puts it, "of deliberately withheld meaning, of progressive and partial and delayed disclosure"—is a movement away from order and coherence. It is no accident that every one of Faulkner's novels involves one or more of these experiments and that in most of the novels we find them all.

It is important to recognize, also, that the effects of Faulkner's fragmentation of material are usually quite different from those produced by others who have used similar techniques. In works like *The Ring and the Book* and the Japanese film *Rashomon* various perspectives are thrown upon the same central event. In *Mrs. Dalloway* and *Ulysses* the seemingly unconnected experiences and events are occurring at the same time or on the same day. That is, either the event, time, or point of view is held constant. In *The Sound and the Fury, As I Lay Dying*, and *Absalom, Absalom!* on the other hand, none of these is constant. The various narrators touch upon a few of the same events, but the selection of events seems determined essentially by the particular interests and obsessions of the narrator. In *The Sound and the Fury*, for example, neither Benjy's nor Jason's narration throws light on the incest theme which dominates the section narrated by Quentin. Quentin, on the other hand, is dead before many of the events take place which are crucial in the lives of Benjy and Jason. In *Absalom, Absalom!* the various narrators emphasize different aspects and periods of Sutpen's history. As a result, the reader feels less sense of pattern and equilibrium than in the first-named works, is less able to group his thoughts and feelings about a common center.

Particularly indicative of Faulkner's intentions is the fact that when he does present explicit interpretations of events or ana-

lytic commentaries on them he always takes pains to make them
either suspect, inconclusive, or incoherent. On many occasions
he will narrate or describe an action in perfectly conventional
and logical sequence, but his interpretive or philosophic passages are almost invariably disordered. I think we can go so
far as to say that the more explanatory or intellectual the content, the less the coherence. The dominant characteristic, in
fact, of Faulkner's intellectuals—it is they, of course, who offer
most of the interpretations—is their tendency to be incoherent.
The most intellectual character in Faulkner's novels, and probably his favorite commentator, is Gavin Stevens, a Ph.D. from
Heidelberg. And, as has been generally recognized, it is his
statements which usually provide the greatest resistance to rational understanding. Here, for example, is a part of his final
commentary, the final explicit commentary of any sort, on the
meaning of the events in *Intruder in the Dust*. Gavin is talking
to his nephew Charles Mallison, who has been chiefly responsible for saving the Negro Lucas Beauchamp from being
lynched.

What's out yonder in the ground at Caledonia Church was Crawford Gowrie for only a second or two last Saturday and Lucas
Beauchamp will be carrying his pigment into ten thousand situations a wiser man would have avoided and a lighter escaped ten
thousand times after what was Lucas Beauchamp for a second or
so last Saturday is in the ground at his Caledonia church too, because that Yoknapatawpha County which would have stopped you
and Aleck Sander and Miss Habersham last Sunday night are right
actually, Lucas' life the breathing and eating and sleeping is of no
importance just as yours and mine are not but his unchallengeable
right to it in peace and security and in fact this earth would be
much more comfortable with a good deal fewer Beauchamps and
Stevenses and Mallisons of all colors in it if there were only some
painless way to efface not the clumsy room-devouring carcasses
which can be done but the memory which cannot—that inevictible
immortal memory awareness of having once been alive which exists
forever still ten thousand years afterward in ten thousand recollec-

tions of injustice and suffering, too many of us not because of the room we take up but because we are willing to sell liberty short . . . for the sake of what we call our own which is a . . . license to pursue each his private postulate of happiness and contentment regardless of grief and cost even to the crucifixion of someone whose nose or pigment we dont like and even these can be coped with provided that few of others who believe that a human life is valuable simply because it has a right to keep on breathing no matter what pigment its lungs distend or nose inhales the air and are willing to defend that right at any price, it doesn't take many three were enough last Sunday night even one can be enough and with enough ones willing to be more than grieved and shamed Lucas will no longer run the risk of needing without warning to be saved. [*ID*, 243–244]

Fortunately Faulkner has other voices besides that of Gavin. But these other voices do not negate or encompass Gavin's so much as stand in suspension with it.

Probably the most crucial indication of Faulkner's intentions is the fact that the endings of all his novels not only fail to resolve many of the tensions and meanings provided in the novels but also seem carefully designed to prevent such resolution. Above all, they leave unresolved the question of the meaningfulness of the human efforts and suffering we have witnessed, whether the sound and the fury is part of some larger design or whether it has signified nothing in an essentially meaningless universe. To read a Faulkner novel is to struggle to integrate and resolve a bewildering number and variety of impressions and suggestions. It is, and it is meant to be, a struggle without end.

The Sound and the Fury

The Sound and the Fury presents various parts of the history of the Compson family in four discontinuous sections, each of which is written from a different point of view and a different point in time. These temporal positions are not sequential; they run April 7, 1928; June 2, 1910; April 6, 1928; and April 8, 1928. In addition, within each of the first three sections there is a continual shuttling back and forth in time, ordered largely by the mental associations of the narrators, who are the idiot Benjy, the sensitive and romantic but neurotically obsessed Quentin, and the practical, materialistic, and self-pitying Jason. The first section is especially fragmented and difficult to embrace, since its narrator cannot distinguish time and has not developed with time, and shows his inability to understand any abstract relationships by omitting all connective tissue between his sentences.

As suggested above, this mode of presentation prevents us from organizing our impressions about any single center and induces a general sense of tension and disequilibrium. Apart from this, however, we reach the end of the first three sections with certain more specific uncertainties and tensions of thought and feeling. For one thing we are not sure what attitude to take toward the disintegration of the family. In the first two sections, Benjy and Quentin report events in such a way that we see and feel their pathetic rather than ludicrous or ironic side. The "sassprilluh" drinking scene, for example, could easily have been presented with the same comic gusto we find in "The Spotted Horses." Instead the emphasis is upon Benjy's discomfort and upon the unhappy effect of T. P.'s laughter on Quentin. We are somewhat aware throughout the first two sections that Benjy is subhuman and that his suffering is not of an order that evokes the highest kind of sympathy, and Quentin's posturing and extreme romanticism at times seem comic, but essentially we are led to see them both as suffering individuals, to feel considerable compassion for them, and to take their predicaments very seriously. In the third section, however, narrated by Jason, the tone is essentially comic and satiric. Not only does Jason come through as a largely comic character but his narration tends to bathe the whole Compson history in a somewhat comic light, which at least temporarily blinds us to the poignancy and pathos of it. We are much more

detached than in the earlier sections, less serious. We want to
see Jason made a fool of, and we are not especially moved by the
plight of his niece Quentin. Had the novel ended with this
section we would view the Compson history largely with a
sense of grim amusement, as a tale of sound and fury signifying
that the human condition is essentially hopeless and not worth
much thought or compassion.

Our response is further complicated by our conflicting feelings about most of the characters. We have sympathy for
Benjy but can never forget that he is an idiot, who is oblivious
to everyone's needs but his own, and that efforts to please or
comfort him are in a sense futile. We can recognize that he is
to some extent a measure or "moral mirror" for the other characters in that we can judge them in relation to their treatment
of him and his response to them, but he is hardly an adequate
measure since he is apparently as comforted by firelight or
golfers as he is by Dilsey or Caddy. And if we admire Benjy's
direct and uncomplicated responses to experience, his ability to
sense evil, and his loyalty and see these as a celebration of
primitivism on Faulkner's part, we must at the same time remember that Benjy is as much incapacitated as his mother or
Quentin, or Emily Grierson for that matter, by his utter inability to let go of the past.

We admire Caddy for her devotion to Benjy but recognize
that she is at the same time willful and domineering and does
abandon Benjy. We are puzzled somewhat by her utter sense of
defeat after her affair with Dalton and by her willingness to
marry Herbert. This seems another example of a Faulkner
character acting in precisely the way which will lead to the
most self-torment. Nor are we ever really enlightened about
her character. We learn that she is concerned about her daughter Quentin's welfare, but not concerned enough to do anything serious about it. In the section narrated by Jason we watch
her suffer but gain little insight into why she behaves as she does
or how she feels beyond the moment.

We are likewise puzzled and confused by Quentin. We sympathize with him but at the same time feel that he suffers as much from a pathological condition which calls for psychiatric care as from a tragic human dilemma which can claim our entire compassion. We recognize the decency and even nobility of many of his feelings but also a certain amount of posturing, and we recognize that in his own way he is as self-centered as Benjy. Finally, I think, we are mystified by him. I suppose no suicide is ever fully comprehensible to those who choose to live, but Quentin's is especially difficult to understand. We know a great deal about his state of mind after he has decided to die, and we know many of his feelings about Caddy and her wedding, but we never see him moving toward or reaching the decision to take his life. In the Appendix Faulkner tells us that Quentin loved death, and Mr. Compson offers various explanations of Quentin's motivation, but these do not satisfactorily explain why two months after his sister's wedding, without any vacillation or hesitation, or even strong feelings of depression, he takes his life. He has written letters to his roommate and his father, but Faulkner does not let us see these. Our last glimpse of him brushing his teeth and then his hat leaves our questions unresolved.

Even toward Jason we have conflicting feelings. In some ways he is a monster, and in many ways he is a fool, and yet, as Faulkner says in his Appendix, he is in some ways "the first sane Compson since before Culloden." He is full of a grandiose self-pity, but it is not entirely unwarranted, for many a better man would consider himself cursed if he had to cope with Mrs. Compson, Quentin II, and Benjy. Although he fails utterly to recognize Dilsey's worth, his estimate of the other Negroes is not entirely unjust. Luster, for example, takes care of Benjy after a fashion but spends as much of his time tormenting him as pacifying him. And if Jason is unjustifiably cynical about all human actions, this permits him to see through his mother in ways that we relish. Still further complicating our response is the fact that he does in a sense support the Compson family, that he does seem to make a more satisfactory sexual adjustment than any of the other Compson children, and that he has a sense of humor, albeit a distorted and paranoiac one. Working most against any resolution of feeling toward him are his violent headaches, which compel a certain sympathy for him and which suggest that he, too, is a suffering neurotic.

Dilsey and Mrs. Compson provide the least irresolution in our responses. We consistently admire Dilsey's decency, loyalty, and stoicism, and we disdain with equal consistency Mrs. Compson's foolishness and self-pity. Yet even these reactions are somewhat qualified, for Mrs. Compson is too silly to be seriously despised, and Dilsey spends much of her time nagging, scolding, and threatening both the Compson children and her own, and she is, in the last analysis, ineffectual.

Besides being unsettled by these various and often conflicting feelings, we are groping at the end of the third section for some larger perspective, context, or pattern under which to view and interpret the unhappy events we have been witnessing. Faulkner has suggested a number of these. The title has suggested that there is no pattern, that the events have no significance, and Mr. Compson's nihilistic philosophy reinforces this, as does the apparently chaotic order of events. Opposed to this, however, is our natural disinclination to accept such a view, and our awareness of Faulkner's at least partial approval of Benjy, Quentin, Caddy, Mr. Compson, and Dilsey, and his disapproval of Mrs. Compson, Jason, and Herbert. There is also our recognition of several more or less recurrent motifs which encourage us to search for pattern and significance within and beneath the sound and fury. But the search has sent us in varying directions, none of which has been clearly or conclusively marked.

Some of the events and emphases have seemed chiefly in accord with a socioeconomic antithesis between an old and new culture of the general sort pointed out by the O'Donnell, Cowley, and Warren line of criticism. Up to a point we can see in Mr. and

Mrs. Compson, Quentin, and the Blands the remnants and cor-
ruptions of a traditional society which is in contrast with a root-
less money-centered culture more or less typified by Jason,
Luster, Herbert, and the carnival, with its performer on the
musical saw and its dehumanized young man with the red tie,
who runs away with Quentin II. To some extent one cannot
avoid making some such schematization. On the other hand, there
is much to keep one from being content with it. One cannot
help feeling that most of the problems and difficulties of Benjy,
Caddy, and Quentin are clinical rather than sociological; they
seem driven more by peculiar personal need than by larger forces.
Quentin's hatred of Herbert seems closely related to the schematization, and the Dalton Ames episode seems partially so,
but the strongly urged incest motif does not, nor does Caddy's
seemingly compulsive promiscuity. Jason's materialism and fi-
nancial chicanery and generally pragmatic attitude fits in, but
his headaches, his persecution complex, and his concern for
stability and decorum do not. We can view Quentin II as a de-
teriorated version of Caddy and thus as a measure of the two cultures, but she, too, seems driven by inner compulsion rather
than by a cultural situation.

To the extent that we do accept some such opposition between
an older and newer order we are disturbed by the impossibility of
choosing between them. Our sympathies, like Faulkner's, are
with the old, but the best representatives of it in this book are
a drunkard, a suicide, and a lost and lonely woman. Between
what they are and what Jason is there seems no middle ground
offered. Dilsey's decency suggests that there can be something
better, but the kind of answer her presence implies is rather
special and ambiguous and finally seems independent of a sociological schematization.

We have been encouraged, also, to seek patterns in several
other directions. Some of the events and emphases have suggested
interpretation in terms of clinical and even specifically Freudian
psychology. We have been strongly encouraged, also, as various

critics have pointed out, to interpret events in relation to Christian myth and ideology, in relation to concepts of time, and in relation to Shakespearian tragedy. As with the old-versus-new-order motif Faulkner has emphasized each of these aspects enough to tempt us to consider it as a possible framework for ordering the fragmented story, but he has not emphasized any one consistently or clearly enough for us to accept it as a center. We are unsettled, of course, not only by this intermittent quality of the individual motifs but by the number and variety of the possible interpretations we must hold in suspension.

The final section of the book, narrated from an omniscient and objective point of view, begins with a focus and emphasis that seem to offer a kind of implicit interpretation and resolution, one in accord with the sentiments and mood of Faulkner's Nobel Prize speech. The strong emphasis on Dilsey's fortitude, decency, and Christian humility and on her comprehensive view of time, as numerous critics have pointed out, provides a context for the unhappy events, a perspective from which to view them and a way to feel about them. On the other hand, this episode does not so much offer a synthesis or interpretation as a general vantage point and degree of moral affirmation. It does not help us to understand most of the particulars of the Compson story any better, to illuminate, say, the character and motives of Quentin and Caddy. Nor does it in any but a peripheral way relate to the socioeconomic context of the story. Although it asserts the relevance of Christianity to the story it does not really clarify the nature of that relevance nor make clear how seriously we are to take the Christian context. I think this occurs partly because Faulkner so strongly emphasizes the peculiarly Negro aspects of both the Easter service and Dilsey's responses and partly because the crucifixion-and-resurrection motif is such a general one. This motif can serve as an ironic or moral commentary on virtually any kind of evil or decadence and therefore does not especially illuminate the meaning of any particular variety. Furthermore, although there have been throughout the book recurrent al-

lusions to the crucifixion and resurrection and recurrent symbolic suggestions of them, the actual difficulties of the Compson's have not been sufficiently presented in Christian terms to
enable us to see how the Christian motif is really applicable to
their predicament. Nor is there any clear connection in the episode between the emphasis on the crucifixion and resurrection
and Dilsey's repeated choral commentary, "I seed de beginnin,
en now I sees de endin" (p. 313). Nevertheless, whatever the
episode leaves unclear or unresolved, its tone and general tenor
do provide a general way of looking at and feeling about the
story and a sense of resolution.

But—and it is a very crucial "but," which most interpreters
of the novel have ignored—the emphasis on Dilsey and her
trip to church is at the beginning of the final section and is only
one of several emphases in that section. It is followed by the
lengthy description of Jason's vain and tormenting pursuit of
Quentin, which provides a very different perspective, mood, and
set of feelings. We are back in a realm of sound and fury, even
of melodrama. We do not see Jason from the large perspective
we have just shared with Dilsey, but respond to his frustration
and defeat with a grim amusement and satisfaction only slightly
leavened by pity. We cannot view his defeat as affirmative, for
the "heroine" who has eluded him seems equally doomed. It is
true that we might draw a sharp contrast between the ways Dilsey and Jason spend their Sunday and between Dilsey's sense of
Christian acceptance and Jason's violent and impatient paranoia,
and we might go on to contrast her slow and decorous walk to
church with his frenzied dependence on the automobile, and
these contrasts can be related to the general contrast between
traditional and traditionless cultures. Here again, however, one
cannot quite understand the relevance of the contrast except as
generalized ironic commentary. Nor do we, I think, actually feel
this contrast while reading this section. Essentially Dilsey and
her church have receded into the landscape and seem barely relevant to Jason's predicament.

The final part of the last section emphasizes Benjy's misery and the callousness and swagger of Dilsey's grandson, Luster, as he torments Benjy, first by taking his bottle, then by shouting "Caddy," and finally by driving around the square in the wrong direction. We are reminded for a moment of Dilsey's decency and faith but only to feel its ineffectualness, for neither she nor the church service has touched Luster. The book closes with the carriage ride of Luster and Benjy—with our attention focused on a young Negro whose main desire is to show off and on an idiot, capable of serenity or anguish but little more than that. Faulkner emphasizes Benjy's terrible agony as Luster throws his world into disorder by going around the square in the wrong direction. Jason comes rushing across the square, turns the carriage around, and hits both Luster and Benjy. Benjy becomes serene again as the carriage moves in its usual direction and things flow by smoothly from left to right "each in its ordered place."

It is a powerful ending and a fitting one in its focus on Benjy and its application to the general theme of order and disorder running through the novel. But it is an ending which provides anything but a synthesis or resolution, and it leaves us with numerous conflicting feelings and ideas. We are momentarily relieved and pleased by the cessation of Benjy's suffering, but we are troubled by the fact that it has been achieved by Jason, who cares nothing for Benjy and is concerned only with maintaining an external and superficial decorum. We can hardly draw any real satisfaction from the serenity and order, because the serenity is the "empty" serenity of an idiot and the order is that demanded by an idiot. The general tenor of the episode is in accord with Mr. Compson's pessimism rather than Faulkner's Nobel Prize speech, for everything in it suggests the meaninglessness and futility of life.

This final scene does not negate the moderate affirmation of the Dilsey episode, nor does it really qualify it. Rather it stands in suspension with it as a commentary of equal force. We feel and are intended to feel, I think, that the events we have witnessed are at once tragic and futile, significant and meaningless. We cannot move beyond this. Nor does the final section help us to resolve whether the Compsons were defeated essentially by acts of choice or by a kind of doom, or whether the doom was chiefly a matter of fate or of psychological aberration or of socioeconomic forces. It is worth repeating that if we do accept as a primary motif the opposition between an older and newer culture we face the impossibility of choosing between them.

In short, the ending seems designed not to interpret or to integrate but to leave the various elements of the story in much the same suspension in which they were offered, and to leave the reader with a high degree of emotional and intellectual tension.

As I Lay Dying

In *As I Lay Dying*, as in *The Sound and the Fury*, Faulkner presents his material in highly fragmented form. The book is divided into fifty-nine sections ranging in length from five words to seven pages. Each section presents a first-person description or statement by one or another of fifteen characters. The shift of point of view, as Aiken puts it, is "kaleidoscopically rapid." Moreover, some of the statements are conscious expressions, some unconscious; some are in character, some obviously beyond the capacities of the speakers (e.g., pp. 379, 384, 392). Inevitably there are great variations in tone. Characters and events appear sometimes heroic, sometimes tragic, sometimes farcical, sometimes naturalistic, sometimes highly distorted. Further complexity is provided by the fact that the dominant or at least most frequent point of view is that of Darl, who is part seer, part madman, and finally seems to go completely mad.

The story line or sequence of events is clearer than in *The Sound and the Fury*, and since the story revolves about a journey and a mission it has a certain unity which the earlier book lacks. Moreover, the presence of Addie, both as a living force and as a corpse, does, for a while, provide the novel with a center of sorts, and many of the actions and tensions within and between characters can be loosely related to her and to her antithesis between "words" and "doing." Still one approaches the end of the book with a great many uncertainties.

One is uncertain about the qualities of some of the important characters and about how to feel toward them; one is puzzled by the meanings of many of the events; one is far from sure what the book is chiefly about, and above all one is uncertain to what extent one has been watching an epic or tragedy or farce. This is worth illustrating at some length. For, although *As I Lay Dying* is one of Faulkner's slighter books, its very slightness and comparative simplicity enable us to see more clearly what Faulkner is after.

Addie, as a number of critics have pointed out, is surely the primary key to any understanding of the novel, and I would agree in part with Mrs. Vickery's assertion that the central problem of the novel is "Addie, not as mother, corpse, or promise but as an element in the blood of her children which they must integrate whether she lives or dies. Within her we must seek their motivation, their knowing and doing." [3] Addie's life and attitudes do illuminate the novel to some extent, but it is in many ways a very hazy and fitful sort of illumination.

In the first place, we do not get a good look at her until two-thirds of the book has passed. It is true that various characters, especially Cora, have now and again given brief clues about her character, but these have been very few and very general. Various members of her family indicate that she was important in their lives, but they do not show us or tell us how. Indeed, their failure to think about her and to remember things about her is such as to affront verisimilitude, and it is hard not to feel that Faulkner has deliberately sought to keep her a shadowy and mysterious figure.

[3] "*As I Lay Dying*," in *Two Decades*, pp. 191–192.

In the second place, the picture she gives of herself when
finally we do meet her is far from clear. We understand that
she is a tormented and frustrated person and that she is especially
tormented by the gap between reality and the words people use
to talk about it. We understand, also, how horrible it must
have been for her to be married to Anse, who was nothing but
words. And we can understand that her attachment to the il-
legitimately and passionately conceived Jewel would be peculiarly intense and tight. But there is much about her that is
much less clear.

We are given little insight, for example, into why she was so
full of hate and misery even before she met Anse, why she hated
her pupils, and why she found life and teaching so horrible that
"I would hate my father for having ever planted me" (p. 461).
We know that her father felt that "the reason for living was to
get ready to stay dead for a long time" (p. 461), and we know
that she felt that her kin had all been in some sense dead, but we
are given none of the details which might help us to understand
why her torment is so great. The nature of her torment is also
perplexing. What seems at first to torment her is a terrible loneliness of both flesh and spirit. She hated her pupils because they
seemed so separate from her and unaware of her. She would
beat them, thinking "with each blow of the switch: Now you
are aware of me! Now I am something in your secret and selfish
life, who have marked your blood with my own for ever and
ever. And so I took Anse" (pp. 461–462). She tells us that

> In the early spring it was worst. Sometimes I thought I could not
> bear it, lying in bed at night, with the wild geese going north and
> their honking coming faint and high and wild out of the wild dark-
> ness, and during the day it would seem as though I couldn't wait for
> the last one to go so I could go down to the spring. And so when
> I looked up that day and saw Anse standing there in his Sunday
> clothes, turning his hat round and round in his hands, I said:
> "If you've got any womenfolks, why in the world don't they
> make you get your hair cut?" [p. 462]

It would seem clear that she chose Anse to fill her longings for union and connection, to end her isolation. Thus we might expect that her shock and horror would come when she learned that Anse could not satisfy these needs. Instead, what seems to shock and dismay her, above all, is the experience of pregnancy. "So I took Anse. And when I knew that I had Cash, I knew that living was terrible and that this was the answer to it. . . . I knew that it had been, not that my aloneness had to be violated over and over each day, but that it had never been violated until Cash came" (p. 463–464). But she goes on to say that "her aloneness had been violated and then made whole again by the violation: time, Anse, love, what you will, outside the circle" (p. 464). And she suggests quite clearly that once born Cash is inside the circle and that having him is satisfying to her.

All this is rather puzzling. First of all, we do not know why pregnancy should be so horrifying to her. Secondly, it had seemed earlier that what she had wanted above all was to have her aloneness violated. Yet here she seems to want anything but that, seems to cherish the aloneness, sees Cash as something which enables her to preserve that aloneness.[4] At any rate, we are led to believe that after the initial shock of becoming a mother she found the relationship with the baby Cash meaningful and satisfying. She implies that she enjoyed nursing him and that there was a real rather than merely verbal bond between them. We might well assume that she would want more children. But we read: "Then I found that I had Darl. At first I would not believe it. Then I believed that I would kill Anse. It was as

---

[4] It is possible that when Addie says, "And when I knew that I had Cash, I knew that living was terrible and that this was the answer to it," she means that the experience of pregnancy and motherhood was a satisfying thing which made her realize how terrible other aspects of life were. And it is possible that despite her use of the word "violation" she means that the violation by Cash was meaningful and satisfying. But such an interpretation raises as many problems as it solves, and it makes even less comprehensible her horror when she discovers she is pregnant with Darl.

though he had tricked me, hidden within a word like within a paper screen and struck me in the back through it" (p. 464). Mrs. Vickery explains her violent reaction on the grounds that "she and Anse have diverged too far for that birth to have been possible." There is no evidence, however, that she had become further apart from Anse than she was when she conceived Cash. Again we wonder why being pregnant should be so terribly horrifying to her. It is hard to know also what her attitude is toward Cash and Darl. Some of her statements imply that she accepts them both, as she had accepted Cash, as a part of herself. She says, "I was three now" (p. 465), and immediately afterward thinks of Cash and Darl without implying any difference in feeling toward them. Even after her affair with Whitfield but before the birth of Jewel she says, "My children were of me alone, of the wild blood boiling along the earth, of me and of all that lived; of none and of all" (p. 467). Yet elsewhere she says "I gave Anse the children. I did not ask for them" (p. 465), and she seems to equate them with Anse when she says that she would refuse to let Anse make love to her "just as I refused my breast to Cash and Darl after their time was up" (p. 466). Most perplexing of all is her statement after the birth of Jewel, who is fathered by Whitfield. "I gave Anse Dewey Dell to negative Jewel. Then I gave him Vardaman to replace the child I had robbed him of. And now he has three children that are his and not mine" (p. 467). Here Darl seems to become Anse's child while Cash remains her own.

It can be argued that I am asking for coherence from a woman who is to a large extent an incoherent and inconsistent creature, one who rejects the validity of words. Certainly her narration can and must be explained and defended on those grounds. My point is that, whatever the dramatic justification for it, this "center" of the book is by no means a clear one, and can at best provide a hazy illumination for the novel as a whole. It may help us to understand, on a symbolic level at least, Jewel's fury and torment, but it throws little light on the characters of Cash and Darl. Cash has a mind which is above all orderly and prosaic. Darl is poetic and on the edge of madness. Yet the circumstances of their births, which presumably explain their characters and problems, were virtually the same.

Another problem we face when we try to see Addie as the center of the novel is our ignorance about her actual behavior toward various members of the family. We are told that Jewel was clearly her favorite, that she whipped and petted him more than the others and saw him as her cross and salvation, and we know that she was willing to be deceitful at times in order to feed and protect him, and we know that she could bake well, but that is all. We have no way of knowing what her determination to "clean her house" after her affair with Whitfield means in terms of her attitudes and behavior toward the family. Except for the brief and not especially illuminating scenes upon the discovery of Jewel's acquisition of the horse and on her deathbed, we do not see her. And, as I said earlier, none of the other members of the family tell us anything specific about her.

Finally, she does not help us to understand the meaning of the trip to Jefferson. The crucial passage is carefully ambiguous: when she becomes pregnant with Darl she first wants to kill Anse.

But then I realized that I had been tricked by words older than Anse or love, and that the same word had tricked Anse too, and that my revenge would be that he would never know I was taking revenge. And when Darl was born I asked Anse to promise to take me back to Jefferson when I died, because I knew that father had been right, even when he couldn't have known he was right any more than I could have known I was wrong. [p. 464]

Why should she want to be buried in Jefferson because her father was right in his belief that "the reason for living was to get ready to stay dead a long time"? The syntax does not make clear whether the promise is the revenge, but, if we assume so, in what way is it a revenge? It is true that the trip does make Anse aware of her in a sense and that it does force him to act, although not very much. On the other hand, that action does provide him with a new set of teeth and a new wife. Has the revenge, then, been successful or unsuccessful? But the obscurity of her motives in exacting the promise leaves unclear an even more important question. How meaningful was the journey and all the effort which went into it? Are we to feel that it made any difference whether her body reached Jefferson or not? Was all the effort dedicated to achieving (or failing to achieve) a revenge? Does the book prove her father right or wrong?

However we read the passage above, how are we to relate it to her statement to Cora that Jewel "is my cross and he will be my salvation. He will save me from the water and from the fire. Even though I have laid down my life, he will save me" (p. 460). Jewel does save her corpse from water and fire but for what salvation, especially if she is going to Jefferson because her father is right or to revenge herself on Anse.

We are faced also with the problem of how to feel toward Addie. There is much to make us feel sympathetic: the force and sincerity of her narration, the horror of being married to Anse, her obviously painful repentance and effort to set her house in order, the clear contrast between her and Cora, Dr. Peabody's sympathy for her, Vardaman's sense of loss. Yet Faulkner also makes us feel that she is a proud and bitter woman and that she as much as anything else is responsible for the hatred and pain within the Bundren family.

After Addie, the most important character in the book is Darl. Not only does he provide more of the narration than any other character and possess the richest consciousness and greatest amount of awareness, but the dominant emphasis at the end of the book is on Darl's committment to the insane asylum at Jackson. Indeed, the emphasis on this is so great and that on the actual burial of Addie so meager that one might well argue that Darl and not Addie is at the center of the book. At the least, we can say that an understanding of Darl is essential for an understanding of the book. Here again however, there is much that is ambiguous and perplexing. No matter how hard we search, he remains essentially a mystery. Clearly Faulkner wishes him to be.

The crucial question, of course, is the nature and extent of his madness. For on this rests our reaction to his incarceration at Jackson. And our interpretation of the book as a whole must depend on how we view that incarceration—whether we see it as a justified or even necessary event or as a terrible and needless cruelty.

Unquestionably Darl is queer in certain ways, and he is seen as queer by numerous characters. The fact that Cora sees him as the most decent and normal member of the family is further testament to his peculiarity, for almost everything Cora thinks or says is clearly wrong. Further evidence of his queerness is provided by his laughter in the wagon at the outset of the trip, by his apparent hallucinations at the coffin shortly before he sets fire to Gillespie's barn and, of course, by the setting of the fire itself. That Darl's mind is disordered is also suggested by the disorder and incoherence of parts of his narrations. But since many of Faulkner's characters are incoherent and since Faulkner uses fragmentation of thought as a structural device, one cannot conclude too much from this.

What is perplexing is the nature and degree of Darl's queerness. Unquestionably he has certain powers of clairvoyance. He knows about Dewey Dell's affair with Lafe and her resulting pregnancy; he is aware of the circumstances of Jewel's birth; and he knows that Addie is going to die. Yet these seem to be the only matters about which he is clairvoyant. One feels he ought to have had more inkling of his own fate, especially since it was within the minds of so many members of his family. There is, it is true, a slight suggestion that he may have been aware of it in his comment to Cash:" 'I thought you'd 'a' told me. It's not that I' " (p. 514). But Faulkner characteristically leaves this crucial sentence unfinished, and we cannot be sure what Darl had in mind.

Throughout most of the journey Darl appears reasonably sane, as sane, certainly, as any other member of the family. His own descriptions of events, including the lengthy one of Jewel's acquisition of the horse and of the fire, itself, are lucid and well organized, and so is his conversation with Cash before they cross the river. His conduct during the crossing and during the fire, if selfish and cowardly, is sensible enough. After the fire, as the family enters Jefferson, he seems far and away the most sane of the group in his efforts to keep Jewel from entering a pointless fight and in his anxiety to get Cash to a doctor. Moreover, his narration of the family's arrival in Jefferson is completely lucid, so lucid and normal that one is completely unprepared when immediately after the end of that narration we learn that the family has decided to send him to Jackson.

Apart from the comments of others that he is queer, there has been little to prepare us for his firing of the barn and his seemingly complete madness on the train to Jackson. His laughter at the beginning of the trip is a bit strange, but it is an understandable and even justifiable reaction under the circumstances. His intense and continual awareness of Jewel, and his frequent taunting of Jewel seem somewhat obsessive, but no more than do Dewey Dell's awareness and hatred of Darl, and Jewel's fury and hatred toward anyone and everyone. The only evidence of insanity, as opposed to mere queerness, is his behavior at Gillespie's. There, before the fire, he tells us that he hears his mother speaking in the coffin, and he takes Vardaman to listen. On the face of it this seems utter madness. Yet one does not, I believe, actually feel this. Perhaps this is because so much of the Bundrens' behavior has seemed on the verge of madness and because Darl's report of Addie's talking has a metaphorical rather than literal quality. After the fire Vardaman reports that Darl is lying on top of the coffin crying. This, too, is seriously abnormal; but again in comparison with the actions of other members of the family it appears relatively insignificant. The only behavior which would warrant his incarceration is the actual setting fire to the barn. We must assume, finally, I think, that he did start the fire, but there is much about the episode that is perplexing. We are given no certain evidence that Darl did start the fire. He, himself, never once even so much as hints that he had anything to do with it. Vardaman, the only witness to the act, in general a highly unreliable witness, says only that he "saw something," something which Dewey Dell told him he must never tell anyone. Later Cash suggests quite clearly that what Vardaman did see was the setting of the fire, and we accept this, but with some discomfort and uncertainty, especially because Darl behaves so sanely afterwards.

Nor are we clear about Darl's motives for starting the fire. Unquestionably his purpose is to burn the coffin. But whether he does so chiefly out of hatred for Jewel or out of a desire to give his mother a clean and peaceful end is problematical. The former is suggested by his taunting of Jewel shortly before the fire (pp. 494–495) and by Cash's remark that it was in a sense the value of Jewel's horse that Darl tried to burn up (p.510); the latter is suggested by Darl's statements to Vardaman that Addie was calling on God to hide her away from the sight of man and by Cash's

But I thought more than once . . . how it would be God's blessing if He did take her outen our hands and get shut of her in some clean way, and it seemed to me that when Jewel worked so to get her outen the river, he was going against God in a way, and then when Darl seen that it looked like one of us would have to do something, I can almost believe he done right in a way. [p. 510]

Moreover there is the question whether Darl's action is in accord with the will of God as Cash implies, or whether, as Addie has said earlier, it is Jewel's actions which are to be seen as the right and necessary ones.

No doubt Faulkner means to suggest all these possibilities, and there is no reason why the motivations and interpretations need be less ambivalent and complex than I have suggested. But our inability to resolve these questions about the fire prevents us from resolving our notions about Darl's sanity or insanity, and this in turn helps to prevent us from resolving the meaning of the book.

We cannot decide whether Darl's clearly evident insanity on the train to Jackson is a proof of his insanity and of the necessity for incarcerating him or whether it is a result of shock and horror at his family's treatment of him. The latter is suggested by his completely sane behavior from the time of the fire to the time when the family jumps on him and by the fact that he does not begin to laugh uncontrollably until Cash indicates that he, too, favors incarcerating him. That the incarceration is warranted is suggested by the extremity of his madness on the train. Even his ravings on the train set up conflicting responses in the reader, for the quality and tone of his laughter and reiterated *Yes*'s are highly ambiguous. Terrible and bitter torment is suggested by some of his thoughts, especially by his question to himself, "Why do you laugh? . . . Is it because you hate the sound of laughing?" Yet our last glimpse of him, as he visualizes his own future, carries a note of peace and even affirmation.

Darl is our brother, our brother Darl. Our brother Darl in a cage in Jackson where, his grimed hands lying light in the quiet interstices, looking out he foams. "Yes yes yes yes yes yes yes yes." [p. 527]

All this is terribly important, for if we can feel that Darl was insane or that he is better off in an asylum we can view the family's whole action as necessary and not entirely inhumane, despite the fact that Jewel's and Dewey Dell's motives were chiefly those of hate. And we can accept as sane and valid Cash's mildly questioning acceptance of Darl's fate and take some comfort in his final words about Darl: "I would think what a shame Darl couldn't be here to enjoy it [the new Mrs. Bundren's gramophone] too. But it is better so for him. This world is not his world; this life his life" (p. 532). To the extent, however, that we feel that Darl was not insane or that his life in the asylum will be one of torment, the action of the family becomes monstrously inhumane, and we must view Cash and virtually all he says about Darl with terrible irony.

To the extent that one sees Darl as mad, an inevitable alien to this world, the whole journey can take on a partly heroic quality, be seen as a task accomplished against almost insurmountable odds, Darl being part of the odds. To the extent that one sees him as a victim of hate and stupidity, the family's achievement becomes ugly and horrible, a triumph of Jewel's and Dewey Dell's hatred and of Anse's self-indulgent ineptitude. If Darl was essentially insane, one can smile a little at the closing lines of the book as Anse presents his new teeth and new wife. If he was not, it becomes one of the most grim and cynical endings in literature.

Obviously one does not and cannot make a choice, nor is it possible to find some middle ground. Clearly Faulkner means us to have all these sets of feelings about Darl and about the family's action. Moreover, Faulkner keeps us sharply conscious of these feelings to the very end by having Cash muse at length about Darl's sanity and behavior, by dramatizing the physical attack on Darl, by having Vardaman repeat and repeat that Darl went crazy and that Darl is his brother, by presenting Darl's own ravings on the train, and by having Cash remind us forcibly of Darl's condition at the end of the next to the last paragraph of the book.

Had the emphasis on Darl's fate clearly dominated the end of the book, we would have felt essentially in command of the meaning of the book. For although we would remain puzzled about some things and although our response would be the ambivalent one I have described, we would have a center about which to group our thoughts and emotions. The ending, however, is a far more complex affair than I have so far indicated, for Darl's fate is only one strand of it.

Among other things we have the problem of how to view Anse and the fact that he is triumphant at the end, the only character who seems to have gained anything by the journey. Much of the time he appears as an essentially comic character, a one-dimensional caricature of shiftlessness, ineptitude, and self-pity. How else can one think of a character who says, while staring at the corpse of his wife a very short time after her death: "God's will be done. . . . Now I can get them teeth" (p. 375), and whose speech consists largely of the sort of reiterations that define a Dickens minor comic character.

Working against this view, however, are several other recurrent suggestions. There is the suggestion that Addie's death is a healthy liberation for him, as well it might have been, in view of her contempt for him. At her funeral "his face is different. . . . He looks folks in the eye now, dignified, his face tragic and composed" (p. 399). At the end of the book, when he has acquired a set of false teeth and a new wife, he looks "a foot taller, kind of holding his head up, hangdog and proud too." Then, too, there is the suggestion that there is a wisdom in his passivity and laziness. The end of the book certainly points to this, and so, perhaps, does Darl's description of him as "partaking of that owl-like quality of awry-feathered, disgruntled outrage within which lurks a wisdom too profound or too inert for even thought" (p. 372). Related to this is the not entirely comic reiteration of the idea that Anse is one of the chosen of the Lord and that the Lord takes special care of him (pp. 402, 415). This is suggested not only by various characters and by the fact that his neighbors and even strangers do take care of him but by the unerring instinct which leads him to the house of the new Mrs. Bundren. As Cash says three times, "It was like he knowed" (pp. 512–513).

There is still another side to Anse, which one must hold in suspension, and which prevents one from viewing him either as a Dickensian comic figure or as a more seriously conceived helpless and inept child of the Lord. There is a ruthless and even vicious quality about him as well, for not only does he steal from his children but he seems completely devoid of any sort of

paternal feelings. Had all his children died on route, one feels
he would have been just as content at the end.

Again we are left not so much with complexity of character
as with differing views of a character which we cannot fully
integrate. This would not be so disturbing were it not that the
book ends on the note of Pa's triumph and that he is the only
character who does achieve any sort of triumph. Thus, depending on how one views Pa, the final paragraph can be seen as
farcical, as a moderately comic affirmation of an effortless trust
of the sort that characterizes Lena Grove in *Light in August*,
or as savagely ironic. In view of the contrast with Darl's fate,
any reading, of course, gives the end an ironic dimension of
some degree.

Still further complexity is given to the ending by the promi-
nence in it of Cash, who narrates both the final section and the
important section describing the attack on Darl. Are we to see
him as a sane and healthy character whose easy acceptance of
Darl's incarceration and of his new mother is a proper response?
Or are we to see his response as pitifully inadequate? His careful workmanship, his courageous behavior crossing the river, his
stoical acceptance of his broken leg, his comparatively compas-
sionate attitude toward Darl, and his philosophizing toward the
end of the book all suggest that we view him not only as the
sanest and most decent member of the family but as a kind of
moral or ethical center, in somewhat the same fashion as we
regard Dilsey in *The Sound and the Fury*. On the other hand,
there is a rigidity and absurdity about much of his thought and
behavior that make it very difficult to see him as such a center.
I am thinking not only of his numbered thoughts and his obsession with the balance of the coffin early in the book but of his
conversation with Dr. Peabody near the end. Even more disturbing is his inability to understand Darl's laughter in response to
his "It'll be better for you" and his deep and earnest conviction
that a little gramophone music is "about the nicest thing a fellow

can have," especially when the gramophone is associated with the duck-shaped woman with hard-looking pop eyes.

One further aspect of the ending compels our attention: the two last sections devoted to Dewey Dell. In the first she encounters the incredibly callous drug store clerk, MacGowan. He answers her request for something to abort her baby by giving her from an unlabeled bottle some liquid which he is aware might be poison and some pills of talcum powder, and then takes her down the cellar to exact his sexual payment. In the second section, which is the next to the last in the book, her father takes from her the ten dollars with which she had hoped to pay for something to cause a miscarriage. In each of these scenes the view of human nature implied is about as cynical as it can be. There is nothing in them which suggests any reason why the world would not be a better place if man were wiped off the face of it. Life, Faulkner seems to be saying, is nothing more than a grim and horrible joke. By his tone in those sections, an essentially comic tone similar to that in the Jason section of *The Sound and the Fury*, he seems to be saying further that it is a joke which might well be regarded with amusement.

As in *The Sound and the Fury*, the ending of *As I Lay Dying*, far from helping us to order or resolve the suspension of multiple suggestions and points of view presented in the book, seems designed to preserve that suspension in all its complexity and even to make it more complex. As in *The Sound and the Fury* both the view of life suggested and the tone to be taken toward it are ambiguous. When at the very end Cash says of Darl "But it is better so for him. This world is not his world; this life his life," we must simultaneously nod in acquiescence and shake our heads in outrage. And even as we read, we cannot decide whether we are nodding because Darl is not good enough for the world or bad enough for it. And we cannot be sure whether Cash understands this ambiguity or whether we are listening to the words of one who has attained a wisdom beyond ours or one who is monstrously blind.

When we read the final paragraph—" 'It's Cash and Jewel and Vardaman and Dewey Dell,' pa says, kind of hangdog and proud too, with his teeth and all, even if he wouldn't look at us. 'Meet Mrs. Bundren,' he says"—we must feel simultaneously that Faulkner is making a kind of comic affirmation and that he is saying that life is so meaningless and even vicious that any kind of affirmation is a mockery.

Finally, the endings of the two books are alike in that the affirmative note in each is not only opposed by other notes but contains within itself an ironic dimension. The order and serenity Benjy achieves is the order of an idiot; the triumph of Pa is in a way equally empty.

Light in August

Judging solely from *The Sound and the Fury* and *As I Lay Dying*, one might conclude that the complexity, ambiguity, and irresolution in Faulkner's work results chiefly from particular structural and stylistic experiment, that they are, so to speak, accidents of technique. *Light in August* reveals quite clearly that much more than this is involved, for neither the style nor the structure of the book in themselves provide any serious obstacle to comprehension. There are, it is true, numerous flashbacks and numerous shifts in event and point of view, but these are clearly marked. And while one is faced with the problem of relating parts of the book to one another there is little problem of deciphering the parts. The complexities lie elsewhere.

Let me begin with Professor Holman's excellent description of the general contents and organization of the book.

Light in August consists of three major and largely separate story strands, what Irving Howe has called "a triad of actions." These strands are the story of Joe Christmas, his murder of Joanna Burden, and his death, together with long retrospective sections that trace his life in considerable detail from his birth to the night of Joanna's

death; the story of Gail Hightower, his reintroduction into life
through Lena Grove and Joe Christmas, and his death, together with
retrospective and narrative sections on his marriage and his min-
istry; and the story of Byron Bunch and Lena Grove, of her search
for the father of her illegitimate child, and of its birth. These strands
are tied loosely together by the accident of time, some interchange
of dramatis personae and by the almost mechanical device of having
characters in one strand narrate events in another. Lucas Burch, the
father of Lena Grove's bastard child, is Joe Christmas' helper and
would-be betrayer. Byron Bunch, Lena's loving slave, is a friend of
Hightower, narrates much of the Joe Christmas story to Hightower
and is himself the retrospective narrator for a good deal of Hightower's early story. Joe Christmas' grandmother attempts, with
Bunch's assistance, to persuade Hightower to save her grandson, and
Joe turns to Hightower in the last moments of his life. Hightower
assists at the birth of Lena's child, and Joe's grandmother confuses
Lena with her daughter Milly and Lena's child with Joe as a baby.
However, these links are not sufficient to tie the triad of actions
into "a single action that is complete and whole."

A certain mechanical unity is imposed upon the novel through
Faulkner's establishing the action of the story in the ten days between Joe Christmas' killing Joanna Burden and his being killed by
Percy Grimm. However, the significance of these present actions
is to be found in the past, and the bulk of the novel actually consists
of retrospective accounts of that antecedent action. Faulkner attempts to preserve a sense of present action as opposed to antecedent
cedent action by the device of telling in the present tense all events
that are imagined to be occurring in a forward motion during these
ten days, and in the past tense all retrospective and antecedent
events.[5]

There has been considerable debate over the extent to which
the three stories or "actions" are unified, and over the nature of
that unity. Essays have been written arguing that the unity lies
in an opposition between "images of the curve" and "images of
linear discreteness," in the emphasis on Southern Protestantism,

[5] C. Hugh Holman, "The Unity of Faulkner's *Light in August*,"
PMLA, LXXIII (1958), 156–157.

in the emphasis on man's search for community, in the contrast between "the brooding self-conscious, introverted life imposed by modern civilization on both Joe and Hightower and the simple normal virtues of a life close to nature like that of Lena and . . . Byron," and in the analogies and contrasts with the Christ story.[6] Professor Holman, who urges this last view, has pulled together a number of these themes and has made what is probably the best case that can be made for the unity of the novel. He writes:

There are three distinct bodies of material in the book: formal Protestant religion, sex, and the Negro in Southern society. Each of the story strands deals predominantly with one of these matters but contains the other two in some degree. The story of Joe Christmas is centered on the problem of the Negro in Southern society; the Gail Hightower story is centered in the Protestant church; and the sex element is the controlling factor in the story of Lena Grove, her search for the father of her child, and Byron Bunch's love for her. The interplays of these materials among these separate story strands help to knit the parts of the novel into a whole, but these bodies of material and the stories constructed from them find their most meaningful thematic expression as contrasting analogues of the Christ story.[7]

Certainly the themes and threads these critics have pointed to are in the novel, and certainly there are connections between them, but the connections are far more tenuous, the themes and emphases far more numerous, and the meanings far more ambiguous than any of these critics imply. Moreover, each of the individual stories raises important questions which are not resolved. Let us begin with these.

The story of Lena Grove, with which the book begins and ends, has generally been seen as a pastoral frame for the novel, and Lena and Byron have usually been viewed as providing a

[6] For a list and brief characterization of these essays see Holman, p. 155, notes 1, 2.

[7] Holman, p. 157.

norm of sanity and natural behavior against which the violence
and perversions of the other stories can be measured. Certainly
there is much to compel such a view. Lena's full-bodied health,
serenity, and faith in the natural order of things, and her pleasure
in life, are in sharp contrast to the fanaticism, barrenness, anguish,
or despair that mark most of the other major characters. Hightower, "remembering the strong young body from out whose
travail even there shone something tranquil and unafraid" thinks
that she will have many more children—*"The good stock peo-
pling in tranquil obedience to it the good earth; from these hearty
loins without hurry or haste descending mother and daughter.
But by Byron engendered next"* (p. 356)—and he goes on to
suggest that obedience and relation to earth is perhaps equivalent
to prayer. Byron, until the last chapter of the book at least, is
clearly a norm, if not an ideal, of generosity and unpretentious
decency, perhaps the most clearly virtuous of any of Faulkner's
characters. His religion, unlike that of McEachern, Hines, and
Hightower, is a peaceful modest affair; each Sunday he quietly
and unobtrusively goes to a country church to lead the choir.

On the other hand, there is much which works in opposition
to this view. Lena unquestionably has a kind of wisdom, but
she is deeply mistaken about the character and intentions of
Lucas, whose emptiness and falseness are completely and immediately apparent to everyone else who encounters him. When
Mrs. Armstid warns her that Lucas will run away if she finds
him, she answers, "I reckon a family ought to be all together
when a chap comes. Specially the first one. I reckon the Lord
will see to that" (p. 18). About this, too, she is terribly wrong,
unless one is to consider as a being together the forced and brief
encounter between Lena and Lucas just before he flees.

Numerous critics have seen Lena as a sort of earth-mother
symbolizing the basic natural order, and Faulkner has said re-
cently, "It was her destiny to have a husband and children and
she knew it, and so she went out and attended to it without asking help from anyone. . . . She was never for one moment

confused, frightened, alarmed." [8] There is, however, another, far
more trivial side to Lena. One of the first things we learn about
her is that on trips to town she would ask her father to stop the
wagon at the edge of town so she could walk the rest of the way
in "because she believed that the people who saw her and whom
she passed on foot would believe that she lived in the town too"
(p. 3). After breakfast at the Armstids she is very proud of the
fact that she "et polite." Nor is her treatment of Byron in the
last chapter particularly natural or admirable, especially when one
remembers her easy acceptance and high valuation of the worthless Lucas. Nor is it true that she was never for one moment confused, frightened, or alarmed. She is distinctly confused and
frightened by Mrs. Hines' confusion and her own confusion
about the identity of her child and its father (p. 359), and she
is very much alarmed when she believes Byron has gone away
for good. While it is true that she didn't explicitly ask help from
anyone, she is not unlike Anse Bundren in her dependence on
others and her expectation that help will be provided. This
expectation is not completely unself-conscious, Faulkner suggests several times. [9]

It can be argued, of course, that without some of the characteristics I have just pointed to Lena would lose all verisimilitude
and become pure symbol, much as Eula Varner is in *The Hamlet*. This is true, but it is important to recognize these aspects of
her character when one proposes her as a norm or ideal.

But Faulkner undermines this view of her in a more important
way—by reducing her to a flat comic character at two crucial
points in the book. At the end of the first chapter as she approaches Jefferson, where she hopes to find the father of her
child, her only response is; "My, my, . . . here I aint been on
the road but four weeks, and now I am in Jefferson already. My,

[8] Jean Stein, "The Art of Fiction XII: William Faulkner," *Paris Review*, no. 12 (Spring, 1956), 50.

[9] See, for example, the description of the way she passes and notes the
Armstid wagon and then waits for it (pp. 6–10).

my. A body does get around" (p. 26). And at the very end of the book, after having tormented Byron terribly with her apparent indifference to him, and seemingly unconcerned about his clearly visible pain, she comments: "My, my. A body does get around. Here we aint been coming from Alabama but two months, and now it's already Tennessee" (p. 444).

We are left finally, I think, with the kind of ambiguity about her which is suggested by the description of her face as having "either nothing in it, or everything, all knowledge" (p. 379), an ambiguity often encountered in Faulkner in the phrase "at once empty and profound."

Even harder to reconcile with the view of Lena and Byron as norm is the reduction of Byron in the last chapter to a purely comic character. Not only has he been presented as the highest representative of man and conscience throughout the book, but in the latter part he has grown in stature by taking more responsibility for the people around him than he ever had before. Moreover, more than any other character, he has been involved in all three stories. Yet in the final chapter Faulkner makes us see him chiefly as an ineffectual and ridiculous little man, so defeated and humiliated by Lena that the narrator of the section becomes "downright ashamed to look at him, to let him know that any human man had seen and heard what happened" (p. 441). It is true that both we and the narrator continue to feel sympathetic toward him, but we can hardly feel respect.

Perhaps better than any other of his creations, Joe Christmas illuminates Faulkner's general methods and intentions. I spoke earlier of Faulkner's tendency to push beyond farthermost limits. His equation of Joe Christmas and Christ is another example of this. For by doing so he has made, so to speak, an oxymoron the center of his book. Many writers, of course, have used themes of redemption through violence, and some have hinted at relationships between criminal outcasts and certain aspects of Christ. Faulkner has gone far beyond this. On the one hand, he compels us by dozens of means, many completely explicit, to think of Joe Christmas as Christ or very much like Christ. On the other, he presents Joe not only as a killer but as an extraordinarily violent man. From the age of fourteen, when he beats up the Negro girl who was to provide his first sex experience, he has physical battles with almost every man and woman with whom he has any relationship. (See above p. 109.) But more than this, Faulkner makes him an exceptionally cold and contemptuous person, remarkably incapable of pity, generosity, or love. It is important to recognize that the equation of Joe and Christ is not chiefly an ironic commentary on his divergence from an ideal, as is, for example, the equation of Bloom and Ulysses in Joyce's book, nor is it simply a grim inversion of the Christ story, for Faulkner makes Joe's battle against the twentieth-century Pharisaic order seem a valid one, suggests divine control of the events leading up to the "crucifixion," implies that Joe in a sense bears our common guilt, and suggests strongly that his "crucifixion" and "ascension" will have a permanent value.

Apart from these two opposed general views of Joe there are several other views and understandings of him we must hold in suspension and seek to reconcile. At times one is led to feel that Joe's primary problem is his Negro blood or belief that he has Negro blood and that it is chiefly this which alienates and destroys him. In the summary of his fifteen years of wandering we are told that he tricked white men into calling him Negro in order to fight them, that he almost kills a prostitute when he discovers she will knowingly sleep with Negroes, and that he becomes "sick" after that and lives with Negroes entirely. During this period he fights Negroes who call him white and lives with a woman "who resembled an ebony carving." Lying in bed with her he tried "to breathe into himself the dark odor, the dark and inscrutable thinking and being of Negroes, with each suspiration trying to expel from himself the white blood and the white thinking and being" (p. 197). But his nostrils "would whiten and tauten, his whole being writhe and strain with physical outrage and spiritual denial" (p. 197). A few hours before he kills

Joanna he flees from the Negro section of town as though it were some "thick black pit" (pp. 99, 101) and reaches the white section with a great feeling of relief. We read:

He could walk quiet here. Now and then he could see them: heads in silhouette, a white blurred garmented shape; on a lighted veranda four people sat about a card table, the white faces intent and sharp in the low light, the bare arms of the women glaring smooth and white above the trivial cards. "That's all I wanted," he thought. "That dont seem like a whole lot to ask." [p. 100]

The immediate context leads us to assume that all he wanted was the conventional life of white people, although there is an important ambiguity here, since his statement also follows one he makes a few pages earlier which relates to a quite different theme: "*All I wanted was peace* thinking, 'She ought not to started praying over me'" (p. 97). During his flight after killing Joanna, he equates the Negro shoes he is wearing with "the black abyss which had been waiting, trying, for thirty years to drown him" (p. 289). Perhaps most important, since it is not simply Joe's own perception, is Gavin Stevens' interpretation of Joe's behavior in terms of white and black blood and his equation of the black blood with violence (pp. 393–394). In the final de-description of Joe, after the castration, we read that

from out the slashed garments about his hips and loins the pent black blood seemed to rush like a released breath. It seemed to rush out of his pale body like the rush of sparks from a rising rocket; upon that black blast the man seemed to rise soaring into their memories forever and ever. [p. 407]

Clearly, in these passages and many others we are strongly urged to interpret Joe's life chiefly in terms of his mixed blood. When we try to do so, however, we encounter a number of problems. During the years he lives with McEachern his difficulties are in no way related to his Negro blood. The McEacherns apparently never suspect it, and there is no evi-

dence that he himself thinks about it until he speaks of it to
the waitress, Bobbie. Even then it does not seem particularly
important to him. Nor does Bobbie's violent rejection of him
seem sufficient to account for his later obsession with the problem. It is true that she makes much of his Negro blood in her
hysterics after the dance hall episode and even calls him "a
nigger son of a bitch" (p. 190), but we do not feel it is this
which bothers her so much as the fact that he has gotten her in
a jam with the police. More important, of course, is how Joe interprets it. But here we get no help from Faulkner, for Joe is
never once shown remembering or thinking about the episode.
We do not know what it means to him, how crucial it was,
and, if it was, in what way. Judging from some of his later
reactions and remarks we are likely to assume its chief effect was
to add to his general distrust of women, a motif I shall elaborate
below, rather than to his sense of his black blood.

Although his Negro blood greatly affects Joanna Burden's
attitude toward him, and although there are moments when he
resents the fact that she thinks of him as Negro, it does not seem
very much involved in his most important responses toward her
or in his decision to kill her. He puts away the thought of
marrying her with the generalized comment: "No. If I give
in now, I will deny all the thirty years that I have lived to make
me what I chose to be" (p. 232), and before he kills her what
clearly obsesses him is the fact that she prayed over him. One
does not feel certain that his relationship with her or his feelings
about it would have been appreciably different had he not felt
himself to be part Negro.

What makes it most difficult to interpret Joe in terms of his
mixed blood, however, is the extent to which Faulkner urges
us to look at Joe's problem in other terms. A number of critics
have urged that we see Joe essentially as victim of narrow or
fanatic Protestantism with its unnatural attitude toward sex.
This theme is clearly dominant in the McEachern episodes

and is prominent in Joe's experience in the orphanage and in his relationship with Miss Burden. More than anything else, probably, Miss Burden's puritan background leads to the actions which make Joe feel he needs to kill her. And I suppose we must believe that it is, in part, a deep resentment of the generally repressive puritan attitude which leads Joe to kill her when she insists that he repent with her for their sexual relations. On the other hand, in each of the sections emphasizing this theme, what upsets Joe most is not the repressive Protestantism so much as the unpredictability and illogicality of the women he is involved with. In the McEachern section this is made completely explicit. Joe resents Mrs. McEachern's secret kindnesses to him much more than he does McEachern's puritanical injustice: "It was the woman: that soft kindness which he believed himself doomed to be forever victim of and which he hated worse than he did the hard and ruthless justice of men" (p. 147).

When we seek to relate the theme of repressive Protestantism to that of Joe's Negro blood, we cannot go very far. Hines' religious and sexual fanaticism is inextricably mixed with a fanatic advocacy of white supremacy; Miss Burden's Calvinism is allied with a fanatic desire to save the Negro. One might link these as more or less comparable perversions, but one can hardly press this relationship as a general theme, since we are told nothing at all about the racial attitudes of McEachern, who is the chief representative of fanatic Protestantism.

Complicating one's understanding of Joe's story still further is the strong emphasis on still another aspect of Joe's life—one which has so far been largely overlooked by commentators— his generally unsatisfactory experience with women and sex. Early in the book Faulkner describes Joe as "too young yet to escape from the world of women for that brief respite before he escaped back into it to remain until the hour of his death" (p. 106); one could make a good case that Joe's chief problem was not nearly so much his black blood or repressive upbringing as that world of women.

His life is largely a series of disastrous relationships with women. At the age of seven he is shocked and bewildered by the dietitian in the orphanage. During the ten years following he rebels against the secrecy and softness of his foster mother, Mrs. McEachern. He is severely shocked twice by the waitress, Bobbie, with whom he believes himself in love, first by the discovery that she is a whore and then by her furious rejection of him when he comes to marry her after killing McEachern. Later he beats a white prostitute almost to death and becomes "sick" for two years after discovering that she will sleep with Negroes. His body and spirit both rebel when he tries to live with a Negro woman as man and wife. And he suffers repeated shocks from Joanna Burden. More than this, some of his reactions to women and natural female functions are almost pathological. At the age of fourteen, when his turn comes to lie with a Negro girl whom a group of boys have engaged for sexual purposes, he goes berserk, kicks and hits the girl, and fights with the four boys until they run away. "None of them knew why he had fought. And he could not have told them" (p. 138). When he learns that women menstruate, he is so disturbed that he feels a need for some ritual acceptance of it, which he achieves temporarily by killing a sheep and bathing his hands in the blood of the dying animal. Several years later, when on his first date with Bobbie she tells him she is menstruating, he is so horrified that he runs away from her and vomits. Part of what infuriates him about Joanna Burden is his belief that she tricked him by lying about her age and *"about what happens to women at a certain age"* (p. 93). When she wants him to go to college, he beats her and tells her over and over that what is wrong with her is that she has become too old to want sex anymore (pp. 242–243). Twice when women feed him he throws the food on the floor, and at some point in his life he becomes so determined to avoid a woman's services that he cannot stand to wear buttons she has sewed on. He goes to the extent of taking his clothes from the family wash before she could replace the missing buttons. "When she foiled him he set himself deliberately to learn and remember which buttons were missing and had been restored. With his pocket knife and with the cold and bloodless deliberation of a surgeon he would cut off the buttons which she had just replaced" (p. 93). On the night before he kills Joanna he stands beneath her window, curses her, and using his hand as a knife, knocks off the last button on his clothing. He sleeps that night in a stable. On the way to it he thinks aloud: " 'Why in hell do I want to smell horses?' Then he said, fumbling: 'It's because they are not women. Even a mare horse is a kind of man' " (p. 95).

Faulkner also suggests that his discovery that Bobbie was a whore had much to do with determining his nature and fate (pp. 173–174), and it is immediately after her rejection of him that he enters the transient and violent course that he runs for the next fifteen years.

Finally, by persistently tying together Joe's relations with women and the eating and rejection of food, Faulkner seems to be suggesting that much of Joe's problem is that he never had a mother and can find no satisfactory substitute.

To a considerable extent we can relate this general theme with the racial one, for most of Joe's difficulties with women directly or indirectly involve his Negro blood, and we can make connections between his sexual difficulties and his repressive Protestant upbringing, although with some difficulty since Faulkner never clearly suggests a causal relationship between the two and since almost all the characters in the book, including Lena, come from somewhat similar backgrounds. But there is little we can do to relate this view of Joe with the view of him as Christ. We are somewhat troubled, too, by the question of how much weight to put on these various interpretations. In his madness old man Hines easily combines all these views of Joe's experience, and Joe, himself, in the same breath, so to speak, often expresses his consciousness of his tainted blood and his resentment of women and never attempts to distinguish between them. As readers, however, we are groping for some understanding and interpretation beyond this, some way of organizing these various views of Joe, of moving beyond the general feeling, the feeling we have about uninterpreted life itself, that there is a highly complex set of relationships which we cannot quite grasp.

Again, however, Faulkner clearly wishes to prevent such a movement and seeks if anything, in the final chapters of Joe's story, to complicate our responses further. First of all, Joe, himself, remains almost completely opaque. In the final chapter of his story, describing his capture, imprisonment, escape, and execution, we see him only from a distance, and in the chapter describing his flight after the murder of Miss Burden he is never shown thinking directly about the murder or in any but the most general terms about the meaning of his former or present actions. As he enters Mottstown to give himself up, we read that

he is entering it again, the street which ran for thirty years. It had been a paved street, where going should be fast. It had made a circle and he is still inside of it. Though during the last seven days he has had no paved street, yet he has travelled farther than in all the thirty years before. And yet he is still inside the circle. "And yet I have been farther in these seven days than in all the thirty years," he thinks. "But I have never got outside that circle. I have never broken out of the ring of what I have already done and cannot ever undo." [p. 296]

We accept this, I think, but we do not know at all clearly in what sense he has gone farther or how that going farther relates to his previous problems. We know that he has attacked a Negro congregation and cursed God from the pulpit. We can interpret this as a parallel of Christ's cleansing of the Temple and as a general act of defiance, but it does not suggest any kind of progress or change, especially in view of his flippant attitude afterward, as he thinks about cutting a notch in the bench leg he has used as a weapon and flips a cigarette toward the ter- rified Negroes in the bushes with the comment "Have a butt, boys" (pp. 284–285). We know also that he has felt himself to be outside time, that he was terribly hungry for a while and then no longer hungry, that knowing the day of the week be- comes more important than food. We can infer that some kind of softening has taken place when instead of asking for food with the harsh words he can feel "marshalling in his mind" he finds himself asking quietly what day it is and then saying "thank you" (p. 290). An even deeper change is suggested when he is remembering a kind of Last Supper in a Negro cabin and thinks, "And they were afraid. Of their brother afraid" (p. 293), and when he realizes later that the reason he feels at peace is that he doesn't "have to bother about having to eat any- more" (p. 295).

Beyond this there is no illumination or resolution of the previously developed themes. We understand that Joe is tired of running and struggling, but as far as we can tell he has been led to this only by physical weariness and by the compulsive awareness (imposed only by the Christ theme) that on Friday he must give himself up. The suggestion, made by his use of the word "brother," that he has accepted his Negro blood is so fleeting and so undeveloped that we cannot really feel he has achieved any resolution of this problem. This is especially true since the chapter ends with an emphasis on the Negro-smelling shoes which suggest his earlier view of his Negro blood and the Negro world as a black pit.

Our reaction to this chapter is complicated by the tone Faulkner uses to describe the futile activities of the sheriff and his posse and bloodhounds, for his satiric treatment of them gives the whole affair a cops and robbers atmosphere, with a dash of Mack Sennett thrown in, and compels us to delight in Joe's ability to outwit his pursuers.

In the final chapter of Joe's story Faulkner goes far out of his way to prevent us from resolving or ordering our understanding of Joe or of the meaning of his life experience. Throughout the chapter he keeps Joe entirely in the background. We see him only for a moment and then at a distance. We have no direct knowledge of what he is thinking or feeling. Furthermore, Faulkner introduces two new characters, Gavin Stevens and Percy Grimm, and devotes the major part of the chapter to the actions and emotions of the latter. It is true that the chapter opens with various speculations about why Joe ran to Hightower's house after escaping and why, once there, he let himself be executed without fighting back. But these are presented clearly as uninformed speculations and are so general and so unrelated to the specific questions we have about Joe that they offer no real illumination. Their effect, and clearly this is Faulkner's intention, is to leave our questions unresolved. It baffles our imagination, just as it baffles Gavin Stevens (who does not believe that anyone could reconstruct the scene) to see how Mrs. Hines could have convinced Joe that Hightower offered a kind of sanctuary, and Stevens' interpretation of Joe's final actions and whole life in terms of alternately ruling white and black blood is so general and mechanical that it can hardly be taken seriously. Nor can it be related satisfactorily to the view of Joe as Christ. Moreover, like most of Stevens' "explanations," it ceases to be comprehensible or coherent when one reads it closely. Perhaps most important, to the extent that we accept Stevens' equation of the black blood with violent and evil acts and accept Joe's own feeling that the black blood is a tainted part of himself, we are accepting the racial attitudes of all the mad and vicious characters in the book. We face this same dilemma if, as Faulkner sometimes encourages us to do, and as Professor Holman has suggested, we view Joe's black blood as a kind of equivalent of original sin, of man's common guilt.

By devoting the major part of the chapter to Percy Grimm, Faulkner not only preserves the suspension he has established but complicates it further. We can relate Grimm to one theme of the Christmas story by viewing him essentially as another kind of zealot and add him to the list of fanatics who have already contributed to Joe's destruction. But Faulkner also compels us to take a far more complex view of him.

Although his patriotism is bigoted, fanatic, and ambitious, he seems at first to be sincerely interested in providing an orderly and dignified military atmosphere which will symbolize the spirit of the United States as he conceives it. He succeeds to the extent that the town comes to accept him "with respect and a little awe and a deal of actual faith and confidence, as though somehow his vision and patriotism and pride in the town, the occasion, had been quicker and truer than theirs" (p. 400). Had it been left up to him he would have escorted Joe with a squad of men so that he could not escape. Yet it is he who departs completely from all order and rule by castrating Joe.

At the same time we must see Grimm on a symbolic level as Joe's assigned and somehow fitting executioner. Here, too, Faulkner provides several suggestions. He describes Gimm as moving with "the implacable undeviation of Juggernaut or Fate" (p. 403). But he also describes him in Christian terms as running "as though under the protection of a magic or a providence" (p. 404), as exhibiting "that serene, unearthly luminousness of angels in church windows" (pp. 404–405), and as crying out with a "voice clear and outraged like that of a young priest" (p. 406). Finally, he describes him several times as a pawn obedient to "whatever Player moved him on the Board" (p. 405).

The chapter, and the story of Joe, ends immediately after the castration with the suggestion that Joe is finally at peace and that the memory of him will remain forever with those who watched him die. It is an effective ending, and one feels that somehow Joe's life and death were significant. But I do not think we can close in at all on the nature of that significance. Apart from our unresolved questions about Joe's character and

motives and about who and what is responsible for his fate, we
are left with questions about the execution and castration. How
are we to interpret Joe's peacefulness? Simply as relief that he
doesn't have to run anymore, or as the achievement of some
more full and serious acceptance of his fate? Are we to view
the castration as a perversion on Grimm's part or as a fitting
and somehow necessary part of Joe's fate and a necessary aspect
of the crucifixion ritual? If the latter, how are we to square it
with the emphasis elsewhere in the book on the importance of
natural sexual attitudes and behaviors? How seriously are we
to take Joe's "ascension" and the suggestion that he has performed a redemptive function? The heavy emphasis on the
Christ parallels in the last two chapters and the tone of the
descriptions of his "ascension" and of the effect on his execu-
tioners suggests we give it weight. Yet it is hard to see what in
Joe's life or end, apart from the shock of seeing him castrated,
would cause him "to rise soaring into their memories forever
and ever" (p. 407). We cannot help but see the ending also as
a travesty upon meaningful ritual or religious experience,
especially since Faulkner chooses to end the scene with the
scream of the fire siren.

Perhaps the clearest illustration of Faulkner's desire to provide ambiguity is provided by the ending of the Hightower
story. Up until that point the character of Hightower and the
meaning of his story are reasonably clear. The only serious
problem we have had is to understand and accept his obsession
with his dead grandfather and the galloping cavalry. What
makes it hard to understand and accept is that it does not, except
in the retrospect passages and at isolated moments, seem to play
any part in his conversation or thought. At no point in his
numerous conversations with Byron or in his thought about
the problems Byron presents, do we see any evidence of the
obsession. Yet we must believe—Faulkner is perfectly clear on
this point (pp. 53–56, 65)—that it was the obsession that pre-
vented him from succeeding either as a minister or a husband.

As the story progresses, however, we tend to forget about the obsession almost completely, since there is no evidence of it between pages 66 and 408. We come to see Hightower as a man who has abdicated not only his obligations as a minister but all human responsibilities, a man who wants only peace and seclusion and, as he himself puts it, is "not in life any more" (p. 263). His problem, clearly, is to come back into life. All Faulkner's emphasis is on this, on his fright and resistance as Byron becomes involved and seeks to involve him, on his own recognition that he does have obligations, and on his gradual acceptance of those obligations.

The story appears to reach a climax and resolution as Hightower achieves a sense of "purpose and pride" after having taken the responsibility of delivering Lena's child and then goes so far as to perjure himself in an effort to save Joe Christmas.

But Faulkner adds one more chapter. In it he describes Hightower's memories and thoughts several hours after the killing of Joe Christmas. It opens with the suggestion that Hightower has not really changed, for he is waiting at the window just as he had in the past for the vision of the galloping cavalry. We then learn something about Hightower's family background, which explains to some extent why he came to idealize and identify with his dead grandfather, a lusty, swaggering man on the order of Sutpen or Colonel Sartoris, and which ties in somewhat with the opposition of natural versus fanatic or distorted attitudes which has informed other parts of the book. I say "somewhat" because Hightower's father, although initially a fanatic abolitionist and unduly zealous minister, becomes, before Hightower's birth, a reasonably sane and practical man and because the action of the grandfather which obsesses Hightower is hardly a natural or unself-conscious one. Nor is it even clearly a heroic one, for it ends with the grandfather being shot while stealing a chicken in a hen house.

The main weight of the chapter is on Hightower's growing realization of the extent of his failure and guilt as minister and husband, a failure due primarily, he recognizes more and more clearly, to his obsession with his grandfather. He seems to accept that it is he, himself, who is responsible for the shame and death of his wife: "After all, there must be some things for which God cannot be accused by man and held responsible" (p. 427). As the chapter progresses, Faulkner suggests by his imagery that Hightower is drawing closer and closer to some final realization about himself. Immediately following the passage just quoted we read that "thinking begins to slow now. It slows like a wheel beginning to run in sand, the axle, the vehicle, the power which propels it not yet aware" (p. 427). As he continues to trace his failure, the wheel slows further, then even more: "Thinking is running too heavily now; he should know it, sense it. Still the vehicle is unaware of what it is approaching" (p. 429). He is described as feeling a gathering "as though for some tremendous effort" (p. 429). We are given a fragment of his thought: ". . . revealed to my wife my hunger, my ego . . . instrument of her despair and shame . . ." (p. 429), ellipses Faulkner's). Then "a sentence seems to stand fullsprung across his skull, behind his eyes: *I dont want to think this. I must not think this. I dare not think this*" (p. 429). The sweat begins to pour from him.

Surely no writer could do more to prepare for and promise illumination and resolution. Finally, it seems to come:

Out of the instant the sandclutched wheel of thinking turns on with the slow implacability of a mediaeval torture instrument, beneath the wrenched and broken sockets of his spirit, his life: "Then, if this is so, if I am the instrument of her despair and death, then I am in turn instrument of someone outside myself. And I know that for fifty years I have not even been clay: I have been a single instant of darkness in which a horse galloped and a gun crashed. And if I am my dead grandfather on the instant of his death, then my wife, his grandson's wife . . . the debaucher and murderer of my grand-son's wife, since I could neither let my grandson live or die . . ."

The wheel, released, seems to rush on with a long sighing sound. He sits motionless in its aftermath, in his cooling sweat, while the sweat pours and pours. The wheel whirls on. It is going fast and smooth now, because it is freed now of burden, of vehicle, axle, all. [pp. 429–430, ellipses Faulkner's]

The released wheel suggests that there has been resolution and makes us feel it. The diction and syntax of the quotation sug-gests it: the "then, if this is so . . . then . . ." suggests a cause-and-effect relationship. But the second clause is a *non sequitur*. The "and I know" suggests self-understanding, but it is fol-lowed by a highly fanciful metaphor which, if anything, con-tradicts the suggestion that he is an "instrument." Another logical sequence is suggested by "and if . . . then. . . ." This time the logic is indeed unassailable, but it is used to extend the highly figurative and alogical equation of himself with his own grandfather, an equation which both he and we have already established. We wonder now whether we have observed a moment of tragic illumination or an escape into fantasy and confusion. The remainder of the chapter complicates our im-pressions further. The released wheel image, "freed now of burden, of vehicle, axle, all," has suggested strongly that what-ever the nature of his final resolution, Hightower is empty and at peace. But apparently he is not, because a moment later we read "then it seems to him that some ultimate dammed flood within him breaks and rushes away" (p. 431). Yet even then there is still conflict within him, for he thinks he should pray but does not try, and there is still self-pity and even more sur-prising, self-deception. "I wanted so little. I asked so little. It would seem . . ." And there is apparently honor and pride, for the final paragraph begins:

It is as though they [the phantom galloping Confederate soldiers] had merely waited until he could find something to pant with, to be reaffirmed in triumph and desire with, with this last left of honor and pride and life. [p. 431]

He has his vision of the galloping figures thundering past. The tone is excited and triumphant, seeming to suggest that the vision is a kind of final reward, and it seems to be equated with strength and honor and life. But this vision, and the obsession that brings it, has been clearly associated with Hightower's failure to come to terms with himself and his world, and in his presumable recognition of his guilt before the final release of the wheel, he himself has recognized this.

We are left puzzled, therefore, not only about the nature and degree of Hightower's self-realization but about how to feel about it. The rhetoric and placement of the final vision compel us to view it as an affirmative and triumphant end for Hightower. It is, after all, what he has been waiting for. At the same time it seems anything but triumphant and affirmative when we consider that this very vision is a kind of madness which has emasculated and destroyed him and that his welcoming of it means he has again retreated from himself and the world.

This final chapter of the Hightower story is puzzling, too, in that it does not, except most indirectly, develop or extend the theme of detachment and involvement which governs the body of his story. At no point does Hightower think about the return to life he experienced previously, nor is there any evidence that that return was of any consequence. The story ceases to be about a man whose chief problem is to find a way back into life and becomes essentially the story of a man with an obsession. True, the obsession is what led him away from life, but the emphasis here is on the obsession itself, and we feel finally that we are viewing a pathological figure rather than a tragic one.

Each of the stories then is ambiguous or unresolved in certain important respects, and none focuses clearly or consistently on a single theme. Obviously it will not be easy to grasp the relationships between them, especially since Faulkner makes no effort to pull the stories together at the end of the book. In fact, he is careful to keep them separate. At the end of the book we read in order the endings to the Christmas story, the Hightower story, and the Lena Grove–Byron Bunch story. These endings are in separate chapters, and each is clearly and distinctly an ending to only one of the stories. More than this, except for the ending to the Christmas story, which does include an important action of Hightower, none of these endings either involve characters from the other stories or make any direct comment on the other stories or in any direct way illuminate the meanings of the other stories. In the Hightower ending, apart from the brief note that the faces of Byron, Lena, Joe, and Grimm are among those Hightower sees in his dying moments, there is no mention even of the recent events in Hightower's life which connect him to the other stories. Clearly Faulkner is seeking to achieve this separation, is willing even to sacrifice verisimilitude, for this ending is set just a few hours after Joe has been shot in Hightower's house, and it is difficult to believe that Hightower would so completely ignore that event. The ending of the Lena Grove story, which ends the book, is even more detached from the other stories. Indeed, were it not for the furniture dealer's passing comment that Lena must have been in Jefferson when "they lynched that nigger," there would be nothing whatsoever even to remind us of the other stories. Again it would seem that Faulkner is being very careful to keep the endings separate. Faulkner, no doubt, has several reasons for presenting the final chapter from the point of view of the furniture dealer; surely one of them is that he has no knowledge of any of the events which have taken place in the book, and this makes it easy for Faulkner to leave them in suspension.

As in *The Sound and the Fury* and *As I Lay Dying*, Faulkner complicates our final responses further by juxtaposing varied tones as well as varied kinds of material: the tone of the first two endings is serious and intense; the tone of the third is largely playful.

As in *The Sound and the Fury* and *As I Lay Dying* we are left with highly mixed feelings about the significance and worth of the human agony and struggle we have witnessed. We are encouraged to see Joe's crucifixion as both a meaningful apotheosis and a parody of one. We must feel that Hightower's suffering has led to ennobling self-knowledge and that it has led nowhere but back into his obsession. And if at first glance the final chapter seems to provide a kind of comic affirmation, the final effect is far more complex than that. In the first place, the comic tone puts the "affirmative" material in a realm completely sealed off from the world of the other events we have witnessed, a realm which none of the other major characters could possibly enter, and one therefore largely irrelevant when we consider their plights. It does not in any sense provide an alternative way of life or alternative set of attitudes for Joe, Hightower, or Joanna Burden; and even Byron in that realm becomes a comic figure. Moreover, the ideal or norm that Lena represents is hardly a full or adequate one. For one thing, her virtues are almost inseparable from her intellectual limitations; for another, she is too much like Anse Bundren in her self-absorbed and ruthless pursuit of her objectives. Hightower is not simply expressing his own fear of life when he thinks of Byron as her husband and says "Poor boy" (p. 356). The final words in the book, her "My, my. A body does get around. Here we aint been coming from Alabama but two months, and now it's already Tennessee" are delightful, but they are delightful partly because they are such an absurdly inadequate commentary on her experience, to say nothing of the other experiences in the book. These complexities in our view of Lena are especially important, because no matter how one interprets the book one must use Lena as a kind of measuring rod for the other characters. As such she is a provocative but hardly constant instrument.

Finally, as in *The Sound and the Fury* and *As I Lay Dying* we are left with a suspension too varied and complex to organize into any clear pattern. We can, of course, discover a great many relationships between the three stories and between parts of the individual stories, and we can, as a number of critics do, trace various themes which recur with some frequency throughout the book. None of these themes, however, as I hope this analysis makes evident, governs enough of the book or resolves enough of the problems in the book to provide any over-all sense of unity. They, too, come to form part of the insoluble suspension, for they cannot be clearly related to one another.

For example, we cannot quite bring together the strong suggestion in the Hightower section that man fails when he retreats from the world or ignores the needs of his fellows and the celebration of Lena's detached, self-centered, and sometimes hardhearted pursuit of her personal destiny. Whatever one thinks of her, surely her detachment from the world is as great as Hightower's. Nor does the theme of responsibility relate very closely to Joe's story, for it is when Joanna does for the first time become concerned about Joe's welfare that she destroys him and herself. Indeed, much in Joe's story would seem to suggest that zealousness or too great concern with the welfare of others is the chief evil. If we push the theme of Protestant rigidity and intolerance, what are we to make of Joe's, and I think Faulkner's, preference for the ruthless McEachern over his soft and generous wife. Nor can the theme of Protestant bigotry be closely related to Joe's obsessive concern with his Negro blood or to his execution by Percy Grimm. If we try to understand Joe and Joanna and Hightower in relation to their loveless or empty or distorted family backgrounds, we discover that Lena's origin was hardly more promising. If we try to see the Lena story as celebrating healthy sex and fecundity in opposition to the guilt-ridden and barren passion of Joanna or see her as representing the virtues of plain ordinary unalienated people, "the good stock," we must contend with the largely unsympathetic treatment of the ordinary unalienated population of Jefferson. And we must contend with the bleak description of the world from which Lena comes, a "labor- and childridden" world in which her sister-in-law "for almost half of every year . . . was either lying in or recovering" (p. 5), a world which has sweated out of her brother all "softness and gentleness and youth . . . and almost everything else except a kind of stubborn and despairing fortitude and the bleak heritage of his bloodpride" (p. 5). Concurrent with whatever particular theme we explore, we must hold in suspension the feeling that what dominates much of the book is sheer inexplicable madness and obsession. Hightower, Joanna, McEachern, Hines, Grimm, and Joe himself are all people with pathological obsessions, while both the dietitian and the waitress react to Joe with a hysteria bordering on madness. I do not think it is going too far to see a kind of madness even in Lena's stubborn and single-minded search for the father of her child. But at the same time one cannot escape the feeling that Faulkner is also saying that the characters do have free will and the obligation to choose more wisely than they do.

One can loosely group a considerable number of the themes and events in terms of a broad antithesis between rigid, perverted, or distorted attitudes toward religion and sex on the one hand, and on the other, natural attitudes more or less exemplified by Lena Grove and Byron and given a degree of explicit expression by Hightower. Or one can group them in terms of their relation to a broadly conceived image of Christ, as Professor Holman has done. But such groupings are so general and so removed from the actual effects of the structure and rhetoric of the book that they are not particularly helpful. They provide a way of side-stepping rather than ordering the actual complexities of the book. For they stand up only so long as one ignores most of the ambiguities and varied and conflicting emphases which provide the essential character of the book; that is, they provide a possible framework for ordering certain aspects of the book, but they do not illuminate the book itself.

Absalom, Absalom!

No brief description can suggest the extent and variety of the complexity of *Absalom, Absalom!* Harvey Breit, who considers it Faulkner's greatest work, says of it:

> The story is handed around in space from narrator to narrator something as a football is by a skillfully deceptive backfield; and it is handed around in time, so that the focus shifts without warning from the son's time to the father's time to the grandfather's time. The technique employed in relating the narrative is that of a system of screens and obstacles, "of deliberately withheld meaning," as Conrad Aiken wrote, "of progressive and partial and delayed disclosure." And the endless, unsyntactical, nefarious sentences are here to challenge and plague and puzzle and dazzle.[10]

Further complexity is added by the fact that none of the narrators is really trustworthy or entirely consistent with the others in his reports or interpretations.

William R. Poirier points out that Rosa and Mr. Compson are untrustworthy narrators because of their attitudes or faulty information, but he sees Quentin and Shreve as trustworthy narrators whose narrations provide an "ordering" of the story.[11]

---

[10] *AA*, p. x. See Hoffman and Vickery, *Two Decades*, pp. 24–25, for a brief summary of comments about the "Anti-Narrative" of *Absalom, Absalom!*.

[11] " 'Strange Gods' in Jefferson, Mississippi," in *Two Decades*, pp. 228–230, 238.

They have more information, it is true, and presumably want to make sense out of the story, but to conceive of their narration as an "ordering" is to ignore its form—its discontinuities, screens and obstacles, its shift of focus away from Sutpen, and its utter inconclusiveness—and to overlook Faulkner's explicit reminders that what they say is true and not true.[12] To speak of Quentin and Shreve's activity, as Poirier does, as an attempt to order and to understand or as demonstrating "an act of humanistic faith" [13] is to disregard all traditional meanings of the words "order," "understand," and "humanism."

Apart from the complexity provided by the general scrambling of events and shifting point of view, there is, also, the problem of the great number and variety of events reported, for the story is not only about Sutpen but about the Sutpen dynasty, which includes the history and legacy of Charles Bon. Indeed, the material is so rich and varied, the thematic suggestions are so numerous, and the questions one is left with are so many that even an analysis of the sort just presented for *Light in August* would require far more space than can be justified. And there is little point in providing such an analysis, for if there is a reader who does not approach the end of this novel with the bewildering suspension of elements I have insisted Faulkner always provides, nothing can show him that such are Faulkner's effects. I do not think it an exaggeration to say that there is scarcely a character in the book toward whom we can avoid having ambivalent feelings and that there is scarcely a theme appearing anywhere in Faulkner's writing which does not shape part of his presentation here.

At the very end of the book there are, in effect, four commentaries on the meaning of the whole Sutpen story. The first is provided by the picture of the last Sutpen, the idiot boy Jim Bond, lurking around the ashes and gutted chimneys that are

[12] See, for example, p. 280.
[13] " 'Strange Gods,' " in *Two Decades*, p. 243.

the remnants of Sutpen's mansion, howling until someone would
drive him away (p. 376). The second is provided by the end of
Mr. Compson's letter, the first part of which we have read two
hundred odd pages earlier (pp. 173–174). Here Faulkner again
suggests there will be resolution:

It [the letter] was becoming quite distinct; he would be able to
decipher the words soon, in a moment; even almost now, now, now.
[p. 377]

But the letter is obviously and carefully ambiguous and irrelevant so far as any ordering of the story is concerned. The
third commentary is that of Shreve, who summarizes the story
with brutal and flippant absurdity:

"So it took Charles Bon and his mother to get rid of old Tom, and
Charles Bon and the octoroon to get rid of Judith, and Charles Bon
and Clytie to get rid of Henry; and Charles Bon's mother and
Charles Bon's grandmother got rid of Charles Bon. So it takes two
niggers to get rid of one Sutpen, dont it?" [pp. 377–378]

He then observes that everything is taken care of except,
"You've got one nigger left. One nigger Sutpen left," and he
briefly erects this Negro into a symbol of Southern guilt (p.
378). Following this he revels in paradox: The Jim Bonds
conquer the western hemisphere and turn white, but still remain
Jim Bonds,

"and so [note again the pseudo logic] in a few thousand years, I
who regard you will also have sprung from the loins of African
kings. Now I want you to tell me just one thing more. Why do you
hate the South?"

And the final commentary:

"I dont hate it," Quentin said, quickly, at once, immediately; "I
dont hate it," he said. *I dont hate it* he thought, panting in the cold
air, the iron New England dark; *I dont. I dont! I dont hate it! I dont
hate it!*

It is difficult to conceive of an "ending" that would provide less ordering and resolution. Not only is there no resolution on a cognitive level, but we are also confronted with the differing tones of the four commentaries, and the terrible emotional ambivalence of Quentin's final outburst. We "end," then, with a psychological oxymoron of simultaneous love and hate, with internal conflict and self-contradiction. It is an intense and powerful ending and a proper one to seal off and preserve the bewildering suspension of elements the book has presented. But it is also a pitiful ending. It is pitiful in that Shreve and Quentin seem to have been so little instructed by their immense labor of imagination. It is pitiful (and among many other things, perhaps, Faulkner is saying this, too) in its varied assertions that so much energy, effort, and pain have come to so little: to a lone idiot, an ironic letter, a brutally flippant commentary and act of cruelty to a roommate, and a cry of bewildered pain. It is pitiful, too, because by it, Faulkner again demonstrates his unwillingness or inability to step beyond the sanctuary of the paradox, to make, himself, as do a number of his characters, the clarifying "gesture," the clarifying "humanistic act of faith."

When we have finished the book, and obviously Faulkner wishes this effect, we feel much as Quentin does—emotionally and intellectually bewildered. In answer to a question about the meaning of the book we must answer much as Quentin does when Shreve asks him whether he understands the South.

"I dont know," Quentin said. "Yes, of course I understand it." They breathed in the darkness. After a moment Quentin said: "I dont know." [p. 362]

We don't know to what extent we have watched a tragedy, the story of a great man whose destruction of himself and his house is due essentially to flaws in character; to what extent a naturalistic drama in which morality and human guilt are irrelevant and the destruction a result of hereditary, economic, and social forces beyond the control of any of the characters; to what extent a grim and pointless joke to which the fitting commentary is the howling of the last Sutpen, who is an idiot.

Ever since Faulkner's assertion in his Stockholm address that man will endure and prevail, much emphasis has been placed on the affirmative aspects of his vision. How ambiguous an affirmation this is becomes clear if we stop for a moment to remember what most visibly and clearly endures in the novels so far discussed. In *The Sound and the Fury*, Dilsey "endures" but so, even more visibly, do Jason and the idiot Benjy. And the last image of humanity in the book is that of Benjy. In *As I Lay Dying* the Bundren family endures, and it does include Cash, who can up to a point be viewed affirmatively, but Darl, probably the most fully human of the Bundrens, has not endured, and the Bundren who most clearly prevails, and who provides our last glimpse of humanity, is the shiftless and parasitic Anse. In *Light in August* we can draw comfort from the fact that it is Byron and Lena who endure, but a highly qualified comfort in view of their reduced and flattened appearances when we last see them. In *Absalom, Absalom!* what endures of the Sutpens is a howling idiot; Quentin, the inheritor, so to speak, of the Southern past, barely endures at the end of the book and commits suicide not long afterward.

Worth noting, also, in this connection, is the darkness in Faulkner's vision that comes from the fact that the agony of his characters almost never leads them or those who outlive them to any wisdom or understanding of their own or the human condition. Even Hightower, who more than any other character does experience an illumination, draws no real comfort or peace from it and at the end retreats again into the obsession which has destroyed him.

The four novels just commented upon have generally been considered Faulkner's best and most characteristic. Faulkner's other books reveal the same general intentions and produce the same general effects. There are interesting differences, of course, in the stories and themes, but the books are all governed at bottom not nearly so much by any particular theme or interpretation as by the desire to create and maintain highly complex and largely irresolvable suspensions.

The Hamlet; Go Down, Moses; The Town

It is significant that for four of his books—*The Unvanquished*, *The Hamlet*, *Go Down, Moses*, and *The Town*—Faulkner has chosen a form that lies somewhere between that of the novel and that of a collection of short stories. For it is a form which allows the reader to speculate about the relationships between the stories but does not require any sort of integration or resolution. It is significant, also, that except for *The Unvanquished*, each of these books ranges in tone from high seriousness to farce and that each book ends in such a way as to complicate one's response to the rest of the book.

At the end of *The Hamlet* we must wrestle with the new knowledge that even the shrewd and detached Ratliff becomes so crazed by avarice that he, too, can be victimized by Flem, and we must try to relate to the many views we already have of Frenchmen's Bend the heavily underscored vision of the madness of Henry Armstid. If we have found in the treatment of some of the local farmers a degree of affirmation of man's nature, we must set it against the final glimpses Faulkner gives us of humanity: the farmers and their families coming in their wagons to spend the day watching the now completely insane Armstid endlessly dig for buried treasure; Armstid's wife slipping a pail of food to him through the fence as though to an animal; young boys tormenting Armstid; and Flem Snopes, impassive as always, watching for a moment, spitting, and moving on into town.

The final story of *Go Down, Moses*, up to a point, is a fitting epitaph for the book, for it shows in the fate and portrait of Samuel Beauchamp, a racketeer and killer who has lost all roots and values, an ultimate form of the deterioration of the old South. In his old grandmother's determination to bring his body back and the assistance the town gives her a kind of continuity is established between the old order and the present-day inheritors of its fragments. On the other hand, we are disturbed by the complete disappearance from the scene of Ike McCaslin, who has dominated the preceding stories, by the ambiguity as to whether the evils focused upon are essentially the result of the slavery system or of the enforced breakdown of that system, and by the portrait of Molly, who seems in part a representative of a valuable tradition and in part an obsessed old woman. Her refrain that Roth Edmonds sold her Benjamin to Pharaoh is at once a partly true and a woefully inadequate interpretation of his fate. Her strength and sense of purpose are ennobling and make her seem larger in a sense than Gavin Stevens or the newspaper editor. But her desire to have it all written up in the paper, a desire which we do not learn until the end, suddenly and sharply cuts her stature to something well beneath theirs and again associates enduring and prevailing with mental limitation. As always the efforts we have witnessed seem both significant and pointless.

The Town ends with a chapter which introduces four new Snopes—the half-Indian, scarcely human children of Byron Snopes. The contrast between them and Flem, who is now president of the bank, and the fact that he gets rid of them show us how far Flem has moved toward a kind of respectability, and their expulsion marks, as Ratliff puts it: "the last and final end of Snopes out-and-out unvarnished behavior in Jefferson, if that's what I'm trying to say" (p. 370). But the tone of the section stands in sharp discord with the serious and even tragic overtones of the preceding section dealing with Eula's suicide and the fate of her daughter and does nothing to clarify the significance of Flem's victory and of Eula's and de Spain's defeat. It does not help us to know whether Eula and de Spain are destroyed because they have committed mortal sin by violating valid and real moral law or because they have violated merely the bigoted tyranny established by "incorrigible and unreconstructible Baptists and Methodists" (p. 307); whether Eula's death is a necessary and justified retribution or the terrible waste of something brave, pure, and clean; whether the outcome of events is primarily a matter of doom and fate or of human will and choice. Nor does the ending help us to understand the opaque and inscrutable Flem, who is at the center of the book, or to help define what Snopesdom really is. By making the children half-Indian, Faulkner leaves ambiguous the extent to which we can regard them, so to speak, as prototype Snopeses, and at the very end of the book he complicates our whole feeling about the intractability and innate viciousness of Snopesdom by suggesting, though tenuously, that perhaps all they need is to be treated with some humanity and kindness. For when Ratliff and Charles Mallison offer the children fruit and candy, we see them behave for the first time in an orderly unfurtive way. The last sentence of the book reminds us of a minor mystery: whether the smallest Snopes is a boy or a girl.

The Wild Palms

Two other of Faulkner's novels—*The Wild Palms* and *Requiem for a Nun*—are experiments in the juxtaposition of dissimilar and largely unrelated material.

In *The Wild Palms*, as initially published, Faulkner alternates the chapters of two completely self-contained stories, which have since been published separately. Considered individually, the stories are among Faulkner's less complex structures, although neither can by any means be described as having a simple structure or meaning. The story of the tall convict is on one level a straightforward adventure narrative. It gains a certain complexity, however, from the long and complex sentences by which it is narrated, from the prison scenes by which it is framed, and from the fact that it is in the third person even though conceived as the convict's own report of his experiences. This last technique allows Faulkner to convey a double view by juxtaposing images of the convict sitting quietly in his bunk with images of his agonizing struggle in the flood. It also enables him at least to seek another double effect: that of immediacy and aesthetic distance. The adventures are narrated throughout the work as vividly and concretely and with as much force as Faulkner can manage. At the same time Faulkner explicitly tells us that the convict's narration gave the events "a quality more dreamily furious than any fable behind proscenium lights" (p. 171) and

seemed to reach his listeners as though from beyond a sheet of slightly milky though still transparent glass, as something not heard but seen—a series of shadows, edgeless yet distinct, and smoothly flowing, logical and unfrantic and making no sound. [p. 174]

The chief complexity, however, is provided by the varied tones taken both toward the adventures and toward the convict, himself. The treatment of the adventures ranges between heroic, burlesque, and naturalistic; the convict is presented as both hero and butt of some cosmic joke (pp. 264–265); he is a symbol of human folly (pp. 23–25) and of human dignity and decency (pp. 165–166). His struggle is magnificent; his reward is a good cigar and ten additional years in prison, to which he says simply, "All right. . . . If that's the rule" (p. 331). Altogether we can by no means take the story simply as comedy; on the other hand, we cannot quite take it or the convict seriously. Faulkner clearly wants us to do both, just as we are to recognize simultaneously the heroism, folly, and futility of the convict's struggle.

The story of Charlotte and Wilbourne, apart from the opening chapter and a considerable number of Faulknerian sentences, is a relatively straightforward narration. It is one of Faulkner's few works which close on a decisive note: Wilbourne's finally crystallized realization that between "grief" and "nothing" he prefers grief, that he can at least retain the memory of his experiences with Charlotte. But with respect to the meaning of those experiences or of their disastrous outcome, this "realization" is irrelevant, and Faulkner leaves unresolved to what extent that outcome is to be blamed on society, upon the confused and oversimple romanticism of the rebels, and upon their sheer stupidity. Like most of Faulkner's heroes and victims, Wilbourne seems to have learned nothing from his harrowing experiences.

The most apparent relationships between the two stories are those of antithesis. A relatively actionless narrative about two lovers seeking a kind of purity and freedom is set against an action-packed narrative about a man who is caught in a Mississippi flood, a man who wishes to give up freedom for security. In the first narrative, a man kills the woman he loves; in the second a man is forced to take responsibility for a woman he does not love. In the first, the relationship between the man and woman is, above all, sexual; in the second, the man and woman never have sexual relations. The first man, trained as a doctor and using surgical instruments, performs an abortion on his beloved which results in her death. The second man, ignorant and untrained, using a tin can, helps the woman he does not love to deliver a child. The tone of the first narrative is serious. More than any other of Faulkner's stories with the possible exception of *Absalom, Absalom!* its conception and movement are tragic. It ends on a note of high seriousness with Wilbourne's "between grief and nothing I will take grief." The over-all tone of the second story is grimly humorous. Its basic conception is comic. It ends with the tall convict's superbly inadequate commentary on his experience: "Women!"

Once we move beyond these rather obvious contrasts and ironies, however, the relationships we can find between the

stories are limited only by our own ingenuity. Even if we see
both stories as primarily focused upon problems of freedom
and restraint and of the individual's relationship to society, the
implications of each story, alone, with respect to these problems
are so ambiguous and complex that the consideration of the
two stories together simply adds further loose ironic overtones
to impressions that already consist largely of ironic overtones.
More than this, whatever coherence or clarity either story
might have by itself is destroyed by the persistent interruption
by the other story.

Again Faulkner ends his work in such a way as to leave unresolved the meaning of his stories and to make ambiguous the
significance and worth of the human struggle he has depicted.
The heroes of both stories endure and in a certain sense prevail,
but both end up in prison. The convict has demonstrated a kind
of simple strength and decency that compels admiration, but
he is reduced at the end to an almost entirely comic or at least
absurd and obsessed character, whose final summation of his
experience—and in a sense of the whole book, since the book
ends with it—is the single word "Women!"

Requiem for a Nun

In *Requiem for a Nun,* three sections of sweeping, grandiose,
historical panorama narrated in thick, long, flowing sentences
are alternated with the acts of a play, a thin closet drama constructed largely of short, terse, nervous statements. The narrative sections provide a rich and complex historical and
thematic context for the play but do not directly illuminate it
or resolve the questions it raises. Rather it makes the play itself
a part of a larger and more complex suspension of elements.

More than most of Faulkner's works the play itself focuses
on a single problem: Temple Drake's effort to deal with her
pain and sense of guilt over her failure as a mother and wife and

to face the prospect of suffering for her failure for the rest of
her life. And there is a considerable degree of plot resolution
in the clear indication at the end that she will try to make a
life with her husband and child, although we are left with many
doubts as to whether she will be successful.

What is left unresolved, for both Temple and the reader, is
whether there is any point to her suffering, whether the pain
of going on "tomorrow and tomorrow and tomorrow" (p.
210) is "for anything" (p. 211). The Negro murderess, Nancy,
has absolute faith that it is, but she is completely incapable of
answering any of Temple's or Gavin Stevens' or the reader's
numerous questions as to the nature and content of her belief.
As Nancy follows the jailor back to her cell, Temple tries
once more:

TEMPLE
(quickly)

Nancy.

(Nancy doesn't pause. Temple
continues, rapidly)

What about me? Even if there is one [a heaven] and somebody
waiting in it to forgive me, there's still tomorrow and tomorrow.
And suppose tomorrow and tomorrow, and then nobody there,
nobody waiting to forgive me—

NANCY
(moving on after the Jailor)

Believe.

TEMPLE

Believe what, Nancy? Tell me.

NANCY

Believe.   [p. 283]

As Temple walks off stage, she is still questioning: "Anyone
to save it [her soul]. Anyone who wants it. If there is none,
I'm sunk. We all are. Doomed. Damned" (p. 286). There is
just enough ambiguity and paradox in Gavin Stevens' answer
to undercut the affirmation it seems to contain: "Of course we

are. Hasn't He been telling us that for going on two thousand years?" (p. 286).

The emphasis on Nancy's sacrifice and devout faith provide the book with a strongly affirmative note, but Faulkner leaves in considerable doubt just what is being affirmed apart from the fact that man is capable of self-sacrifice and of enduring pain. And the affirmation is again qualified by its association with mental limitation and a kind of madness. For Nancy's way of saving Gowan and Temple and one of their children was to kill the other child. The affirmation is further qualified by our knowledge that the marriage that Nancy has given her own and a child's life to preserve is, and undoubtedly will remain, an empty and loveless one. While it is clear that her actions have in a sense saved Temple from running away, it is not clear what she has been saved for. Gavin Stevens at one point says that what is being affirmed is "that little children, as long as they are little children, shall be intact, unanguished, untorn, unterrified" (p. 211), but Temple is much less concerned with this than with her own soul, and there is little evidence that by staying with Gowan she can provide her child with that sort of security.

The remaining novels of Faulkner's mature period vary widely in form and subject, but all of them in some crucial way are ambiguous and unresolved.

Sanctuary

In a sense the ending of *Sanctuary* provides the greatest degree of resolution of any of Faulkner's novels in that it completes the picture of horror, emptiness, and futility the novel has painted and does nothing to counteract the feeling we get from the rest of the book that life is grim and pointless. On the other hand, it does nothing to provide the book with a center or to help us to understand it. It is true that the biography of Popeye focuses some attention on the urban, mechanical, root-

less, and loveless environment which produced him and suggests a sociological interpretation of his character and fate, but
there is also much which suggests that his problems are entirely
pathological and have nothing to do with his environment; nor
does anything we learn reduce his complete opaqueness. Indeed,
the description of his behavior after he is arrested emphasizes
and in a sense cherishes this opaqueness. And if we have taken
the book at all seriously, this final description does complicate
our response somewhat, for in it Popeye becomes partly a
comic figure and, insofar as he retains his tough and impenetrable manner to the last, a partly heroic one.

Temple, too, remains opaque. At the very end of the book
we glimpse her face, "sullen and discontented and sad" (p.
379)—nothing more. What her harrowing experiences have
meant to her, if anything, we have no way of knowing.

One can hardly speak of affirmation in connection with this
book, but it is worth noting that the most sympathetically
treated character, the one placed most sharply in opposition to
Popeye is Tommy, a half-wit.

But all this is to take the book too seriously, I think, for,
whatever its power and whatever Faulkner managed to do in
his rewriting of it, it remains to a large extent a potboiler and
is shaped at bottom by Faulkner's intention to write "the most
horrific tale I could imagine" (p. vi).

Pylon

Structurally, *Pylon* is the least complex of Faulkner's works
for it has relatively few shifts in point of view and time and has
considerable unity of time, place, and action. Thematically,
however, it is among the most complex and ambiguous of Faulkner's books and offers one of the clearest illustrations of Faulkner's intentions and methods. In it we are encouraged to
interpret events in terms of an opposition between the natural

and mechanical or man and the machine, in terms of most of
the themes urged in *The Waste Land* and other early poems of
Eliot, in relation to Christian myth, and in terms of an opposition between the purposefulness and heroism of the fliers and
the aimlessness of the "moiling" humanity in the town and at
the airport, who keep getting in the fliers' way.

We must, on the one hand, view the fliers as a peculiarly
damaged and dehumanized form of being:

> They aint human. It aint adultery; you can't anymore imagine two
> of them making love than you can two of them airplanes back in
> the corner of the hangar, coupled. . . . Cut him and it's cylinder
> oil; dissect him and it aint bones: it's little rockerarms and connect-
> ing rods. [p. 231]

It is even suggested at times that they are so dehumanized that
their behavior is incomprehensible to humans and that any
human who tries to make contact with them will be seriously
hurt. At the same time they frequently exhibit a quixotic type
of honor and generosity and a vitality which reminds one of
the Southern aristocrats of Yoknapatawpha county and which
makes them seem far more human than any of the other inhabitants of the Waste Land depicted in the book, especially
since many of the latter are shown as callously exploiting or
mocking them. Unlike other victims of the Waste Land, Shumann is governed from childhood by a clear sense of purpose.
Moreover, Shumann demonstrates the very highest kind of
humanity by choosing to use the last of his control over his
burning plane to avoid hitting the other planes and to plunge
into the lake instead of the crowd. We must see Laverne as a
peculiarly desexed and defeminized product of the machine age
and as having an erotic force not unlike that of Eula Varner,
as a symbol of maximum promiscuity and of peculiar loyalty.
There is much to suggest that Shumann's actions are governed
essentially by a passion for machines and speed which began in
his childhood; there is also much which suggests that he was

driven essentially, especially in the races we watch, by the need for money.

We are explicitly urged to view the reporter as a scarecrow out of Eliot's "The Hollow Men" and as Prufrock. But far from being governed by indecision and inability to act, he is driven by an obsessive interest in the fliers and a passion for Laverne, and he, more than anyone else, makes the decisions and performs the actions which lead to Shumann's death. We must see him also as "patron (even if no guardian) saint of all waifs, all the homeless the desperate and the starved" (p. 183), not only because of Faulkner's explicit statement, but because he alone does care for and seek to understand the fliers. Yet we cannot ignore the suggestion that his actions may be motivated almost entirely by his desire for Laverne.

The ending leaves these questions about character and motivation unresolved. The reporter suffers but never tries to think about the meaning of what has happened. Although he says again and again that Laverne hasn't understood, he is incapable of communicating either to himself or others what it is she hasn't understood. Above all, the ending leaves unresolved the significance of the events. That Shumann's death was a meaningful and necessary act is strongly suggested by the emphasis on the crowds who watch the hunt for his body, by the fact that his death marks the end of the cheap confetti ritual of the Mardi gras and the beginning of Lent, in which the crowd is decorous and quiet "as though the very brick and stone had just recovered from fever" (p. 267), and by the various suggestions that the trip to Dr. Shumann's is to some degree a movement out of the Waste Land. On the other hand, we are made to feel it was all pointless, by the callousness of the chorus of card-playing reporters; by the extent to which Shumann has destroyed his father, whose bitter cry that "nothing is worth anything but peace, peace, peace" (p. 306) is more a travesty than a parallel of the Shantih, Shantih, Shantih which ends Eliot's The Waste Land; by Dr. Shumann's misinterpretation and burning of the money, which was not, as he thought it was, a sign of deception and selfishness but of the generosity of several characters; and by the fact that no one seems to gain anything but pain as a result of Shumann's death.

At the very end of the book we read two news stories about Shumann's death. The first, pieced together by a copy boy from copy torn up by the reporter, contains nothing but phony sentiment. The second, written by the reporter and left on the editor's desk under an empty whiskey bottle, conveys only the reporter's anger and bitterness. Beneath it was written "savagely in pencil":

I guess this is what you want you bastard and now I am going down to Amboise st. and get drunk a while and if you dont know where Amboise st. is ask your son to tell you and if you dont know what drunk is come down there and look at me and when you come bring some jack because I am on a credit. [p. 315]

The reporter clearly is unable to make sense out of his experience, and we are in much the same predicament. That Faulkner wants us to be and thinks we should be is strongly suggested several times in the book. On one occasion he writes:

As the cage door clashed behind him, the editor himself reached down and lifted the facedown watch from the stack of papers, from that cryptic staccato crosssection of an instant crystallised and now dead two hours, though only the moment, the instant: the substance itself not only not dead, not complete, but in its very insoluble enigma of human folly and blundering possessing a futile and tragic immortality:

FARMERS BANKERS STRIKERS   ACREAGE
        WEATHER POPULATION

Now it was the elevator man who asked the time. "Half past two," the editor said. He put the watch back, placing it without apparent pause or calculation in the finicking exact center of the line of caps, so that now, in the shape of a cheap metal disc, the cryptic stripe was parted neatly in the exact center by the blank backside of the greatest and most inescapable enigma of all. [p. 85]

Later, after rendering an even longer list of headlines, he speaks of them as "the fragile web of ink and paper, assertive, proclamative; profound and irrevocable if only in the sense of being profoundly and irrevocably unimportant" (p. 111).

Faulkner seems to be saying here not only that life is enigmatic and that it is at once futile and tragic, but that its immortality or enduring quality is dependent upon its folly, blundering, or unimportance, an emphasis which must be set against the more sanguine one of the Stockholm address. What will "endure," he seems to suggest throughout *Pylon*, is man as a moiling purposeless mass, man as he exists in the city:

By looking back he could still see the city, the glare of it, no further away; if he were moving, regardless at what terrific speed and in what loneliness, so was it, paralleling him. He was not escaping it; symbolic and encompassing, it outlay all gasolinespanned distances and all clock- or sunstipulated destinations. It would be there—the eternal smell of the coffee the sugar the hemp sweating slow iron plates above the forked deliberate brown water and lost lost lost all ultimate blue of latitude and horizon; the hot rain gutterfull plaiting the eaten heads of shrimp; the ten thousand inescapable mornings wherein ten thousand swinging airplants stippleprop the soft scrofulous soaring of sweating brick and ten thousand pairs of splayed brown hired Leonorafeet tigerbarred by jaloused armistice with the invincible sun: the thin black coffee, the myriad fish stewed in a myriad oil—tomorrow and tomorrow and tomorrow; not only not to hope, not even to wait: just to endure. [pp. 283–284]

Intruder in the Dust

In some respects *Intruder in the Dust* is probably the least complex and least unresolved of Faulkner's novels. Its plot is relatively uncomplicated, it focuses quite consistently on the theme of the white man's responsibility toward the Negro, and it casts very little doubt upon the necessity, propriety, or justice of Chick's effort to save Lucas. Still its final effect is essentially similar to that of the other novels. Faulkner achieves this effect by providing an unusually high degree of structural and stylistic complexity; by tangling us continually in the elliptical and ambiguous rhetoric of Gavin Stevens; by making Chick's motivation exceedingly complex; by keeping the Negro, Lucas, largely opaque; by giving Lucas some white blood and other atypical Negro characteristics; by making Lucas throughout the book a partly comic character; and by making us feel that the cause of most of the action is to a large extent nothing more than Lucas' almost absurd inability or unwillingness to tell either Gavin or Chick what he knows about the killing. Above all, he achieves it by an ending which greatly complicates our responses.

First of all, the emphasis at the end shifts from the boy, Chick, and the problem of white-Negro relations, to the town square and the evils of mechanization and standardization. The county population, which had been portrayed as essentially human and potentially moral and decent as well as potentially ugly and violent, is now shown as a clotted mechanized mass immersed in carbon monoxide and amplified sound. This shift in emphasis not only provides a broad new theme which we must try to relate to the events we have already witnessed and raises many new questions about the meaning of those events, but makes us feel that perhaps the whole effort to save Lucas was really quite pointless.

This feeling is strengthened by many other aspects of the final chapter: by the strong suggestion that the county will quickly forget what has happened and will learn nothing from it; by the unpromising picture of Aleck Sander, who had helped to save Lucas, standing in the Square in a "flash Saturday shirt and a pair of zoot pants and a handful of peanuts or bananas" (p. 237); and by Gavin Stevens' cynical argument that the American loves nothing but his automobile. It is true that Chick does not accept the argument and that Gavin tells him to go on refusing to accept it, but the force of the argument remains, though in suspension with its antithesis. It is also true that shortly afterward Gavin seems to affirm the value of saving Lucas and of continuing to perform such acts, but that affirmation is embedded in a highly ambiguous and incoherent passage (pp. 242–244) which also suggests the futility of such acts.

What most forcibly makes us question the significance and value of Chick's effort and most complicates the book is the reduction of Lucas in the final chapter to an almost entirely absurd and comic character or, if some readers will not grant that much, the exclusive emphasis at the end on Lucas' more comic and eccentric qualities. It is true that these qualities have been shown throughout the book, but always in such a way as to permit us to see him in considerably more than a merely comic light. In the final chapter he becomes almost entirely comic. Since this aspect of the book has been entirely ignored, let me elaborate.

Lucas is a man who one week before was almost lynched for a crime he had not committed. He was saved only because a boy, Chick Mallison, and an old lady, Miss Habersham, were willing to go to desperate and dangerous lengths to prove his innocence. He walks into the office of Gavin Stevens, who has also played some part in saving him and who has secured his release from prison,

tieless and even collarless this time except for the button but with an old-time white waistcoat not soiled so much as stained under the black coat and the worn gold loop of the watchchain—the same face which he [Chick] had seen for the first time when he climbed dripping up out of the icy creek that morning four years ago, unchanged, to which nothing had happened since not even age—in the act of putting the toothpick into one of the upper waistcoat pockets as he came through the door, saying generally,

"Gentle-men," and then to him: "Young man—" courteous and intractable, more than bland: downright cheerful almost, removing the raked swagger of the hat: "You aint fell in no more creeks lately, have you?" [pp. 240–241]

Lucas has to be forced, much as a child might, into thanking Miss Habersham, and he resists, much as a child might. Gavin is quite sure, and so are we, that the only way he will get to Miss Habersham with the flowers Gavin has provided is for Charles to drive him there. Lucas gives in grudgingly. When Lucas and Charles return (and characteristically Faulkner reports nothing of this scene in which these two chief and deeply related characters are alone together), Lucas tries to pay Gavin, who has officially been his lawyer. Gavin will accept only two dollars, for the expense of replacing a fountain pen point he broke because of exasperation while trying to make sense out of things Lucas told him.

"Two dollars?" Lucas said. He blinked twice again. Then he blinked twice again. "Just two dollars?" Now he just blinked once, then he did something with his breath: not a sigh, simply a discharge of it, putting his first two fingers into the purse: "That dont sound like much to me but then I'm a farming man and you're a lawing man and whether you know your business or not I reckon it aint none of my red wagon as the music box says to try to learn you different:" and drew from the purse a worn bill crumpled into a ball not much larger than a shrivelled olive and opened it enough to read it then opened it out and laid it on the desk and from the purse took a half dollar and laid it on the desk then counted onto the desk from the purse one by one four dimes and two nickels and then counted them again with his forefinger, moving them one by one about half an inch, his lips moving under the moustache, the purse still open in the other hand, then he picked up two of the dimes and a nickel and put them into the hand holding the open purse and took from the purse a quarter and put it on the desk and looked down at the coins for a rapid second then put the two dimes and the nickel back on the desk and took up the half dollar and put it back into the purse. [pp. 245–246]

When Gavin complains that he is a quarter short, Lucas picks up the quarter and takes a sack of fifty pennies from a second "almost elbow-deep section" of the purse. Gavin makes him count these, and when he has done so and has wiped his hands and stands "again intractable and calm and not looking at either of them" Gavin says, "Now what? . . . What are you waiting for now?" The book ends with Lucas' answer: "My receipt."

On a symbolic and thematic level this reply and much of the final chapter is apt and effective in that it deals with the problem of repaying moral obligations; in that it points out that the efforts made in Lucas' behalf in no way even the score between Negro and white or even reduce the white man's obligation and guilt; in its suggestion, which the book in part bears out, that the Negro has little reason to trust the white man; and in its complexly ironic recapitulation of the opening chapter, in which Charles tries to pay Lucas for having fulfilled a normal human obligation.

But by ending on this comic note, by emphasizing throughout the final chapter the comic and eccentric aspects of Lucas, and by making his response so completely inappropriate to the situation as we perceive and feel it, Faulkner radically affects our perspective on the whole story. Not only must we add a comic perspective to those we already have, we must grapple with the feeling that what has been saved is something less than a fully human man. For what largely characterizes Lucas in the final chapter and provides the comedy is his lack of the very quality which most defines the human being—the ability to understand what has happened to him. Since the town has learned nothing and Lucas has learned nothing, and there is not even a hint of a change in the relationship between Lucas and Gavin and Lucas and Charles, we must feel that all the effort and turmoil were in a sense futile.

In one further way the ending complicates our response.

Much in the book has implied that the South is guilty because it has perceived and treated the Negro as nigger rather than man. This, quite specifically, is the cause of Chick's shame and need to repay. At the end of the book we are encouraged, as we are by Gavin's reiteration of the word "Sambo" earlier in the book, to view Lucas as nigger rather than as man. Like Shylock at the end of *The Merchant of Venice* and Jim at the end of *Huckleberry Finn*, Lucas is reduced to the kind of stereotype whose fate does not compel serious concern. We are not at any point in the book made quite as fully conscious that Lucas is human as we are of the humanity of Shylock and Jim, but the opening chapter has much the same kind of effect as Shylock's "Do I not bleed" speech and Jim's lecture to Huck about "trash," and Charles makes the identical discovery about Lucas that Huck makes about Jim, a discovery Faulkner underscores by repetition and italics both:

She had just died then. That was why he [Lucas] *didn't see me. That was why he didn't have the toothpick:* thinking with a kind of amazement: *He was grieving. You don't have to not be a nigger in order to grieve.* [p. 25; see also p. 161]

In the final chapter the emphasis is solely on those characteristics of Lucas which separate him from us, which have fooled Charles and other white men into believing a Negro is not sufficiently human to grieve or to grieve for. Our final glimpse in the book is at a character asking for a receipt for two dollars which he has paid for having his life saved.

Again Faulkner has ended in such a way as greatly to complicate our responses to his book and our understanding of it. Again we find that the affirmative elements in the book have been opposed by alternative sugestions and by tone. Again a kind of triumph, indestructibility, and endurance has been associated with a degree of mental limitation and peculiarity and with a comically inadequate response to experience.

A Fable

A Fable offers peculiarly impressive evidence that the characteristics of Faulkner's writing I have been pointing to are fundamental in his work. It does so in part because it retains most of those characteristics even though it differs from Faulkner's other work in many other respects and in part because it deals explicitly with some of the ideas and attitudes governing those characteristics.

Most simply stated, the book presents on the literal level a variety of events that are related in some way to a mutiny and temporary cessation of combat which occurs in France several months before the end of World War I. On the symbolic or even allegorical level, it presents a re-enactment of Christ's Passion. The exact re-enactments of specific events of the Passion Week and in Christ's life are relatively few, but there is elaborate and extensive paralleling of a looser sort between the life of Christ and the life of a corporal, who with twelve disciples engineers the mutiny and is executed for it. The corporal's chief antagonist is the Supreme Commander of the Allied Forces, usually referred to as "the old general," who is the corporal's father. On the symbolic level he is part God, part Pontius Pilate, part Caesar, and part Satan.

The re-enactment and the general conflict between the corporal and general provide the novel with a certain degree of unity and serve as a kind of center insofar as all the other characters and events can be related to them. Faulkner furthers this sense of unity by using the days of the week to title his sections and by confining his description of present action to the period between Monday, when the mutiny occurs, and Sunday, when the corporal's dead body disappears.

But the book is far more diffuse and complex than this suggests. It is made so partly by Faulkner's usual involuted time

sequences, flashbacks, and shifts in tone and point of view and
by a more than usually intense and involuted style and partly
by his usual juxtaposition and alternation of several more or less
independent stories. Some of these stories operate chiefly on
the literal level, others chiefly on the allegorical. Moreover, the
corporal is by no means the central figure in the book, nor can
the re-enactment of the Passion be considered the central action.
Actually the old general plays a far more prominent role than
the corporal, and even he is less in the foreground than the
English battalion runner, who does not have an allegorical role
in the Passion or a direct role in the mutiny, although he is
deeply affected by both. But even he is not focused upon sufficiently to provide a center. There are also extensive emphases
on the story of General Gragnon, who commands the division
which contains the mutinous regiment; upon the story of
Levine, a British pilot who commits suicide; upon the story of
the corporal's half-sisters Marthe and Marya; and upon the
story of the Reverend Sutterfield, the English groom, and the
stolen race horse. This last, much of which was written earlier
and published separately as *Notes on a Horsethief,* is related
only peripherally to the mutiny and, as we shall see, greatly
extends and complicates the meaning of the book. Faulkner also
devotes much attention to the mass of people filling the area
from which the mutinous regiment was recruited and where it
has been imprisoned, so much attention that the mass itself
must be viewed, so to speak, as a character. This mass of people
also serves as a kind of choreographic chorus and at times as a
symbol of mankind.

Although these various stories are related mechanically, in
that they all tie in to some degree with the mutiny and temporary peace, they are not sufficiently integrated with it or with
one another to produce any comfortable sense of unity or
pattern.

Further complexity is provided by Faulkner's continual
shifting between literal and symbolic levels. In Faulkner's other

works the symbolism is largely a matter of overtones. His
characters are essentially concrete persons who may or may
not be viewed as symbolic. Even Joe Christmas is essentially a
realistic character and need not be seen as Christ. In *A Fable*,
however, as the title suggests, the symbolic level is far more
persistently and elaborately enforced, so much so that the cor-
respondences sometimes become almost allegorical. The effect
is somewhat like that produced by the later books of *The Faerie
Queene*, in which literal and allegorical figures exist side by side.
Only it is more complex, since the distinctions are less clear
and firm. The characters are allegorical in varying proportions
and move freely between their literal and figurative roles.

Still further complexity is provided by the amount of paradox
we are confronted with. For example, the corporal, whom we
must view as Christ, is a completely secular being, a man not
only without dogma or theology but without any religion or
religious concern whatever. He is described as being "utterly
free of compassion" (p. 17). On the other hand, the chief
symbol of love and passion, who like "Adam and Lilith and
Paris and Helen and Pyramus and Thisbe and all the other
recordless Romeos and their Juliets" takes part in "the world's
oldest and most shining tale" (p. 153) is a vicious, foul-mouthed
stable groom and later racketeer whose response to virtually any
attempt to communicate with him is a curse and who viciously
kicks and beats the runner when the latter talks too long and
enthusiastically about the mutiny. To grant him the status of
man, Faulkner suggests, "was merely to accept Darkness' emis-
sary in the stead of its actual prince and master" (p. 158). The
runner, who is probably the most important and indomitable
symbol of man, gives up his commission and rejoins the rank
and file, because he hates man and wants to be able to stop
having hope for him.

Finally, much in the book is simply and obviously mysterious.
We are given no understanding of how the corporal and his
squad bring about the mutiny. Nor can we assume any rational

explanation, because Faulkner suggests quite clearly that they do not ever preach or advocate. Some do not even speak French. On one occasion, just before a kind of "Last Supper," Faulkner describes the faces of the squad as "harassed, but absolute, one in whatever it was—not trust exactly, not dependence: perhaps just one-ness, singleness" (p. 340). The corporal, himself, is essentially opaque. We understand that he is calm and somehow above or beyond the petty or temporary struggles about him and that he accepts rather than judges men, but he remains essentially a mysterious figure as both man and symbol. The old general, too, who among other things disappeared for thirteen years and spent part of that time in a Tibetan lamasery, is essentially a mystery if we try to comprehend him as a single human being. We are encouraged sometimes to see him as an utterly cynical and disillusioned old general, sometimes as an omnipotent and omniscient figure who has the deepest faith in man and governs all things for the best, sometimes as a victim of his circumstances, sometimes as an empty figurehead, as "gaudy as a child's toy" (p. 333), sometimes as kind and merciful, and sometimes as utterly without mercy, someone whom man not only does not need but needs to be protected from. One general says of him: "If I were evil, I would hate and fear him. If I were a saint, I would weep. If I were wise, and both or either, I would despair" (p. 230). We cannot understand him any more than we can understand God, and obviously Faulkner wishes it to be that way. Somewhat baffling, also, is the crucial decision of the generals to continue the war. We understand to some extent their fear of chaos and of letting the common soldiers understand their power, but in presenting the meeting of the generals Faulkner focuses almost entirely on the character, attitudes, and mannerisms of the Prussian general and merely refers to an earlier part of the meeting at which the matter was discussed directly. When asked to ratify the agreement formally the old general says simply, "What agreement. . . . Do we need an agreement? Has anyone missed one?" (p.

309). Perhaps most mysterious of all is the origin and nature and purpose of Reverend Sutterfield's untranslatably titled association: "*Les Amis Myriades et Anonymes à la France de Tout le Monde.*"

As in Faulkner's other works, we cannot embrace the meaning of the book, at least once we try to go beyond the bare generalization that the book is about man's heroism and folly and capacity to endure. First of all, we are encouraged to interpret events in three rather disparate ways: in terms of various struggles within mankind between the common man and his rulers; in terms of problems of faith and sacrifice; and in terms of man's capacity to endure. Moreover, the complexity and ambiguity within each of these general conceptions is such that they, too, become suspensions of alternative views and suggestions rather than integrated wholes. It is worth looking at these various alternatives in some detail, for they provide a kind of summary of the ideas and attitudes which I believe govern virtually all of Faulkner's works.

The struggle within mankind is sometimes presented in largely Marxist terms, with the old general representing the hierarchy of civil and military vested interests and the corporal representing the common man who is manipulated, exploited, and destroyed by the ruling classes. This view is given explicit statement by the narrator, by the quartermaster general, and by several other characters, and it is dramatized by the ranks of corporal and general, by the equation of the corporal with ancient English bowmen and miners in coal towns back of Pittsburgh (pp. 276–277), and by the fact that the mutiny and temporary peace is achieved solely by privates. The runner is unable to approach the corporal and his men or to find out what is going on because he was once an officer. Related to this view, but not entirely in accord with it, is one which regards the conflict as between those who desire grandeur and glory and those who desire merely peace and the right to pursue the simple unpretentious activities of everyday life. The corporal

is a farmer, and his followers have peasant faces; the crowd of
friends and relations of the mutineers is described as sweeping
over the military "irresistible in that passive and invincible
humility . . . [with] a humbly and passively contemptuous
disregard, like martyrs entering an arena of lions" (p. 5). And
there is much else to make us feel that all would be well if man
were simply left alone, to make us see the mutiny, as the quartermaster general does, simply as the expression of "the simple
unified hope and dream of simple man" (p. 331), to make us
cherish man's humble and passive qualities, and to make us feel
that man is corrupted and destroyed above all by the ideal of
"fatherland" and by the slogans of glory that so infuriate the
runner: "They shall not pass. My country right or wrong. Here
is a spot which is forever England" (p. 436).

At the same time, however, we are compelled to see the
struggle in a radically different light, showing man as a moiling,
chaotic, spiritless mass which desperately needs order and direction, which has, in fact, a "deathless passion for being led,
mystified, and deceived" (p. 349). This view is forcefully expressed not only by various generals (see pp. 30, 53) but by
what seems to be the narrator's voice as he celebrates

that titanic congeries of the long heroic roster who were the mile-
stones of the rise of man—the giants who coerced compelled di-
rected and, on occasion, actually led his myriad moil: Caesar and
Christ, Bonaparte and Peter and Mazarin and Alexander, Ghenghis
and Talleyrand and Warwick, Marlborough and Bryan, Bill Sunday, General Booth and Prester John, prince and bishop, Norman,
dervish, plotter and khan, not for the power and glory nor even
the aggrandisement; these were merely secondarily concomitant and
even accidental; but for man: by putting some of him in one motion
in one direction, by him of him and for him, to disjam the earth,
get him for a little while at least out of his own way. [p. 181]

This view is further enforced by Faulkner's frequent emphasis
on the chaotic and purposeless movements of the crowd around
Chaulesmont, its sympathy for General Gragnon, who wants

to shoot the whole regiment, and its fury at Marthe, Marya, the corporal, and the runner; by the old general's argument that he is continuing the war as an alternative to chaos (p. 331); by the celebration of heroism and passion in the story of the stolen race horse; and by the fact that the runner, the groom, the sympathetically conceived Picklock, and even the corporal, all have medals for valor.

On other occasions we are urged to view man not so much as a humble mass or directionless "moil" but rather as a creature driven essentially by greed. The group commander argues that greed is responsible for the war and for the creation of "the captains and the colonels," while the quartermaster general sees rapacity as a source and essence of civilization and immortality:

"Rapacity does not fail, else man must deny he breathes. . . . Not just France, but all governments and nations" [which ever left their mark] "had sprung from it and in and upon and by means of it became forever fixed in the amazement of man's present and the glory of his past; civilization itself is its password and Christianity its masterpiece, Chartres and the Sistine Chapel, the pyramids and the rock-wombed powder-magazines under the gates of Hercules its altars and monuments." [pp. 259–260]

He goes on to argue that "it is in and from rapacity that he gets, holds, his immortality" (pp. 260–261). This view is further supported, among other ways, by the emphasis on the groom's moneylending operation, by Polchek's Judas-like betrayal of the corporal for money, and by the extent to which money plays a part in the switching of bodies which puts the corporal in the coffin of the Unknown Soldier.

Not entirely in accord with any of these alternative views is one which regards the old general not as champion of glory or power but simply as the realist, and the corporal not as representing the sane humble desires of common man but as the idealist, or, as the old general puts it, "I champion of this mundane earth which, whether I like it or not, is; . . . you champion of an esoteric realm of man's baseless hopes and his

infinite capacity—no: passion—for unfact" (p. 348). Insofar as
we take such a view, we must see man's hopes and the corporal's
sacrifice as good and as a triumph over the generals and also
see them in the cynical terms of the group commander: "Yes,
let them believe they can stop it, so long as they dont suspect
that they have. . . . Let them believe that tomorrow they
will end it; then they wont begin to ponder if perhaps today
they can. Tomorrow. And still tomorrow. And again tomorrow" (p. 54).

Less prominent, but strongly suggested by the emphasis on
the old general's intelligence and articulateness, by the story
of the stolen race horse, and by the arguments of the tempter
priest is an opposition of head and heart in which the corporal
and man represent the latter. On the other hand, the most indomitable representative of man, the runner, is an intellectual
whose heart is not at all an admirable or trustworthy instrument.

The second major theme of the book—that of faith and
sacrifice— is complicated in part by the complex and unresolved
aspects just mentioned, for, without any clear understanding of
what the corporal stands for, we cannot answer the questions:
Faith in what? Sacrifice for what? Clearly Faulkner does not
wish us to, for at no time does he allow the corporal to express
his beliefs in any but the most oblique and inconclusive way. To
the elaborate arguments and temptations of the old general he
simply reiterates, "There are still ten." By this he affirms the
value of his squad's faith and trust in him and the necessity for
him not to betray it, but does nothing to clarify the nature of
the faith. Nor are our questions answered by what the corporal
is and does, for we see very little of him and that little tells us
only that he is a simple, unpretentious man with a kind of elemental human dignity and serenity. We are baffled when we try
to reconcile this supreme serenity and acceptance of things and
of men as they are with his role as leader of the mutiny or to
reconcile his exemplification in action of common sense and
decorum with his role as sacrificial hero. Most baffling of all is

the presumably important episode at the end of the meeting between the old general and the corporal. In this episode the
corporal gives dignity back to the hysterical Pierre Bouc by the
command "Be a soldier" after failing to have any effect with the
commands "Be a man," and "Be a Zsettlani" (p. 356). One expects something quite different from either a Christ or a leader
of a mutiny for peace.

The other exemplar of absolute faith or "innocent and invincible affirmation" (p. 204), the Reverend Sutterfield, is very
much like Nancy in *Requiem for a Nun*, who "believes" but
cannot answer what she believes. He leaves the runner, who
comes for help, as baffled and frustrated as Nancy leaves Temple
Drake. In a sense he seems to believe in and to accept everything: that laughter and tears are the same to God, that "Evil is
a part of man, evil and sin and cowardice, the same as repentance
and being brave. You got to believe in all of them, or believe in
none of them. Believe that man is capable of all of them, or he
aint capable of none" (p. 203). He can assent to the runner's
statement that the important thing is just to believe and hope,
and his Society seems founded simply to enable people to "sit
together in the anguished room and believe and hope" (p. 202).
Yet he can also assent to the runner's argument that what enables man to go on is

"his integrity as a creature tough and enduring enough not only not
to hope but not even to believe in it and not even to miss its lack;
to be tough and to endure until the flash, crash, whatever it will be,
when he will no longer be anything and none of it will matter any
more, even the fact that he was tough and, until then, did endure."
[p. 203]

Perhaps even more indicative of Faulkner's intentions, since
no faith is ever fully explicable, is the extent to which he makes
ambiguous the validity, value, and meaningfulness of the faith
and sacrifice. On the one hand, we must feel that Sutterfield's
faith is admirable, for it gives him an utter serenity and enables

him to perform what amount to virtual miracles. At times we are led to view it as a more valid response to life than the runner's anguished one. On the other hand, we are made to feel that his faith in the groom's redeemability is unwarranted and even ridiculous and to suspect his whole view of the groom as having little relation to reality. We must give considerable assent when just before they are both killed, the groom shouts, "What did I tell you? Didn't I tell you to let me alone?" (p. 321). Moreover, Sutterfield, like the corporal, is destroyed, while the runner, motivated by "indomitable despair," continues to endure. The deaths of both the groom and the priest, who fails to tempt the corporal, seem at once meaningful and pointless. The groom achieves a moment of humanity as he says "we" and not "I" for "the first time in his life probably" (p. 321), but he does not realize he has said it and in the next moment, his last one, says "I" again and repudiates Sutterfield. The priest seems to have a moment of peace and hope as he thinks, "*He was nailed there and He will forgive me*" (p. 370), but his last sound is "a thin sweet crying of frustration and despair" (p. 370). The soldiers who join the runner's abortive pacifist action have a moment of "dawning and incredulous hope" and then are shelled and destroyed.

These are comparatively minor events. The ironies and ambiguities involved in the corporal's sacrifice are far more complex. We must, of course, view his sacrifice as profoundly meaningful. Even apart from his equation with Christ there is much to make us see him as a kind of savior and to see his martyrdom as a triumph. Even the old general insists on this: "If I gave him his life tonight, I myself could render null and void what you [the quartermaster general] call the hope and the dream of his sacrifice. By destroying his life tomorrow morning, I will establish forever that he didn't even live in vain, let alone die so" (p. 332).

On the other hand, there is much to make us feel that the sacrifice has been utterly meaningless and futile and even to make it seem a horrible travesty of Christ's sacrifice. For one thing, there is no indication anywhere that the martyrdom has any effect at all on the course of the war or on man's future attitudes or behavior. As far as we can tell, this Christ leaves no heritage behind him and no active disciples. At the end of the book the world is paying homage to the dead old general while the corporal lies unrecognized in the coffin of the Unknown Soldier. The corporal's symbolic resurrection is accomplished by a shell blast as the war begins again. Even if we are to assume that by his martyrdom the corporal kept alive man's hope for peace and man's belief that he could attain it, we must in part view that accomplishment in the cynical terms of the general known as Mama Bidet, who believes that as long as men have hope for tomorrow they will not seek to change anything today. Finally, one must also share Irving Howe's view of the re-enactment as

one of the most desperate and radically bleak visions of human experience that any novelist in our time has advanced. The very idea of a *re-enactment* is itself utterly desperate. To conceive of a Second Coming which is essentially a repetition of the original agony; to see the Christ figure as again scorned by the crowds, again betrayed and deserted by his followers, again crushed by the state; and most terrible of all, to conceive of a Christ who knows he is doomed, who offers neither hope nor a belief in the idea of hope—all this, if not heresy or even blasphemy, implies a vision of despair that completely undercuts the assumptions of both our liberal culture and of Christianity itself. For Faulkner, Christ now seems to signify the Crucifixion without the Redemption; or perhaps it is that the crucifixion has become a Redemption.[14]

The third major theme of *A Fable*—man's capacity to endure —is in one sense not at all complex, for there is no serious challenge in the book to the assertion that he will endure. What this assertion means, however, is left unclear, for the word

[14] "Thirteen Who Mutinied: Faulkner's First World War," *The Reporter*, X (Sept. 14, 1954), 44.

"endure" is a rich and ambiguous one and Faulkner plays on each of its chief meanings: "to put up with," "to suffer," and "to persist in time." Left unclear, also, is how much man's ability to endure is related to the corporal's sacrifice or to man's capacity to hope and believe, how much to his capacity to go on without hope, how much to his instinctive drive to survive and reproduce.

Nor is it clear how affirmative an assertion it is. At the end of their interview, the old general offers the corporal a final temptation—mere life itself, arguing that "nothing—nothing—nothing—not power nor glory nor wealth nor pleasure nor even freedom from pain, is as valuable as simple breathing, simply being alive" (p. 350). He then places this in antithesis with the "baseless dream" the corporal represents, an antithesis somewhat in accord with the quartermaster general's idea that man endures "not because he is immortal but immortal because he endures" (p. 260). The corporal answers, "Dont be afraid. . . . There's nothing to be afraid of. Nothing worth it" (p. 352). The general answers: "Afraid? No no, it's not I but you who are afraid of man; not I but you who believe that nothing but a death can save him" (p. 352). He goes on to argue that man "has in him that which will enable him to outlast even his wars" and the era of enslavement by machines which he is about to enter. The general then presents at length a partly terrifying, partly comic vision of this era, which ends with man crawling shivering out of his burrow to watch the battle of the last two machines. And the general concludes:

"Oh yes, he will survive it because he has that in him which will endure even beyond the ultimate worthless tideless rock freezing slowly in the last red and heatless sunset, because already the next star in the blue immensity of space will be already clamorous with the uproar of his debarkation, his puny and inexhaustible voice still talking, still planning; and there too after the last ding dong of doom has rung and died there will still be one sound more: his voice, planning still to build something higher and faster and louder; more efficient and louder and faster than ever before, yet it too inherent with the same old primordial fault since it too in the end will fail to eradicate him from the earth. I dont fear man. I do better: I respect and admire him. And pride: I am ten times prouder of that immortality which he does possess than ever he of that heavenly one of his delusion. Because man and his folly—"

"Will endure," the corporal said.

"They will do more," the old general said proudly. "They will prevail." [p. 354]

Apart from the ambiguities of content and tone in the passage itself, we face the ambiguities of the dramatic context, which leave uncertain to what extent we are listening to the general as general, as Caesar, as Satan, as God. Nor can we determine whether the corporal's "will endure" is an assent to the old general's presentation or merely a momentary participation in its rhetoric. In his Nobel Prize address Faulkner seems in part to reject the general's tone and emphasis when he says:

It is easy enough to say that man is immortal simply because he will endure; that when the last ding-dong of doom has clanged and faded from the last worthless rock hanging tideless in the last red and dying evening, that even then there will still be one more sound: that of his puny inexhaustible voice, still talking. I refuse to accept this. I believe that man will not merely endure: he will prevail. He is immortal, not because he alone among creatures has an inexhaustible voice but because he has a soul, a spirit capable of compassion and sacrifice and endurance.[15]

Although there is much in *A Fable*, even apart from the fact that the corporal does perform his sacrifice, to make us accept the point of view and tone of the Stockholm address and to regard the old general's emphasis as inadequate and partial, there is just as much to make us accept the general's tone and point of view as the inclusive and final one. We cannot choose. The spectacle remains, as always, at once futile and tragic.

The final chapter, entitled "Tomorrow," both implicitly and

[15] O'Connor, *The Tangled Fire*, pp. 147–148.

explicitly recapitulates and reinforces all the complexities and ambiguities that have gone before. The transfer of bodies, which puts what is probably, but not certainly, the corporal's body in the coffin of the Unknown Soldier, occurs in part because of an old woman's obsessive desire to possess the body of her son, in part because of a sergeant's contempt for the desires of his squad, in part because of the squad's desire for money to buy liquor. Both Picklock and the French farmer who sells him the corporal's body are shown as possessing a mixture of avarice and compassion. The scene at the farm of the corporal's sisters emphasizes the serene faith and tolerance and the natural occupations of Marya, but she is a half-wit. Polchek (Judas) is shown as stricken by a feeling of guilt and a need for expiation, but he remains insolent and violent and seems to have no comprehension of the enormity of his betrayal. Moreover, his efforts to gain relief are futile, for the sisters will not take pity on him by accepting his thirty pieces of silver. " 'Go now,' " Marya says in "her serene and unpitying voice. 'Go now. It is not much further. You dont have much longer to despair' " (p. 432).

The visit of the runner—now on crutches, half scar, half man —to get the corporal's medal, suggests that the corporal has left at least one disciple, but one whose imitations of the corporal are always violent and futile gestures leading only to his own destruction. When Marthe asks whether he wants to see the corporal's grave, he answers "What for? . . . He's finished" (p. 431). How much he means by this, we cannot know, for when Marthe objects, Marya answers: "He didn't mean it that way, sister. . . . He just means that Brother did the best he could, all he could, and now he doesn't need to worry anymore" (p. 431). Then she looks at the runner, "serene and unsurprised and unpitying," and says "You like to laugh, don't you." And he does so, "laughing, strong and steady and completely, with that side of his mouth still capable of moving, opening to laugh, the single eye meeting hers—theirs—full and calm and unpitying and laughing too" (p. 431). We learn also that the corporal's wife has gone back to the Marseille brothel in order to support an old grandmother, an act which both Marya and the runner think quite admirable; and we learn that Marthe's husband has died, in a sense, she implies, because he had learned to hope during the temporary peace and "probably decided that he could not bear another peace" (p. 430).

The final scene depicts the burial ceremonies of the old general and shows the whole world following and mourning as his casket is brought to the Arch de Triomphe, under which burns the flame of the Unknown Soldier. We are encouraged to see the old general first as a kind of God and bringer of peace. The day is gray "as though in dirge for him to whom it owed (and would forever) for the right and privilege to mourn in peace without terror or concern" (p. 433). And there is

the dirge of victorious and grieving France, the dirge of Europe and from beyond the seas too where men had doffed the uniforms in which they had been led through suffering to peace by him who lay now beneath the draped flag on the caisson, and even further than that where people who had never heard his name did not even know that they were still free because of him. [p. 435]

Immediately following these lines we hear the ringing cry of the "first man in France: poet, philosopher, statesman, patriot and orator," which violently shifts our perspective: "That's right, great general! Lie always with your face to the east, that the enemies of France shall always see it and beware!" (p. 435).

At this, the runner, "not a man" but an "upright scar, on crutches," bursts from the crowd and lurches into the empty space enclosing the Arch, wearing his filthy dinner jacket on which hang "on their barber-pole ribbons a British Military Cross and Distinguished Conduct Medal, and a French *Médaille Militaire:* which (the French one) was probably why the

French crowd itself had not dared prevent him emerging from
it and even now did not dare grasp him and jerk him back" (p.
435). Grasping the French decoration he cries out:

"Listen to me too, Marshal! This is yours: take it!" and snatched,
ripped from his filthy jacket the medal which was the talisman of
his sanctuary and swung his arm up and back to throw it. Apparently he knew himself what was going to happen to him as soon
as he released the medal, and defied it; with the medal up-poised
in his hand he even stopped and looked back at the crowd which
seemed now to crouch almost, leashed and straining for the moment
when he would absolve himself of immunity, and laughed, not triumphant: just indomitable, with that side of his ruined face capable
of laughing, then turned and flung the medal at the caisson, his voice
ringing again in the aghast air as the crowd rushed down upon him:
"You too helped carry the torch of man into that twilight where
he shall be no more; these are his epitaphs: They shall not pass. My
country right or wrong. Here is a spot which is forever England—"
    Then they had him. He vanished as though beneath a wave, a tide
of heads and shoulders above which one of the crutches appeared
suddenly in a hand which seemed to be trying to strike down at
him with it until the converging police (there were dozens of them
now, converging from everywhere) jerked it away, other police
rapidly forming a cordon of linked arms, gradually forcing the
crowd back while, rite and solemnity gone for good now, parade
marshals' whistles shrilled and the chief marshal himself grasped the
bridles of the horses drawing the caisson and swung them around,
shouting to the driver: "Go on!" the rest of the cortege huddling
without order, protocol vanished for the moment too as they hurried after the caisson almost with an air of pell mell, as though in
actual flight from the wreckage of the disaster. [p. 436]

Finally, rescued and still protected by two policemen, the
runner lies in the gutter of a side street surrounded by a small
crowd. When a voice says, "Maybe he will die this time," he
tries to laugh. Then, helped to spit out blood and shattered
teeth by the old quartermaster general, who has come to his
side, he laughs at the crowd and says, " 'That's right. . . .

Tremble. I'm not going to die. Never.' 'I am not laughing,' the old man bending over him said. 'What you see are tears.' " With this the book ends.

It is a powerful and moving ending and a unifying one in that it repeats, as it were, so many of the themes of the book and reminds us even of the Reverend Sutterfield's notion that God has room for both laughter and tears, that they are all the same to Him, and that He can grieve for both of them (p. 202). But it does not and is not intended to resolve our thoughts and feelings about any of the questions the book has raised. The runner performs an act of defiance which we must view sympathetically and see as just. We must also see it as a futile and empty gesture, a parody of the corporal's quiet and humble revolt, a gesture bringing only the chaos which the old general has argued would be the result of the corporal's victory. And we cannot overlook that it is a symbol of authority, the police, which keeps the crowd from killing the runner. Of man, who will endure, we see the crowd, capable of grief and dignity, of "being led, mystified and decieved" by ritual and patriotism, and of tearing to bits a man on crutches who tells them the truth; we see the runner, defiant and heroic but futile and self-destructive, misinterpreting a sympathetic response, having neither learned nor changed from any of his experiences, laughing; and we see the ineffectual old quartermaster general in tears—tears we must view both as his sympathetic response to the runner's condition and as his answer to the runner's assertion that man will endure.

There is, of course, much more than this to be said about Faulkner's novels, and I certainly do not wish to imply by my emphasis upon their similarities that they are all to be equally valued. I have side-stepped the problem of evaluation and have been as singleminded in my analysis as I have because I believe that by far the most pressing problem, at present, is to understand the kind of entities the novels are. It has been generally recognized, of course, that they are complex and in many respects ambiguous and inconclusive. But there has been little if any recognition of the remarkable extent to which this is true, of the extent to which any particular statement about a Faulkner novel and any particular interpretation of one, to say nothing of interpretation of his vision as a whole, is bound to be partial and inadequate. Interpretation of virtually any novel, of course, involves oversimplification and a degree of distortion, but, if my view of Faulkner is even partially correct, interpretation of his work becomes a peculiarly difficult and hazardous affair and presents Faulkner criticism with serious problems it has so far ignored.

Conclusions

FAULKNER'S ambiguity and irresolution, at bottom, are more a matter of temperament than of deliberate artistic intent, as will be shown later. Up to a point, however, we may understand them as serving or reflecting two general intentions.

The first of these is to achieve powerful emotive and perhaps even hypnotic effects. This intention becomes clear when we understand something of Faulkner's generally irrationalistic attitudes. Conrad Aiken has suggested that what Faulkner is after, in part, is a "medium without stops or pauses," an "image stream" toward which the reader "must be powerfully and unremittingly hypnotized," and Aiken suggests that this intent to hypnotize accounts, perhaps, not only for the length and elaborateness of Faulkner's sentence structure but for his repetitiveness as well.[1] It is likely that the frequent resistance of Faulkner's work to rational analysis also contributes to this hypnotic effect. Some passages from Edward Snyder's *Hypnotic Poetry* strongly suggest that this may be true. Professor Snyder notes that in actual hypnosis the stimuli used "are such as to fix the attention while retarding mental activity," and he concludes that the same retardation of mental activity is helpful in producing the less complete hypnoidal state which he calls

[1] "William Faulkner: The Novel as Form," in *Two Decades*, pp. 141–142.

"emotional trance," a state in which the subject's emotional susceptibility is highly intensified.[2] In his Foreword to Snyder's book, the psychologist James Leuba writes that Snyder has "demonstrated the existence of a type of poetry which owes its attraction to a method of composition, the effect of which is to limit the intellectual activity, i.e., to induce a state of partial trance, and thereby to free in some measure the emotional life from the trammel of critical thinking." [3]

Whether Faulkner actually induces a state of partial trance is not especially important here. And I do not wish to suggest that the spell he puts upon us is deadening or paralyzing. Quite the contrary. It does seem likely, however, that the purpose and effect of much of his presentation is to free the emotional life from the "trammel" of critical thinking, so that like the preacher in *The Sound and the Fury*, who is also in a sense a hypnotist, he might speak directly to the "heart." To some extent, we can say of Faulkner, as McCaslin says was true for God, that he "didn't have His Book written to be read by what must elect and choose, but by the heart" (*GDM*, 260). I do not mean to connect the word "heart" entirely with the words "emotive" or "hypnotic," and Faulkner's own use of the word "heart" is inconsistent, but there is no doubt that he sees the heart essentially as an organ of feeling and as antithetic to the head and that he regards it, not the head, as providing the way to truth. "Ideas and facts," he has said in an interview, "have very little connection with truth." [4] We give ourselves "mind's reason[s]," says Ike McCaslin, "because the heart dont always have time to bother with thinking up words that fit together" (*GDM*, 348).

An even greater distrust of the head is suggested when he speaks of "fact and probability" as "rubble-dross" (*RN*, 261)

---

[2] *Hypnotic Poetry: A Study of Trance-Inducing Techniques in Certain Poems and its Literary Significance* (Philadelphia: University of Pennsylvania Press, 1930), pp. 25, 32–33.

[3] *Ibid.*, p. x.   [4] Stein, "Art of Fiction," p. 49.

and when he equates "that best of ratiocination," to which Quentin and Shreve are dedicated, with Sutpen's dead morality and Miss Coldfield's "demonizing" (*AA*, 280). Jason Compson, whom Faulkner has said he considers the most vicious and detestible of his creations, is in a sense the most logical of his characters. Faulkner describes him as "the first sane Compson since before Culloden. . . . Logical, rational" (*SF*, 16). Faulkner's most sympathetically presented characters, on the other hand, tend to be virtually inchoate or else, like Gavin Stevens, they speak with little regard for rational sequence or organization. And, of course, Faulkner's own style—with its syntactical violations, pseudo syntax, shifting metaphors, and oxymorons —suggests, at the least, a desire to transcend the usual rational processes of comprehension. So does his deprecation of Hemingway for staying within limits and his affirmation of his own and Thomas Wolfe's desire to go beyond this, to attempt the impossible.

Allied with his desire to transcend the usual rational processes is an obvious discontent with the ability of language to convey truth. This is evident not only in his stylistic straining at the limits of language but in his various comments about the chasm between life and print or, as Addie Bundren puts it, between "words" and "doing." Like Addie, he also seems to fear not only that "words don't ever fit even what they are trying to say at" (*AILD*, 463) but that they are empty substitutes for feeling and experience. "sounds that people who never sinned nor loved nor feared have for what they never had and cannot have until they forget the words" (*AILD*, 465).

Much of Faulkner's presentation, I think, is designed to prevent his readers from substituting language and "mind's reasons" for the actual experiences he is trying to suggest. The equation of a single word with a feeling, the suggestion that they can possibly be synonymous, is especially to be avoided. This helps to explain why Faulkner so often begins his descriptions negatively, by saying it was not one thing but another, or describes feelings or conditions as a tension between poles or an approximation of a pole or even something beyond a pole, gives us a term like fear (or love or rage) and then says it was not that but almost that or something beyond that. Perhaps it helps to explain, also, why he uses so many words. Similarly, his oxymorons, synesthetic images, mixed metaphors, pseudo syntax, noncoherent "explanations," and alternate and multiple suggestions, all prevent us from comfortably substituting language and logic for feelings; they all counteract our tendency to construct pigeon holes in order to forget the things we put in them. This same intention, I think, has much to do with the larger and more general ambiguities and irresolution that prevent us from integrating our responses to the novels as wholes. For so long as our reactions are in a suspension rather than in crystallized form, they remain feelings and experiences rather than rational or verbal constructions.

The foregoing would seem to be reasonably safe, though partial, conclusions. But I would like to suggest a further, somewhat more tenuous aspect of Faulkner's irrationalism: his tendency to take and present a somewhat Bergsonian view of both experience and comprehension.

Like Bergson, he often tends to view experience as a state of the whole being or of the self and to conceive of the self as an indivisible internal process which can only be intuited and cannot really be defined either by analysis or images. It is this notion of experience and self which Rosa suggests when she refers to herself as, "not my body . . . but I, myself, that deep existence which we lead" (*AA*, 137). It is this which Faulkner suggests in his frequent descriptions of an experience or act as something participated in by the "whole" or "entire" being. For example, when Joe Christmas tries to feel what it is like to be a Negro he can feel "his whole being writhe and strain with physical outrage and spiritual denial" (*LIA*, 197). Faulkner's presentation often seems in accord also with Bergson's view that "every feeling . . . contains within it the whole past

and present of the being experiencing it." [5] We find Faulkner
again and again using the flashback to add to a feeling or event
the whole past of the being experiencing it. Again and again he
interrupts an important experience not merely to describe one
past event or a few associations called up by the present experience but to recapitulate much and sometimes all of a character's essential past up to that point. His description of
experience as both cumulative and retroactive (*U*, 145) is in
accord with this view.

More significant, however, is Faulkner's attempt to present
this experiencing self through images of motion and tension.
Although Bergson insists that no image can fully express the
nature of the self, he does view the self essentially as motion
and tension. After comparing the inner life to "the unrolling of
a coil" or "a continual rolling up, like that of a thread on a
ball," [6] he writes: "Finally let us free ourselves from the space
which underlies the movement in order to continue only the
movement itself, the act of tension or extension; in short pure
mobility. We shall have this time a more faithful image of the
development of our self in duration." [7] Later he says that "intuition" is as distinct from a summary or synthesis of knowledge "as the motor impulse is distinct from the path traversed
by the moving body, as the tension of the spring is distinct from
the visible movements of the pendulum." [8]

Again and again, as we have seen in Part I, Faulkner presents
important psychological experiences of his characters as sensations of movement or tension of an undefined internal self or as
tensions between the velocities of different parts of the self, as
though the self were a series of motions. His even more frequent
presentations of psychological conditions as generalized states
of quiescence and turbulence and as gatherings and releases,
although not in strict keeping, perhaps, with a Bergsonian view

[5] Henri Bergson, *An Introduction to Metaphysics*, tr. T. E. Hulme
(New York and London: Putnam, 1912), p. 25.

[6] *Ibid.*, pp. 11–12.   [7] *Ibid.*, p. 14.   [8] *Ibid.*, p. 92.

of self, all suggest that he frequently conceives of the self as an indivisible organic and dynamic process and that he views experiences as conditions of that dynamic process rather than as specific and analyzable reactions. What we know about Faulkner's characters, as pointed out earlier, is not their thoughts or specific emotions or even their likes and dislikes so much as their general state of quiescence or turbulence, usually a state of tension. What we witness then in Faulkner's works is in large measure a vision of the dynamics of the human psyche or the process which some psychologists have labeled "primitive sensation," a vision of the quiescences, turbulences, tensions and releases, writhings and strainings of man viewed not from without, as mosaic, but from within, as whole being.

Faulkner often thinks of comprehension in a similar way, seeing true understanding not as intellectual act but as experience—experience again defined as feeling, sensation, and dynamic process of the whole being, something very different from the words and sentences usually used to convey it. This comprehension comes not from disinterested detachment but from involvement, empathy, identity. It is the kind of comprehension Quentin has of part of the Sutpen story, having "absorbed it . . . without the medium of speech somehow from having been born and living beside it, with it, as children will and do" (*AA*, 212–213). It is the kind Judith and Sutpen have of each other "who seem to know one another so well or are so much alike that" they comprehend "without need of the medium of ear or intellect" (*AA*, 122). Will Varner wants "to find out what it must have felt like to be the fool that would need all this [a large mansion] just to eat and sleep in" (*H*, 7). That is, he wants to imaginatively re-experience it. What Rosa, Hightower, and other of Faulkner's narrator's explicitly demand of their listeners is not that they understand or even sympathize in the usual sense so much as feel what happened, share in the experience: hear it, smell it, above all "feel" it. Addie beats her pupils so that her blood in them will run and make them "aware" of her, make her something in their "secret and selfish" lives.

The fullest comprehension of something, Faulkner sometimes suggests, would come not merely from being close to it, feeling it, or even from imaginatively projecting oneself into it, but from a kind of mystical union with it. Thus Quentin and Shreve are finally described not only as riding along with Charles and Henry but as somehow merging with them into a new twosome "smelling the very smoke which had blown and faded away forty-six years ago" (*AA*, 351). Thus Gavin Stevens muses that "by the act of eating and maybe only by that" can man

actually enter the world, get himself into the world: not through it but into it, burrowing into the world's teeming solidarity like a moth into wool by the physical act of chewing and swallowing the substance of its warp and woof and so making, translating into a part of himself and his memory, the whole history of man. [*ID*, 207]

Here again Faulkner's view is close to Bergson's belief that real understanding comes only through "intuition," which he defines as an entering into an object, a coincidence with it, rather than a viewing from without.

The author may multiply the traits of his hero's character, may make him speak and act as much as he pleases, but all this can never be equal to the simple and indivisible feeling which I should experience if I were able for an instant to identify myself with the person of the hero himself. . . . [T]hat which is properly himself, that which constitutes his essence cannot be perceived from without, being internal by definition. . . . Coincidence with the person himself would alone give me the absolute.[9]

It is this kind of comprehension Joe Christmas so desperately seeks as he tries "to breathe into himself the dark odor, the dark and inscrutable thinking and being of Negroes" (*LIA*, 197).

If the essence or inmost self of another person is a dynamic

[9] *Ibid.*, pp. 3–5.

process, the ultimate act of empathy or identity would be to
experience that dynamic process. To empathize would not mean
merely to think the thoughts the other person thinks or to
feel the specific sensory responses he feels; it would mean to
share the movements, quiescences, turbulences, tensions, releases, writhings, and strainings of his inmost self. This, I believe, is the kind of response Faulkner often wants to produce
in the reader. The reader's act of comprehension is not to be
from without, not a detached contemplative or evaluative act,
but rather an empathetic experience, a comprehension from
within. He is not so much to observe and judge characters, as
to feel what they feel, as nearly as possible, to be them. He is to
comprehend as much as possible as Quentin comprehends the
South, through somehow absorbed heritage, and as Quentin
and Shreve come to comprehend Henry and Charles, through
identity. Like Will Varner he is to experience what things and
people "felt like." And since the ultimate act of comprehending
something would be to empathize or identify with its essence,
essence seen as dynamic process, much of the reader's experience
is to be the experience of tensions and dynamic process within
his own being.

It is the degree to which Faulkner provides this last kind of
experience that most marks him off from other modern novelists
who try, as he does, to give their readers an essentially empathetic experience through interior monologues, spiral movement, sensory emphasis, hypnotic repetition, evocative images,
and symbols. And it is this which accounts for much of the
peculiar force of his work. We can say that he produces these
deep inner movements and tensions largely by his persistent
and many-pronged stimulation of the kinesthetic and visceral
senses, but we must understand that the phrase "kinesthetic and
visceral senses" is inadequate here and that there is undoubtedly
a profound kinship between the responses we call "kinesthetic"
and "visceral" and our fundamental sense of life and of our
own being; certainly there is a deep kinship between those

responses and the experiences of the kind of inmost self Faulkner assumes. We must understand, also, that empathy is largely dependent upon such motor and visceral responses.[10]

These responses to Faulkner's work are brought about in part by his continual emphasis on motion, quiescence and turbulence, and tension and release, that is, by the consistency with which the external and internal worlds are presented as dynamic process. They are even more powerfully stimulated by Faulkner's persistent use of certain kinds of antithesis, those antitheses which juxtapose irreconcilable elements and leave the reader with the tension of an impasse and those antitheses which simultaneously suggest movement, activity, or impulse and restraint of movement, activity, or impulse. I am thinking now not only of images like "rapt dynamic immobility," "hanging immobilised by the heels in attitudes of frantic running," or "calm and contained and rigidly boiling," but of the many larger struggles within and between characters and between characters and natural forces, which have the same qualities and effects as such images.

In a more general way the same sorts of deep inner tension are induced by Faulkner's techniques of "deliberately withheld meaning" and "of progressive and partial and delayed disclosure," as Conrad Aiken puts it, and by his long involuted and interrupted sentences and paragraphs, for they continually block or retard the urge of eye and intellect to move forward. It is no accident that Joseph Warren Beach chooses powerful visceral images to describe the effect of these techniques. "Half the time we are swimming under water, holding our breath and straining our eyes to read off the meaning of submarine phenomena. . . . From time to time we come to the surface, gasping, to breathe the air of concrete fact and recorded truth, only to go floundering again the next moment through crashing waves of doubt and speculation." [11]

[10] See note 10, p. 25.
[11] Joseph Warren Beach, quoted in *Two Decades*, p. 29.

Finally, I think, our total response to the novels is to a large extent one of deep and profound tension. For unless we possess an unusually high degree of negative capability, we are not content with complex unresolved suspensions and are deeply frustrated and strained by our inability to integrate our thoughts and feelings. To the extent that the experience of Faulkner's characters has been a matter of powerful inner movements and tensions we are by our own similar responses sharing their experience and thereby, in a Bergsonian sense, most deeply "intuiting" and comprehending it.

To what extent Faulkner is consciously seeking the kinds of effects just described I am not sure. At one time I felt that one could trace in Faulkner's works and public statements a fairly consistent mystical vision very much in accord with Bergson's philosophy, a vision of time being defeated by a process in which the past experience of men, experience understood primarily as tension, is involved with the past and future in the form of tension, a vision, in the largest sense, of the *élan vital*, the life force itself, enduring in time. And I felt that Faulkner's reiterated assertion that "man will endure" was to be understood essentially in those terms, as was his assertion that both the writer and reader were enabled to "say No to death" by means of the capacity of the writer's words to engender "the old deathless excitement in hearts and glands." [12] I have come to feel, however, that, although one can make a case for the existence of such a vision in the works, it is too intermittent and partial, and too often contradicted, to be seen as anything other than one more of the many ideas and themes that lie in loose suspension with one another.

I have dwelt upon the Bergsonian approach to experience and comprehension because, regardless of Faulkner's intention, it seems a valid and illuminating way to look at his works. It explains much of his power and makes the tension he produces in the reader more purposeful and meaningful than it might

[12] *Faulkner Reader*, pp. x–xi.

seem if we see it merely as the consequence of a less specific irrationalism which desires only to prevent us from translating feeling into language or abstract formulations.

Yet even to see a general sort of irrationalism as the governing principle behind Faulkner's works is not entirely satisfactory, for there is too much that it does not explain. Faulkner's ambiguity and irresolution must also be understood as asserting and reflecting a somewhat more intellectual intention and view of life. It is difficult to define this view and almost impossible to draw a dividing line between the view and Faulkner's temperament. Warren Beck has helped to illuminate this view of life:

If Faulkner's sentences sometimes soar and circle involved and prolonged, if his scenes become halls of mirrors repeating tableaux in a progressive magnification, if echoes multiply into the dissonance of infinite overtones, it is because the meanings his stories unfold are complex, mysterious, obscure, and incomplete. There is no absolute, no eternal pure white radiance in such presentations, but rather the stain of many colors, refracted and shifting in kaleidoscopic suspension, about the center of man's enigmatic behavior and fate, within the drastic orbit of mortality. Such being Faulkner's view of life, such is his style.[13]

Karl Zink asserts that "at its best, form in Faulkner's art constitutes a living effort to penetrate and to realize in art an ineffable complexity." [14]

Certainly these critics are right that Faulkner's work often embodies and suggests a view that life is enigmatic and ineffably complex. To a large extent his shifts in tone and point of view, his avoidance of resolution, and his various obstacles to rational understanding may be seen as an effort so to present life and experience as to make facile interpretation impossible. The meaning of the stories of Sutpen and Joe Christmas and

[13] "William Faulkner's Style," in *Two Decades*, p. 162.
[14] Karl E. Zink, "William Faulkner: Form as Experience," *South Atlantic Quarterly*, LIII (1954), 384.

others, Faulkner is saying, is largely ambiguous: Whether they
are free agents or pawns, heroes or villains, is ambiguous, just
as it is uncertain whether the tall convict is a hero or a fool,
whether Darl Bundren is a seer or a madman, and whether the
desperate struggles of the convict, the Bundrens, and others are
tragic or comic, significant or futile. Whether or not there is a
God is also problematical and, if there is, whether he is to be
thought of as Jehovah, Christ, Satan, Joker, Umpire, Chess
Player, or life force. Even about the one certainty—that "man
will endure"—we are to wonder whether he will endure by
virtue of his soul or his folly and whether enduring means
primarily to suffer or to transcend time. These "alternative"
views, we must remember, are usually presented in such a way
that we can neither choose between them nor combine them.
Faulkner does not permit us to think of a character as part hero
and part fool or of events as partly significant and partly futile.
Like the terms of most of Faulkner's oxymorons the "alternatives" remain at once together and apart.

   To say that Faulkner sees and presents life as enigmatic and
ineffably complex is not enough, however; such a description
leaves out important qualities of his feeling about life, qualities
that are inseparable from his view of life.

You get born and you try this and you dont know why only you
keep on trying it and you are born at the same time with a lot of other
people, all mixed up with them, like trying to, having to, move your
arms and legs with strings only the same strings are hitched to all the
other arms and legs and the others all trying and they dont know why
either except that the strings are all in one another's way like five or
six people all trying to make a rug on the same loom only each one
wants to weave his own pattern into the rug; and it cant matter, you
know that, or the Ones that set up the loom would have arranged
things a little better, and yet it must matter because you keep on
trying. [AA, 127]

The words are Judith Sutpen's, but the passage communicates
more clearly than any other, I believe, the essence of Faulkner's

view of life and his feeling toward it. The passage suggests not only the complex and enigmatic qualities of life, but the sense of life as conflict, tension, and frustration, which persistently informs Faulkner's presentation. Above all, it suggests the intense contradictory feelings which, as much as anything else, I think, explain Faulkner's attitude toward life and toward his own art: "It cant matter, you know that, . . . and yet it must matter." It cannot have meaning and yet it must. The statement does not simply describe a dual perspective (sometimes seems to matter, sometimes not) or an uncertainty (may or may not matter) or even a paradox (does and does not matter). The simultaneous "cant" and "must" suggests a desperately divided and tormented perspective, a condition of mind which tries to move simultaneously and intensely toward both order and chaos and which understandably seizes upon the figure which most nearly moves in both directions, the oxymoron.

This division in view and feeling about the meaningfulness of life and effort accounts, undoubtedly, for Faulkner's frequent explicit and implicit coupling of terms like "empty" and "profound," "futile" and "tragic," and for phrases such as "the substance itself [life] not only not dead, not complete, but in its very insoluble enigma of human folly and blundering possessing a futile and tragic immortality" (P, 85), and "profound and irrevocable if only in the sense of being profoundly and irrevocably unimportant" (P, 111). This division helps us also to understand Faulkner's seemingly obsessive assertion and denial of immortality and to account for his often perceptive idiots and incoherent intellectuals. It accounts, in part, for his failure to pursue thoroughly many of the ideas and meanings which he has suggested, even more, for his ability to urge certain meanings intensely and then to ignore them or to contradict them with equal intensity, and also for his use of form both to illuminate and to obscure. It is a view and feeling which, in general, makes it necessary for him to try continuously to affirm and deny, to illuminate and obscure, the meaning of his own artistic creations and the significance of the lives and experiences he presents. It accounts, perhaps, for his inability finally to commit himself and for his ability to treat art both as a plaything and a dedication. Undoubtedly it helps to explain the utterly divergent critical estimates and interpretations of his work. Finally, I believe, it accounts in large measure for the peculiarly compelling and disturbing power of his works, for it reminds us of the similar schizophrenia within ourselves which we have worked hard to bury.

Generally skeptical views of life, or dual perspectives in which life appears in some ways meaningful and in some ways meaningless, are not uncommon, are certainly comprehensible, and have informed much great art, including that of Shakespeare. Metaphysical poetry and Jacobean drama, at times, seem to suggest a division of feeling, as well as of view, about life's meaningfulness, which is as intense as Faulkner's. There is still, however, an important difference. Whatever the tensions and opposing suggestions, explicit or implicit, in a poem by Donne or a play by Webster, one feels behind them, I think, a governing mind which never really doubts the validity of its own ideas and perceptions or the possibility, if not the existence, of a moral universe in which such ideas and perceptions are relevant, which never abandons the effort to order its thoughts and emotions. Like many modern artists Faulkner has no such certainty.

Unlike any other modern of comparable stature, however, Faulkner's uncertainty also embraces his art. Virginia Woolf, Joyce, and even Kafka never seem to have really doubted the validity of art, and they have used it always to resist and to recreate as well as to reflect the dissolving worlds they saw and felt about them. They remain committed to order and reason. There have been some writers and painters, the surrealists and Dadaists, who have not resisted, whose uncertainty or despair has led them to deny reason, whose desperation has led them to protest against disorder with disorder. A part of Faulkner remains intensely committed to art and order and seeks desperately, and of course paradoxically, to find a way by which art can order equally intense convictions that life and art do and do not matter. A part of him is content with disorder.

Finally, however, I do not think we can adequately explain the kinds of tensions and suspensions we find in Faulkner's work except in terms of temperament. At bottom, his works seem governed not so much by a view of life, or by a particular gap in his thought and feeling, or by particular principles of organization as by his temperament, that is, by the particular compound of intellectual and emotional inclinations, tendencies, and responses that characterize his mental life and shape his reactions to experience. It is his temperamental responses, rather than any theories or ideas or particular torments, which he undoubtedly trusts to produce and to order his art. Any work of art, of course, reflects the temperament of its author and in some ultimate sense is governed by his temperament. But in Faulkner's case, the relationship between art and temperament seems far more immediate, direct, and pervasive than is true for most novelists. With most writers we can think of temperament as providing coloring or flavoring or at most as affecting their choice and treatment of material; with Faulkner it becomes an inextricable part of the very structure and meaning of his work. I mean this quite literally—that both the form and meanings of his works are governed much less by any controlling ideas, or themes, or dramatic or aesthetic considerations than by a succession of temperamental impulses and responses. The finished work becomes, in a sense, the record of a process, the record of the artist's struggle with his materials, rather than the record of his victory over his materials. Yet even this way of putting it is misleading, for it suggests a priority to the materials that I do not think they possess in Faulkner's case. To a large extent the materials, themselves, are proliferations which come into being as a direct result of temperamental impulse. In many cases the proliferations become the chief substance of the books.

When asked about the composition of *The Sound and the Fury*, Faulkner answered as follows:

That began as a short story, it was a story without plot, of some children being sent away from the house during the grandmother's funeral. They were too young to be told what was going on and they saw things only incidentally to the childish games they were playing, which was the lugubrious matter of removing the corpse from the house, etc., and then the idea struck me to see how much more I could have got out of the idea of the blind, self-centeredness of innocence, typified by children, if one of those children had been truly innocent, that is, an idiot. So the idiot was born and then I became interested in the relationship of the idiot to the world that he was in but would never be able to cope with and just where could he get the tenderness, the help, to shield him in his innocence. I mean "innocence" in the sense that God had stricken him blind at birth, that is, mindless at birth, there was nothing he could ever do about it. And so the character of his sister began to emerge, then the brother, who, that Jason (who to me represented complete evil. He's the most vicious character in my opinion I ever thought of), then he appeared. Then it needs the protagonist, someone to tell the story, so Quentin appeared. By that time I found out I couldn't possibly tell that in a short story. And so I told the idiot's experience of that day, and that was incomprehensible, even I could not have told what was going on then, so I had to write another chapter. Then I decided to let Quentin tell his version of that same day, or that same occasion, so he told it. Then there had to be the counterpoint, which was the other brother, Jason. By that time it was completely confusing. I knew that it was not anywhere near finished and then I had to write another section from the outside with an outsider, which was the writer, to tell what had happened on that particular day. And that's how that book grew. That is, I wrote that same story four times. None of them were right, but I had anguished so much that I could not throw any of it away and start over, so I printed it in the four sections. That was not a deliberate *tour de force* at all, the book just grew that way. That I was still trying to tell one story which moved me very much and each time I failed, but I had put so much anguish into it that I couldn't throw it away,

like the mother that had four bad children, that she would have
been better off if they all had been eliminated, but she couldn't
relinquish any of them. And that's the reason I have the most tenderness for that book, because it failed four times.[15]

Although we probably cannot accept this as an entirely
literal or accurate account in view of other statements Faulkner
has made about the book,[16] I believe it nevertheless reveals much
about the way his works come into being and about the kind of
entities they are. It does so especially when we remember that
the various narrators do not, as Faulkner says they do, focus
upon the same day or the same occasion and that each section
develops and emphasizes a new set of events, builds a new story.
Faulkner's insistence that he was trying to tell "one story" may
not at first seem in entire accord with the notion that Faulkner's
proliferations become the substance of his books, but it does
fit if we recognize that the "story" was not something Faulkner
had clearly in mind but something he vaguely sensed and was
reaching for. The book, then, as we have it, is in a sense the
record of the process of reaching. We can say the reason he
failed is that, each time he reached, his proliferations and temperamental impulses put the "story" farther out of reach. Interesting also is Faulkner's statement that "there had to be the
counterpoint," a notion I shall comment on later.

Perhaps even more suggestive of how much the proliferations
can overwhelm a germinal idea is Faulkner's insistence that in
A Fable he was "primarily" telling the tragic story of "the
father who had to choose between the sacrifice or the saving of
his son." [17] It is not too much to say, I think, that in the com-
pleted work this story is virtually lost amid the other stories and

[15] *Faulkner at Nagano*, ed. Robert A. Jelliffe (Tokyo: Kenkyusha, Ltd.,
1956), pp. 103–105.
[16] These statements, however, are similar enough to the one quoted to
indicate that it is at least roughly true. See, for example, Stein, "Art of
Fiction," pp. 39–40, and Cynthia Grenier, "The Art of Fiction," *Accent*,
XVI (1956), 172–173.
[17] *Faulkner at Nagano*, pp. 159–160.

other emphases. One even feels that Faulkner has neglected this aspect of the story. As finally presented, in fact, the choice seems entirely the son's.

Probably the most graphic illustration of the process by which Faulkner constructs his stories is the section of *Absalom, Absalom!* in which Shreve and Quentin, giving full vent to their temperaments and emotions of the moment, elaborate upon the Sutpen story: at times they are carried away by a minor detail; at times one or the other becomes too excited to be coherent or to finish a thought or to heed the other's cry of "Wait. Wait"; at times they retrace something they have said and are dis- satisfied with; at times they are horrified, shocked, or amazed at what they have said, or they become lost and confused about where they are going; at times their conflicting attitudes lead them to quarrel and to take conflicting views of the same event or conflicting tones toward it, which they cannot take time to argue out or resolve; at times they simply luxuriate in the spectacle of their own creative process; and they continually keep thinking of one more thing that must or may or might have happened and one more way of interpreting what happened until they have built a structure so complex and involved and so impossible to embrace that they can respond to it only in violent emotional terms. Faulkner, I believe, writes his books in much the same way.

Perhaps all this seems obvious and unnecessary to belabor. Yet it cannot have been obvious if one is to judge from the enormous number of attempts to explain the novels in terms of one or another specific theme or specific aesthetic or strategic intention, or to judge from the apparently overwhelming in- clination of critics to treat the novels as though they entirely resembled *Madame Bovary* and were nothing at all like *Tristram Shandy*.

What is most significant, of course, about Faulkner's novels is not the mere fact that they are largely governed by tempera- mental responses, but the kinds of responses these are. For it is the kind of temperament he has that gives his works their characteristic shape (or shapelessness, depending on how narrowly one conceives the term shape), and that makes the search for the meaning or design of his novels so enticing and yet so futile an occupation.

Obviously it is premature to attempt any full or final analysis of Faulkner's temperament, but I believe this study has shown certain fundamental aspects of that temperament which more than any others determine the form of his novels. One of these aspects is the group of tendencies I have labeled the polar imagination: the tendency to view and interpret experience in extreme terms, to see life and feel it on all levels as composed essentially of pairs of warring entities, and to be fascinated by those especially tense sorts of antitheses in which the opposed entities are in a state of conflict which can neither be ended nor resolved. Clearly, the creative process for Faulkner is in large measure a series of responses by this sort of imagination, a series of movements or leaps from a thing to its opposite, and this process seems to take place regardless of what that thing is—a word, character, idea, or tone. It may even occur with respect to a whole story. When asked about the composition of *The Wild Palms*, he answered that his object was

To tell the story I wanted to tell, which was the one of the intern and the woman who gave up her family and husband to run off with him. To tell it like that, somehow or another I had to discover counterpoint for it, so I invented the other story, its complete antithesis, to use as counterpoint. And I did not write those two stories and then cut one into the other. I wrote them, as you read it, as the chapters. The chapter of the *Wild Palms*, chapter of the *River Story*, another chapter of the *Wild Palms*, and then I used the counterpoint of another chapter of the *River Story*. I imagine as a musician would do to compose a piece of music in which he needed a balance, a counterpoint.[18]

[18] *Ibid.*, pp. 79–80. See also Stein, "Art of Fiction," p. 43.

What is revealing here is not only his desire for a counterpoint but his desire to make it a "complete antithesis" and his need to move back and forth between the two as he goes along. Even if, as is possible, he did not actually write the book that way, his desire to explain it in those terms and to publish the stories in that form is significant. It is also illuminating that, despite his assertion that the primary story is the one about the woman and the intern, he ends the book with the story of the convict. Moreover, the antithesis, or proliferation, comes to seem the dominant and more powerful story. Unlike the musician, who at the end of his composition resolves the counterpoint, Faulkner leaves us simply with the counterpoint itself.

Again and again throughout his work Faulkner obviously feels a need to counterbalance what he thinks or feels with some kind of antithesis. I suspect that he experiences much the same sense of completion and satisfaction from the tension of an unresolved antithesis that most other writers do from harmony and resolution, that like a juggler he feels fulfilled only when his materials are in motion.

It may seem odd at first glance that a polar imagination, which is after all a rather simple and orderly form of imagination, should result in novels as complex and ambiguous as Faulkner's. Yet it is not strange at all when one realizes that the kinds of tense relationships Faulkner keeps establishing must by their very nature remain unexplored and that the effect of an accumulation of antitheses differs greatly from that of a single one. A single antithesis has the sharpness and clarity of a single combat; an accumulation of antitheses much more resembles a war of each against each and all against all, which is chaos. One can see this quite clearly on a small scale when one examines some of the almost unintelligible thoughts and statements of characters like Rosa Coldfield and Darl Bundren and finds that they are essentially accumulations of antitheses.[19] One can see it on a larger scale when one closely examines a complex

[19] See above, pp. 100–101, 105.

whole like *Light in August* and discovers that its scenes consist largely of fairly simple "pairings" in which characters are in antithesis with each other or with a group.[20]

But the polar imagination alone would not account for the immensely varied kinds of ambiguity and irresolution we find in the novels. These can be explained, I think, only by two other aspects of Faulkner's temperament. One is his remarkable fecundity. It is this, of course, which has enabled him to create so rich and varied a fictional world and to provide for his reader such a profusion of effects and suggestions. In a sense he is so busy giving birth that he has no time to train or discipline his children. Too much of the irresolution is deliberate, however, for it to be the result merely of undisciplined fecundity or for it to be explained by his own statement: "I didn't like school and I quit about sixth grade. So I don't know anything about rational and logical processes of thought at all. I didn't have enough mathematics to have a disciplined mind." [21] If nothing else, Faulkner's quite careful consistency about the physical details of his stories and the clearly deliberate irrationality of much that he does make such explanations insufficient.

The other of these two aspects of his temperament is what must be an almost compulsive desire to leave things unresolved and indeterminate. This desire seems quite different from the

[20] Lena–Mrs. Armstid (pp. 15–18); sawmill workers–Christmas (pp. 27–31); sawmill workers–Brown (pp. 31–34); Brown–Christmas (pp. 34–35, 89–91, 239–240); Bunch–Lena (pp. 45–48, 434–444); Hightower–townspeople (pp. 52–62); Bunch–Hightower (pp. 67–88, 261–269, 272–278, 318–320); Christmas–dietitian (pp. 107–109); dietitian–Doc Hines (pp. 110–116); dietitian–matron (pp. 116–118); Christmas–McEachern (pp. 128–134, 139–144, 177–178); Christmas–Mrs. McEachern (pp. 146–147, 181–182); Christmas–Bobbie (pp. 156–157, 160, 162–164, 170–173); Bobbie–Max (pp. 167–168); Christmas–Bobbie, Max, blonde lady, and so on (pp. 185–191); Christmas–Joanna (pp. 210–211, 224–247); sheriff–Negro (pp. 255–256); Christmas–Negro congregation (pp. 281–285); Hightower–Byron, Hineses (pp. 323–328, 334, 338–343); Hightower–Lena (pp. 357–361); Brown–Lena (pp. 376–379); Bunch–Brown (pp. 384–385); Christmas–Grimm (pp. 404–407).

[21] *Faulkner at Nagano*, p. 38.

kind of tolerance for inconclusiveness that has sometimes been called "negative capability." One senses, rather, in both Faulkner's novels and public statements an active unwillingness to close in on things, to narrow or define, to clarify or explore relationships, to commit himself, whether it be to a particular view of a character, particular explanation of an action, or particular meaning of a word. I cannot help feeling that many of his leaps and shifts of ground are as much a way of escaping having to resolve his thoughts or feelings as they are a way of reaching for something farther. It is as though he is determined to avoid clarifying or finishing his ideas, almost as though he feared to take hold of them, to give them full shape or realization, as though in some obscure way he wished to fail so that he would be able to go on trying.[22]

Insofar as there is any single key to understand both Faulkner's mind and work, it is, I believe, his notion and feeling that what is important about life is the act of trying and that completion or success or resolution would mean both an end to trying and a sign that not enough had been tried.

Earlier I suggested that Faulkner's comments to Harvey Breit about contemporary authors indicated that in a very real sense Faulkner was seeking failure, that he saw failure as a kind of measure or objective. In a later interview he makes that attitude quite explicit. He says of Hemingway:

I thought that he found out early what he could do and he stayed inside of that. He never did try to get outside the boundary of what he really could do and risk failure. He did what he really could do marvelously well, first rate, but to me that is not success but failure . . . failure to me is the best. To try something you can't do, because it's too much (to hope for), but still to try it and fail, then try it again. That to me is success.[23]

[22] For another discussion which emphasizes the importance of Faulkner's temperament and divided sensibility see Alfred Kazin, *On Native Grounds* (New York: Reynal and Hitchcock, 1942), pp. 453–470.

[23] *Faulkner at Nagano*, pp. 3–4. The three periods after "failure" appear in the original.

A moment later, in answer to the question "Do you consider human life basically a tragedy?" he says: "Actually, yes. But man's immortality is that he is faced with a tragedy which he can't beat and he still tries to do something with it." [24] If the absolutely crucial thing is to go on trying—if it is the act of trying which gives man his immortality and which even, as Judith Sutpen suggests, makes life matter and gives it meaning —then one cannot really risk success, and failure becomes a kind of success.

I think it is not mere verbal paradox to call Faulkner's effort a "quest for failure." It is a quixotic ideal, certainly. But Faulkner is a Southerner and he has said that he usually reads *Don Quixote* once every year.[25] Earlier I commented on the number of Faulkner's characters who behave in precisely the ways which will prolong their torment and ensure their failure or doom. They, too, seem driven by a quest for failure. This kind of quest is a compelling and moving thing to witness. But it is a tormenting and discouraging thing to have to take part in. That is what, consciously or no, Faulkner makes the reader do. The reader, too, must try and try to grasp the novels and is doomed to fail. The "jigsaw puzzle picture integers" remain always "inextricable, jumbled, and unrecognizable," "just beyond his reach."

Many readers, I am sure, will be dissatisfied and disappointed by these conclusions, and they will go on trying to weave their own patterns on the loom that Faulkner has provided, feeling as Judith Sutpen did, and as part of Faulkner does, that it must be possible to do so "because you keep on trying." That they will keep trying, will face something they "can't beat and still tr[y] to do something with it," would surely win Faulkner's

---

[24] *Ibid.*, p. 4. See also Stein, "Art of Fiction," pp. 29–30, where Faulkner writes that if the artist were really successful in matching his work to his dream of perfection, "nothing would remain but to cut his throat."

[25] *Faulkner at Nagano*, p. 42.

approval, for it is this quality in man which, as he puts it, "gives him his immortality."

What I have tried to assert and make clear is the other side of this terrible paradox: that we as readers are faced with something we "can't beat," that the pattern in Faulkner's world cannot be found, or woven, else the one "that set up the loom would have arranged things a little better."

If Faulkner is right about man's quixotic propensities, and I believe he is, some of my conclusions can never fully be accepted. The most I can hope is that they are not misunderstood.

First, I am not asserting that there is no ordering or unifying principle in Faulkner's art, but rather that the dominant principle is the persistent placement of entities of all sorts into highly tense relationships with one another, relationships which to varying degrees resemble the relationship between the terms of an oxymoron. This is, of course, a curiously complex and puzzling kind of ordering principle, since it contains within itself a kind of disorder and disintegration and works against the attainment of any final, over-all order and unity.

Second, I am not saying that there is no unifying perspective in Faulkner's vision, but rather that his perspective is an intensely ambivalent one and that the ambivalence exists with respect to almost every important aspect of human experience, including reason and the question of whether life and art have any point or meaning. This, too, is a curiously complex and puzzling sort of perspective, for it, too, contains within itself a form of self-destruction, since it allows the artist almost any kind of freedom in his presentation, including the freedom to neglect or negate his own conceptions. Beyond this, Faulkner's art and vision both are ordered chiefly by his temperament and by the persistent patterns of rhetoric and perception described earlier in this book—by his powerful tendency to polarize experience of all varieties and to render it in terms of motion and immobility, sound and silence, quiescence and turbulence, and tension.

This is not to say that his works are devoid of major ordering themes, ideas, values, or attitudes, but rather that they embody a great many of these, that different and often conflicting ones are urged or embodied at various times or at the same time, and that none dominates his work sufficiently or consistently enough to serve as a unifying center. When one looks at his works as a whole, I do not think one can say that they consistently support even the rather loose group of values usually associated with the Christian and chivalric traditions, for in opposition we find a celebration of any and all kinds of dynamic and intense activity. To put it a little differently, Faulkner seems to be saying sometimes that the way in which man endures is terribly important and sometimes that the way does not matter just so long as the process of enduring goes on. Sometimes he makes Christ and Caesar mortal enemies, sometimes quite literally celebrates them in the same breath.

On the metaphysical level, too, there is a fundamental division in his thought, for we can find embodied in his works, as I have suggested, an essentially monistic philosophy which fuses body and mind into "whole being," which sees reality and truth as dynamic, a matter of action, involvement, and emotion, and which makes immortality a continuing process within the world of time and change. At the same time we can find a sharply dualistic view which might roughly be labeled Platonic, a view which dichotomizes body and mind, which sees reality and truth and immortality as static and immutable, and which leads Faulkner to create in his works an extensive realm outside time.

The only major idea, I believe, that he never abandons or seriously undercuts is that man should and must keep on trying whatever it is he must try and that his greatness consists in this.

All this does not mean that there is no point or profit in tracing the various patterns, themes, ideas, and attitudes that recur in Faulkner's novels. But we must come to recognize the extent to which any of these are partial and fragmentary and part of a suspension which will not be resolved.

The reader may well wonder why, despite my admiration for much that Faulkner does and despite my belief that ambivalence is a valid point of view, my tone is often irritable and annoyed. It may seem even stranger when I say that I share much of Faulkner's uncertainty about whether life has pattern or meaning. My irritation comes, I believe, from my feeling that Faulkner's fictional world is in many respects even more ambiguous and complex than the real one and that this is, in part, the result of a deliberate quest for failure. I understand that this will be the least palatable of my conclusions, but I must insist that I mean it quite literally and soberly. I do not mean by it that Faulkner has failed merely because he has been in quest of perfection or of "the impossible" and therefore had to fall short, as one feels was often true of Conrad, for example. I mean that in a very real sense he has seen complexity and inconclusiveness and baffling relationships as both means and end and has welcomed them too easily. He has not always so much fought his way through experience and, after his best efforts to understand and clarify it, arrived at certain ambiguities and paradoxes that represent the farthest he can go. He often seems rather to start with paradoxes and to delight in finding them and in remaining with them. When an enormous number of relatively simple things like faces, movements, and sounds have been described in oxymoronic or paradoxical terms and when numerous insignificant experiences have been presented ambiguously, one is less respectful of the major paradoxes and ambiguities, less certain that they are the result of reaching too far. When virtually every technique of an author is a movement away from coherence and resolution, one cannot easily feel that the final disorder is merely the result of too high an aim. When a writer consistently uses the ends of his novels to put his meanings farther out of reach, there is a sense in which he is not only reaching but is pushing as well. Let me make perfectly clear that I am not quarreling with the use of these techniques or with deliberate disorder as such. What troubles me is the amount of such disorder in Faulkner's work and his degree of reliance upon it, so that, finally, we cannot distinguish between the real mysteries and the manufactured ones. It is difficult, as I have said, to believe that a man can seek failure, though perhaps all men in some sense do so, but if one believes, as Faulkner does, in the crucial importance of endless trying, then failure can become not only a proof that enough has been tried but a need and a quest.

Works Cited

Aiken, Conrad. "William Faulkner: The Novel as Form," *Atlantic Monthly*, CLXIV (1939), 650–654. Reprinted in *Two Decades of Criticism*, edited by Hoffman and Vickery, pp. 139–147.

Backman, Melvin. "Sickness and Primitivism: A Dominant Pattern in William Faulkner's Work," *Accent*, XIV (1954), 61–73.

Beck, Warren. "William Faulkner's Style," *American Prefaces*, VI (1941), 195–211. Reprinted in *Two Decades of Criticism*, edited by Hoffman and Vickery, pp. 147–164.

Bergson, Henri. *An Introduction to Metaphysics*. Translated by T. E. Hulme. New York and London: Putnam, 1912.

Bowling, Lawrence E. "The Technique of *The Sound and the Fury*," *Kenyon Review*, X (1948), 552–566. Reprinted in *Two Decades of Criticism*, edited by Hoffman and Vickery, pp. 165–179.

Breit, Harvey. "A Walk with Faulkner," *New York Times Book Review*, Jan. 30, 1955, pp. 4, 12.

Campbell, H. M., and Foster, R. F. *William Faulkner: A Critical Appraisal*. Norman: University of Oklahoma Press, 1951.

Capote, Truman. "Faulkner Dances," *Theatre Arts*, XXXIII (April, 1949), 49.

Conrad, Joseph. "Heart of Darkness," *Youth and Two Other Stories*. New York: Doubleday, Page, 1912. Pp. 51–184.

Cowley, Malcolm. "Introduction," *The Portable Faulkner*. New York: Viking, 1946. Reprinted in *Two Decades of Criticism*, edited by Hoffman and Vickery, pp. 63–82.

Dos Passos, John. *Manhattan Transfer*. New York: Harper, 1925.

Eliot, George. *Adam Bede*. Library ed.; Edinburgh: Blackwood, 1901.

Faulkner, William. *Absalom, Absalom!* With an Introduction by Harvey Breit. New York: Modern Library, 1951. (First published in 1936.)

——. *As I Lay Dying*. Published together with *The Sound and the Fury*. New York: Modern Library, 1946. (First published in 1930.)

——. *Collected Stories*. New York: Random House, 1950.

——. *A Fable*. New York: Random House, 1954.

——. Foreword, *The Faulkner Reader*. New York: Random House, 1954.

——. *Go Down, Moses*. New York: Random House, 1942.

——. *The Hamlet*. New York: Random House, 1940.

——. *Intruder in the Dust*. New York: Random House, 1948.

——. *Light in August*. With an Introduction by Richard H. Rovere. New York: Modern Library, 1950. (First published in 1932.)

——. *Mirrors of Chartres Street*. Minneapolis: Faulkner Studies, 1953. (Stories and sketches written in 1925 for the New Orleans *Times-Picayune*.)

——. Nobel Prize speech. (Address made in 1950, in Stockholm, Sweden, upon receiving the Nobel Prize for Literature.) Quoted in full in O'Connor, *The Tangled Fire of William Faulkner*, pp. 147–148.

——. *Notes on a Horsethief*. Greenville, Miss.: Levee Press, 1950.

——. *Pylon*. New York: Smith and Haas, 1935.

——. *Requiem for a Nun*. New York: Random House, 1950.

——. *Sanctuary*. With an Introduction by William Faulkner. New York: Modern Library, 1932. (First published in 1931.)

——. *Sartoris*. New York: Harcourt, Brace, 1929.

——. *The Sound and the Fury*. With a new appendix as a Foreword by the author. New York: Modern Library, 1946. (First published in 1929.)

——. *The Town*. New York: Random House, 1957.

——. *The Unvanquished*. New York: Random House, 1938.

——. *The Wild Palms*. New York: Random House, 1939.

Fogle, Richard H. "Empathetic Imagery in Keats and Shelley," *PMLA*, LXI (1946), 163–191.

Grenier, Cynthia. "The Art of Fiction: An Interview with William Faulkner—September, 1955," *Accent*, XVI (1956), 167–177.

Hardy, Thomas. *Tess of the D'Urbervilles*. New York and London: Harper, 1935.

Hoffman, F. J., and Vickery, O. W. (eds.). *William Faulkner: Two Decades of Criticism*. East Lansing: Michigan State College Press, 1951.

Holman, C. Hugh. "The Unity of Faulkner's *Light in August*," *PMLA*, LXXIII (1958), 155–166.

Hopper, Vincent F. "Faulkner's Paradise Lost," *Virginia Quarterly Review*, XXIII (1947), 405–420.

Howe, Irving. "Thirteen Who Mutinied: Faulkner's First World War," *The Reporter*, X (Sept. 14, 1954), 43–46.

——. *William Faulkner: A Critical Study*. New York: Random House, 1951.

Jelliffe, Robert A. (ed.). *Faulkner at Nagano*. Tokyo: Kenkyusha, Ltd., 1956.

Joyce, James. *A Portrait of the Artist as a Young Man*. New York: The Modern Library, 1928.

Kazin, Alfred. "Faulkner: The Rhetoric and the Agony," *Virginia Quarterly Review*, XVIV (1942), 389–402. Reprinted in *On Native Grounds* (New York: Reynal and Hitchcock, 1942), pp. 453–470.

Langfeld, Herbert S. *The Aesthetic Attitude*. New York: Harcourt, Brace, 1920.

Lewis, Wyndham. "Moralist with a Corn Cob," *Life and Letters*, X (1934), 312–328. Reprinted in *Men Without Art* (London: Cassell, 1934), pp. 42–64.

Lowrey, Perrin. "Concepts of Time in *The Sound and the Fury*," *English Institute Essays*. New York: Columbia University Press, 1954. Pp. 57–82.

O'Connor, William Van. "The State of Faulkner Criticism," *Sewanee Review*, LX (1952), 180–186.

——. *The Tangled Fire of William Faulkner*. Minneapolis: University of Minnesota Press, 1954.

O'Donnell, George M. "Faulkner's Mythology," *Kenyon Review*, I (1939), 33–47. Reprinted in *Two Decades of Criticism*, edited by Hoffman and Vickery, pp. 49–62.

Poirier, William R. "'Strange Gods' in Jefferson, Mississippi: Analysis of *Absalom, Absalom!*," *Sewanee Review*, LIII (1945), 343–361. Reprinted in *Two Decades of Criticism*, edited by Hoffman and Vickery, pp. 343–361.

Roth, Russell, "The Centaur and the Pear Tree," *Western Review*, XVI (1952), 199–205.

Sartre, Jean-Paul. "A propos de *Le Bruit et la fureur:* La Temporalité chez Faulkner," *La Nouvelle Revue Française*, LII (1939), 1057–1061; continued, LIII (1939), 147–151. Translated and reprinted as "Time in Faulkner: *The Sound and the Fury*," in *Two Decades of Criticism*, edited by Hoffman and Vickery, pp. 180–188.

Snyder, Edward D. *Hypnotic Poetry: A Study of Trance-Inducing Technique in Certain Poems and Its Literary Significance.* Philadelphia: University of Pennsylvania Press, 1930.

Stein, Jean. "The Art of Fiction XII: William Faulkner" (an interview with Faulkner), *Paris Review*, no. 12 (Spring, 1956), 28–52.

Sutherland, Donald. "Time on Our Hands," *Yale French Studies*, no. 10 (1953), 5–13.

Swiggart, Peter. "Moral and Temporal Order in *The Sound and the Fury*," *Sewanee Review*, LXI (1953), 221–237.

Thompson, Lawrance. "Mirror Analogues in *The Sound and the Fury*," *English Institute Essays.* New York: Columbia University Press, 1952. Pp. 83–106.

Thorpe, Clarence D. "Some Notices of Empathy Before Lipps," *Papers of the Michigan Academy of Sciences, Literature, and the Arts*, XXIII (1937), 525–533.

Vickery, Olga W. "*As I Lay Dying*," *Perspective*, III (1950), 179–191. Reprinted in *Two Decades of Criticism*, edited by Hoffman and Vickery, pp. 189–205.

———. "Gavin Stevens: From Rhetoric to Dialectic," *Faulkner Studies*, II (1953), 1–4.

Warren, Robert Penn. "William Faulkner," *New Republic*, CXV (1946), 176–180; continued 234–237. Reprinted in *Two Decades of Criticism*, edited by Hoffman and Vickery, pp. 82–101.

Zink, Karl E. "William Faulkner: Form as Experience," *South Atlantic Quarterly*, LIII (1954), 384–403.

Index

References to major discussions of characters and works are italicized. For references to characters in Faulkner's works see Characters.